PLURILINGUALISM IN TEACHING AND LEARNING

Assembling a rich and diverse range of research studies on the role of plurilingualism across a wide variety of teaching and learning settings, this book supports teacher reflection and action in practical ways and illustrates how researchers tease out and analyze the complex realities of their educational environments. With a focus on education policies, teaching practices, training, and resourcing, this volume addresses a range of mainstream and specialized contexts and examines the position of learners and teachers as users of plurilingual repertoires. Providing a close look into the possibilities and constraints of plurilingual education, this book helps researchers and educators clarify and strengthen their understandings of the links between language and literacy and offers them new ways to think more rigorously and critically about the language ideologies that shape their own beliefs and approaches in language teaching and learning.

Julie Choi is a Lecturer in Education (Additional Languages) in the Melbourne Graduate School of Education at the University of Melbourne, Australia.

Sue Ollerhead is a Lecturer in Literacies and English as an Additional Language in the School of Education at the University of New South Wales, Sydney, Australia.

PLURILINGUALISM IN TEACHING AND LEARNING

Complexities Across Contexts

Edited by Julie Choi and
Sue Ollerhead

NEW YORK AND LONDON

First published 2018
by Routledge
711 Third Avenue, New York, NY 10017

and by Routledge
2 Park Square, Milton Park, Abingdon, Oxon, OX14 4RN

Routledge is an imprint of the Taylor & Francis Group, an informa business

© 2018 Taylor & Francis

The right of Julie Choi and Sue Ollerhead to be identified as the authors of the editorial material, and of the authors for their individual chapters, has been asserted in accordance with sections 77 and 78 of the Copyright, Designs and Patents Act 1988.

All rights reserved. No part of this book may be reprinted or reproduced or utilised in any form or by any electronic, mechanical, or other means, now known or hereafter invented, including photocopying and recording, or in any information storage or retrieval system, without permission in writing from the publishers.

Trademark notice: Product or corporate names may be trademarks or registered trademarks, and are used only for identification and explanation without intent to infringe.

Library of Congress Cataloging-in-Publication Data
A catalog record for this book has been requested

ISBN: 978-1-138-22847-4 (hbk)
ISBN: 978-1-138-22849-8 (pbk)
ISBN: 978-1-315-39246-2 (ebk)

Typeset in Bembo and Stone Sans
by Florence Production Ltd, Stoodleigh, Devon, UK

For my new friends at MGSE, Sue and Mei

—Julie

CONTENTS

Foreword by Angel M. Y. Lin ix
Preface xiii

1 Introduction 1
  Sue Ollerhead, Julie Choi, and Mei French

Part I: Plurilingual Language-in-Education Policies 19

2 Provision, Policy and Reasoning: The Pluralisation of the Language Education Endeavor 21
  Joseph Lo Bianco

3 Mother-Tongue-Based Multilingual Education in the Philippines: Perceptions, Problems and Possibilities 37
  Priscilla Angela T. Cruz and Ahmar Mahboob

4 Bypassing Unrepresentative Policies: What do Indigenous Australians Say About Language Education? 54
  Rebecca Hetherington

Part II: Plurilingual Student Repertoires 69

5 The Translingual Advantage: Metrolingual Student Repertoires 71
  Emi Otsuji and Alastair Pennycook

6 An Expanded View of Translanguaging: Leveraging the Dynamic Interactions Between a Young Multilingual Writer and Machine Translation Software 89
Sara Vogel, Laura Ascenzi-Moreno, and Ofelia García

7 Keeping the Plurilingual Insight: Visualising the Literacies of Out-of-School Children in Northern Ghana 107
Brendan Rigby

Part III: Plurilingual Classroom Practices and Teacher Perspectives 127

8 Translingual Innovation Within Contact Zones: Lessons from Australian and South African Schools 129
Sue Ollerhead, Mastin Prinsloo, and Lara-Stephanie Krause

9 Plurilingualism and Agency in Language Education: The Role of Dramatic Action-Oriented Tasks 147
Enrica Piccardo and Angelica Galante

10 The Plurilingual Life: A Tale of High School Students in Two Cities 165
Brian Davy and Mei French

Part IV: Plurilingualism in Higher Education Contexts 183

11 Transforming Lexicon, Transforming Industry: University Lecturers as Language Planners in Timor-Leste 185
Trent Newman

12 Challenging the Quiet Violence of a Powerful Language: Translanguaging Towards Transformative Teaching in South African Universities 201
Monica Hendricks and Ntombekhaya Fulani

13 From Linguistic Preparation to Developing a Translingual Mindset: Possible Implications of Plurilingualism for Researcher Education 220
Jane Andrews, Richard Fay, and Ross White

List of Contributors 234
Index 238

FOREWORD

Plurilingualism in Teaching and Learning—Productive Tension in Heteroglossia

The past two decades have witnessed a plurilingual and dynamic turn in applied linguistics. This turn is gaining increasing momentum as poststructuralism is given a new twist by new materiality ontologies and assemblage theory (Clark, 1997; Cowley, 2006; de Landa, 2006; Thibault, 1997) culminating in the recent Distributed Language View (DLV) (Thibault, 2011) and post-humanist applied linguistics, shifting the researcher's focus from the speech/language of the individual and the community to distributed and spatial repertoires (Canagarajah, 2017; Makoni & Pennycook, 2007; Otsuji & Pennycook, 2010; Pennycook, 2016). The DLV emphasises distributed, dynamic repertoires (including both human bodies and non-human objects and artifacts) and disrupts the monolithic view of language as stable, bounded codes (e.g. named languages). Plurilingualism and translanguaging (García & Li, 2014) thus have the potential to disrupt the hierarchy of named languages. However, the notion of plurilingualism is often also exploited by neoliberalist discourses to uncritically celebrate and promote a kind of elite/non-egalitarian multi/plurilingualism dominated by English or other sociopolitically/socioeconomically powerful languages (Kubota, 2014; Lin, 2015). Neoliberalist discourses now demand that the elites of the world will *also* need English in order to participate in a globalised, neoliberalist economy. Multi/plurilingualism then often becomes understood as another language or languages plus English—i.e., an 'English plus' multi/plurilingualism (García & Lin, forthcoming). As the editors of this volume point out, educational policy still privileges 'elite' foreign language learning over maintenance and development of home languages and literacies (Choi and Ollerhead, this volume). Kubota (2014) also makes a strong critique of the trans-, multi-, pluri-, super-diversity discourses pointing out that these theoretical discourses often have little to offer when it comes to addressing issues of inequalities facing linguistic minorities in education and society.

That said, I am still optimistic that the plurilingual and translanguaging turn does have something important to offer, as we can gain insights from the multifarious ways in which the authors of the articles collected in this volume have critically engaged with these complex issues in each of their diverse contexts. What unifies them is the commitment to a candid and critical discussion of how to serve students' best interests amidst all these new competing policy discourses and institutional regimes. Their critical discussions remind me of Hilary Janks' critical exploration of how one might overcome the 'access paradox', which says that providing students with access to the dominant codes perpetuates the domination of these codes in society (Janks, 2004). Janks' (2010) critical literacy synthesis approach proposes that different ways of doing critical literacy follow from different ways of conceptualising the relationship between language and power by foregrounding one or other of the four key orientations: **domination**, **access**, **diversity** and **design**. These four orientations to critical literacy are interdependent and should be integrated in practice. It has very important implications for the application of genre theory (or other kinds of pedagogy) geared towards providing access to the dominant linguistic/academic conventions, styles, registers in education or society:

> Genre theory without creativity runs the risk of reifying existing genres; deconstruction without reconstruction or design reduces human agency; diversity without access ghettoises students. Domination without difference and diversity loses the ruptures that produce contestations and change.... We need to find ways of holding all of these elements in *productive tension* to achieve what is a shared goal of all critical literacy work: equity and social justice. We need to weave them together in complex moves from deconstruction to reconstruction to deconstruction, from access to deconstruction to redesign, from diversity to deconstruction to new forms of access. These different moves need to control and balance one another.
> (Janks, 2010, p. 27; italics added)

What I'd like to highlight is Janks' use of 'productive tension'. The plurilingual, dynamic turn has highlighted tension as an inescapable condition of our existence now. We need to provide students with access to the powerful dominant 'named languages' or genres/conventions through plurilingual pedagogies (Lin, 2013; Lin & Lo, 2017; Lin & He, 2017) and yet we also need to raise students' critical awareness of the domination of these (institutionally stabilised) conventions, registers and named languages while encouraging and validating students' diverse, creative translanguaging acts in the direction of expanding their distributed, emplaced repertoires (Turner & Lin, forthcoming). It is a difficult yet interesting time because there is no easy stipulation of pedagogies but only a constant, reflexive juggling with all these different (competing) goals/orientations in a kind of productive tension—a kind of tension-filled heteroglossia in the full Bakhtinian sense (Bailey, 2012).

Angel M. Y. Lin
The University of Hong Kong

References

Bailey, B. (2012). Heteroglossia. In M. Martin-Jones, A. Blackledge, & A. Creese (Eds.), *The Routledge handbook of multilingualism* (pp. 499–507). London, UK: Routledge.

Canagarajah, S. A. (2017). *The smartest person in the room is the room: Emplacement as language competence*. Keynote speech delivered in the Annual Conference of the American Association for Applied Linguistics (AAAL), 18–21 March 2017, Portland, OR.

Clark, A. (1997). *Being there: Putting brain, body, and world together again*. Cambridge, MA: MIT Press.

Cowley, S. J. (2006). Language and biosemiosis: A necessary unity? *Semiotica, 162* (1/4), 417–444.

De Landa, M. (2006). *A new philosophy of society: Assemblage theory and social complexity*. London, UK: Continuum.

García, O., & Li, W. (2014). *Translanguaging: Language, bilingualism and education*. Basingstoke, UK: Palgrave.

García, O., & Lin, A. M. Y. (forthcoming). English and multilingualism: A contested history. To appear in P. Seargeant (Ed.), *Routledge handbook of English language studies*. London, UK: Routledge.

Janks, H. (2004). The access paradox. *English in Australia, 139*(1), 33–42.

Janks, H. (2010). *Literacy and power*. New York: Routledge.

Kubota, R. (2014). The multi/plural turn, postcolonial theory, and neoliberal multiculturalism: Complicities and implications for applied linguistics. *Applied Linguistics, 37*(4), 474–494.

Lin, A. M. Y. (2013). Towards paradigmatic change in TESOL methodologies: Building plurilingual pedagogies from the ground up. *TESOL Quarterly, 47*(3), 521–545.

Lin, A. M. Y. (2015). Egalitarian bi/multilingualism and trans-semiotizing in a global world. In W. E. Wright, S. Boun, & O. García (Eds.), *The handbook of bilingual and multilingual education* (pp. 19–37). Chichester, UK: Wiley Blackwell.

Lin, A. M. Y., & He, P. (2017). Translanguaging as dynamic activity flows in CLIL Classrooms. *Journal of Language, Identity and Education, 16*(4), 228–244.

Lin, A. M. Y., & Lo, Y. Y. (2017) Trans/languaging and the triadic dialogue in Content and Language Integrated Learning (CLIL) Classrooms. *Language and Education, 31*(1): 26–45.

Makoni, S. and Pennycook, A. (2007). *Disinventing and Reconstituting Languages*. Clevedon, UK: Multilingual Matters.

Otsuji, E. and Pennycook, A. (2010). Metrolingualism: Fixity, fluidity and language in flux. *International Journal of Multilingualism, 7*(3), 240–254.

Pennycook, A. (2016). Posthumanist applied linguistics. *Applied Linguistics*, amw016.

Thibault, P. J. (1997). *Re-reading Saussure: The dynamics of signs in social life*. London, UK: Routledge.

Thibault, P. J. (2011). First-order languaging dynamics and second-order language: The distributed language view. *Ecological Psychology*, *23*(3): 210–245.

Turner, M., & Lin, A. M. Y. (forthcoming). Translanguaging and named languages: Productive tension and desire. To appear in *International Journal of Bilingual Education and Bilingualism*.

PREFACE

The past three decades have seen monumental political and economic changes taking place around the world, resulting in a marked increase in cross cultural contact. Rapid increases in mobility and migration have given rise to a proliferation of terminologies to capture the cultural and linguistic integration that has ensued across communities on a large scale, including terms such as translanguaging (García, 2009), code-meshing (Canagarajah, 2006) polylingualism (Jørgensen, 2008), third spaces (Gutierrez, 2008) and metrolingualism (Otsuji & Pennycook, 2010). This profusion of terms calls for a reconceptualisation of language as system to one of language as an inherently social practice, in which grammars are emergent, performative, mixed and distinctly multimodal (Pennycook, 2012).

The term "plurilingualism" emerged from the Common European Framework of Reference for Language Learning and Teaching (Council of Europe, 2001), which characterised plurilingual competence as the ability to use several different languages for communication. Within this view, people are seen as social actors who have varying degrees of proficiency across a number of languages. These competencies do not sit discretely alongside each other. Instead, together they form a "composite" repertoire of competencies (Coste, Moore & Zarate, 2009, p. 10) that people can draw upon during communication. Plurilingualism has thus come to be seen by most language educators, policy makers, curriculum designers and learners as an essential feature of communities and classrooms.

Plurilingualism in Teaching and Learning: Complexities across Contexts assembles a rich and diverse range of research studies on the role of plurilingualism across a wide variety of teaching and learning settings. It addresses a range of mainstream and specialised contexts, examining the position of learners and teachers as users of plurilingual repertoires, and the opportunities and challenges posed by the different policies, teaching practices, training and resourcing in these environments.

While this book illuminates the possibilities and affordances of plurilingual education, it also makes space for both researchers and educators to clarify and critically reflect upon plurilingual endeavors in their specific contexts. This book is not about advocating for any one position, or 'stance'. It is also not about telling practitioners what to do but about interrogating the possibilities and constraints of a 'plurilingual stance' in different contexts. By seeing how researchers tease out and analyse the complex dynamics that crisscross particular teaching and learning settings around the world, such as the interactions between policy, practices, resources and the positions of different stakeholder groups, the book also encourages educators to analyse their own practices and spaces.

The book is divided into four sections: 1) Language-in-education policies; 2) Plurilingual student repertoires; 3) Plurilingual classroom practices and teacher perspectives and 4) Plurilingualism in higher education contexts.

In each of the 12 chapters, authors will take a close look into the possibilities and constraints in taking up a plurilingual stance within the unique dynamics that constitute particular spaces of teaching and learning. Factors of influence include policies, histories, discourses, pedagogies, practices, resources, and linguistic and cultural repertoires. Through a critical analysis of the context, each contributor will propose pedagogical possibilities s/he thinks are most appropriate for the setting.

The aim of the book is to help researchers, teacher trainers and teachers to think more deeply, rigorously and critically about their orientations, beliefs, values and approaches to language teaching and learning. In drawing out the complex dynamics that assemble in particular teaching and learning settings, we believe teachers will gain clearer insight into the dynamics that flow in their teaching spaces so that they may "develop the knowledge and skill, attitude, and autonomy necessary to construct their own context-sensitive pedagogic knowledge" (Kumaravadivelu, 2001, p. 541). Trendy and new terms are moving at a rapid pace in multilingual studies. This book aims to provide a reflective punctuation point or pause in thinking through the ideas before translating them into practice.

Few books on plurilingualism cover as comprehensive and extensive coverage of the topic. The chapters in this book consider both language and literacy education. While the majority of the chapters will focus on English language learning in different contexts, we also include studies where English is used as a vehicle for teaching content. Furthermore, chapters in this book will address a range of educational contexts such as mainstream and intensive English language settings at different stages of education, including primary, secondary, vocational and tertiary levels. In addition, we give focus to contexts of education which are often sidelined in contemporary discussion of plurilingualism, including de-colonised settings, developing nations, marginalised learners in developed settings.

Most of the chapters in this volume provide a finely grained description of plurilingual interaction, in sites presented as micro-systems embedded within the broader, ideological macro-context of language policy and planning. In this way, the book provides an invaluable contribution to the study of cultural and linguistic diversity in teaching and learning contexts around the globe, providing situated accounts of linguistic, social, political and pedagogical practice.

References

Canagarajah, S. (2006). Towards a writing pedagogy of shuttling between languages: Learning from multilingual writers. *College English, 68*, 589–604.
Coste, D., Moore, D., & Zarate, G. (2009). *Plurilingual and pluricultural competence.* Strasbourg, France: Council of Europe. Retrieved from www.coe.int/t/dg4/linguistic/publications_en.asp?toprint=yes&-40
Council of Europe. (2001).*Common European Framework of Reference for Languages: Learning, teaching, assessment.* Cambridge, UK: Cambridge University Press.
García, O. (2009). *Bilingual education in the 21st century: A global perspective.* Malden, MA: Blackwell.
Guiterrez, K. (2008). Developing a sociocritical literacy in the third space. *Reading Research Quarterly, 43*, 148–164.
Jørgensen, J. N. (2008). Polylingual languaging around and among children and adolescents. *International Journal of Multilingualism, 5*(3), 161–176.
Kumaravadivelu, B. (2001). Toward a post-method pedagogy. *TESOL Quarterly, 35*, 537–560.
Otsuji, E., & Pennycook, A. (2010). Metrolingualism: Fixity, fluidity and language in flux, *International Journal of Multilingualism, 7*(3), 240–54.
Pennycook, A. (2012). *Language and Mobility: Unexpected Places.* Bristol, UK: Multilingual Matters.

1
INTRODUCTION

Sue Ollerhead, Julie Choi, and Mei French

Plurilingualism in Language Studies

Since the beginning of the twenty-first century, the impact of globalisation and new technologies has seen previously isolated linguistic groups come into increasing contact with each other. This has led applied linguists concerned with linguistic diversity and multilingualism to shift away from associating the term *multilingual* with an "enumerative strategy of counting languages and romanticising a plurality based on these putative language counts" (Makoni & Pennycook, 2007, p. 16). Instead of thinking about languages in additive, discrete systems where we have distinct cognitive compartments for separate languages with different competencies for each (see de Jong, 2011; Makoni & Pennycook, 2007 on the 'collateral damage' such embedded notions of language may be perpetrating), languages are thought of as always in contact with and mutually influencing each other, always open to renegotiation and reconstruction, and as mobile resources that are appropriated by people for their purposes (Canagarajah, 2013, pp. 6–7). Thus, increasingly, researchers do not start with languages in language studies but with people, *translingual practices*, places and spaces where communication transcends both "individual languages" and words, thus involving "diverse semiotic resources and ecological affordances" (Canagarajah, 2013, p. 6). This proliferation of new ways of conceptualising linguistic diversity has resulted in the Council of Europe and scholars such as Moore (2006) and Piccardo (2013) drawing a distinction between the terms "multilingualism" and "plurilingualism". While the term "multilingualism" denotes several different languages co-existing in a given physical location or social context, the term "plurilingualism" accounts for the ways in which individuals' linguistic repertoires overlap and intersect and develop in different ways with respect to languages, dialects and registers. Thus, while multilingualism is "the study of *societal contact*", plurilingualism allows us to study the *individual's* repertoires and agency in several languages (Moore & Gajo, 2009, p. 138).

Such a shift has resulted in an explosion of new terminologies that help us to think about language practices in more fluid ways. García & Li Wei (2014) describe *translanguaging* as "the enaction of language practices that use different features that had previously moved independently constrained by different histories, but that now are experienced against each other in speakers' interactions as one *new* whole" (p. 22). Li Wei (2015) also describes translanguaging as "the strategic deployment of multiple semiotic resources, e.g. languages, modalities, sensory cues, to create a socio-interactional space for learning and understanding, knowledge construction and identity negotiation" (p. 32). Jørgensen, Karrebæk, Madsen & Møller (2011) use the term *polylanguaging* to illustrate the [interactional] use of features associated with different "languages", even when speakers know only a few features associated with (some of) these "languages" (p. 33). Rather than assuming connections between language and culture, ethnicity, nationality or geography, *metrolingualism*, as coined by Otsuji and Pennycook (2010), "seeks to explore how such relations are produced, resisted, defied or rearranged" (p. 246). Blackledge and Creese (2010) draw on Bakhtinian notions such as *heteroglossia*, *polyphony*, *double-voicedness*, *dialogue*, and *multivocality* to reflect the notion of simultaneity of multiple meanings, intentions, personalities and consciousness and the traces of a speaker's past, the present context and future desires that are embedded within utterances. Lin (2013) pushes for 'plurilingual pedagogies' in language teaching and learning, "fostering plurilingual competences[,] . . . creating and affirming plurlingual identities and subjectivities" (p. 540). While similar but different in their own ways, scholars in this area of language studies take the overall stance of rejecting notions of language as "the co-existence of multiple linguistic systems [as] discrete, ahistorical, and relatively self-contained" (Bailey, 2012, p. 500). The focus in multilingual studies, as we understand it, now inherently starts with a polyphonic lens that seeks to capture the simultaneity of multiple language use, the inclusion of various semiotic resources, and the socio-political/historical and negotiation processes that shape utterances in a certain point in time and space. "Polycentricity", the crisscrossing of multiple meanings but also multiple belongings (Blommaert, 2005, p. 75) is inherently present in today's studies.

García (in García and Sylvan, 2011) argues that today's multilingual and multicultural classrooms are defined by a "plurality" of language practices. She eschews the notion of pedagogies that cater for specific language groups, instead advocating for a focus on the singularity of individual students within a classroom characterised by multiple linguistic practices. To this end, she espouses Makoni & Pennycook's (2007) term "singularization of plurality—that is, a focus on the individual differences in the discursive regimes we call languages" (p. 386). Certainly, with rising global mobility of many types, the focus for researchers and educators is turning increasingly to extreme linguistic heterogeneity brought about by new immigration patterns into settings previously constructed as monolingual or as having relatively homogeneous multilingual populations.

Multilingualism and Literacy

Within prevailing teaching practices in many mainstream educational teaching settings, additional language learners experience serious challenges in achieving high literacy levels and literacy engagement (August & Hakuta, 1998; Collier, 1992; Cummins, 2000). In Canada, Ashworth (2000) noted that despite multiculturalism being promoted in many educational systems, bilingual children were gradually becoming more at risk of losing their home language rather than developing and maintaining it alongside English or French. This is despite the fact that successive empirical studies over the past century have found that literacy development in two or more languages provides not only linguistic benefits, but also cognitive and social advantages for bilingual/multilingual students (Cummins & Early, 2011; García, Bartlett, & Kleifgen, 2007). Studies have also found that achievement in first language literacy is a key indicator of success in academic literacy in the second language, and that home language maintenance supports second language and academic development (Thomas & Collier, 1997). However, educational policy still privileges 'elite' foreign language learning over maintenance and development of home languages and literacies. In Australia, Eisenchlas, Schalley and Guillemin (2015) state that "the more multilingual Australian society has become, the more assimilationist the policies and the more monolingual the orientation of the society politicians envisage and pursue" (p. 170). In relation to literacy education, there are critiques of literacy education being limited to English monolingual assumptions, and marginalising multilinguals and multilingualism (see Coleman, 2012; Cross, 2011, 2012; Lo Bianco, 2002). According to García (2009), schools need "to recognise the multiple language practices that heterogeneous populations increasingly bring and which integrated schooling, more than any other context", has the potential to liberate (p. 157). To date, however, these research findings have done little to influence multilingual education policy and practice.

In recent years, multilingual literacy researchers have proposed a suite of principles they have found to enhance students' multilingual literacy proficiency. We now understand that bilingual students' cultural knowledge and linguistic abilities are vital for enabling them to engage with academic tasks across the curriculum; teaching practices that draw upon students' identities will lead to their investment in literacy learning; and collaboration between schools and parents from culturally and linguistically diverse backgrounds offers a rich resource for literacy development (see Cummins, 2006; Helot & Young 2002; Hornberger & Link, 2012; Molyneux, 2009). As de Jong and Freeman Field (2010) discuss, teaching strategies from bilingual settings can be adapted to support students in linguistically heterogeneous classrooms. Methodologies associated with research into effective multilingual literacy practices include building upon students' funds of knowledge (Gonzalez, Moll, & Amanti, 2005), and the use of collective pedagogical inquiry frameworks that use teachers/school based researchers and university-based educators/researchers to work together to observe and document pedagogical strategies being made in particular contexts. The case studies serve to document the feasibility of using specific multilingual pedagogical strategies that use students' home languages as valuable resources for learning and teaching.

Theoretical Lenses

A number of theoretical lenses inform research into multilingual literacy practices. The concept of multiliteracies, introduced by the New London Group in 1996 and developed by numerous researchers such as Cope and Kalantzis (2000; 2009), Hull and Schultz (2001), and Pahl and Rowsell (2005), emphasises multimodality as a discerning feature, focusing on the multiple semiotic resources available to students involved in meaning making, including audio, visual, linguistic, spatial and performative. This allows students to extend and adapt their literacy learning by responding to cultural and linguistic diversity and promoting the use of home languages within the classroom.

Another useful framework is that of post-structural theories of identity and the concepts of identity positioning (Toohey, 2000) and identity investment (Norton, 2000). McKinney and Norton (2008) propose that "foregrounding identity and the issues that this raises are central in responding critically to diversity in language and education" (McKinney & Norton, 2008, p.195). Drawing on the notion of identities as temporal, fluctuating, shaped by social context and coming about as a result of membership of specific communities, teaching strategies that harness students' funds of knowledge and draw upon their linguistic and social capital help students to develop a positive learning identity.

Complementing these theoretical frameworks are pedagogies such as the Literacy Engagement Framework (Cummins & Early, 2011), which emphasises engagement in literacy tasks as a necessary condition for literacy achievement. Reinforcing and affirming students' identity positions is crucial in this regard. Thus, activities such as identity texts, which include elements of creativity and cultural expression through multiple modes (e.g. art, drama, animation) allow students to articulate, shape and account for their identities in front of various audiences and engage in feedback and dialog which allows for intercultural sharing.

According to Ntelioglou, Fannin, Montanera, and Cummins (2014), classrooms that facilitate students' use of multiple languages through multimodal texts allow students to select their own multiple linguistic repertoires. In other words, they are able to make meaning through their own choice of medium. Such an approach, or "stance", cultivates learner autonomy, identity investment and literacy engagement (p. 12). When teachers open up instructional spaces for multilingual and multimodal forms of pedagogy, languages other than English are legitimised in the classroom and students' home languages and community connections become resources for learning. Thus, teachers play an important role in not only bringing these ideas to their classroom practices but how they weave the plurilingual into either resource-poor spaces or spaces that have a long-standing monolingual or mono-centric ideological structure, tradition or formal policy.

Literature in TESOL and language education is starting to show examples of teachers taking up a plurilingual stance. Before we turn to the kinds of comments we are beginning to see, we will clarify what *we* mean by teachers taking up a plurilingual stance.

What we Mean by a "Plurilingual Stance"

We base our understanding of what we mean by taking up a plurilingual stance by foregrounding it in Canagarajah's (2011, p.1) statement that, for multilinguals, languages are part of a repertoire that is accessed for their communicative purposes; languages are not discrete and separated, but form an integrated system for them; multilingual competence emerges out of local practices where multiple languages are negotiated for communication; competence doesn't consist of separate competencies for each language, but a multicompetence that functions symbiotically for the different languages in one's repertoire; and, for these reasons, proficiency for multilinguals is focused on repertoire building—i.e., developing abilities in the different functions served by different languages—rather than total mastery of each and every language.

We understand teachers taking up a plurilingual stance typically embody the following beliefs and understandings:

a) Successful learners of English are successful plurilingual learners and communicators, rather than pseudo native speakers.
b) All of a student's language knowledge is part of their single plurilingual repertoire, and languages are not siloed in their mind.
c) Understanding of plurilingual practices such as translanguaging, switching, mixing, translating as the norm.
d) Understanding that language competence is realised in its performance and practice, not as a set of knowledge inside a learner's head.

As a consequence of these ways of thinking about language then, a teacher with a plurilingual stance would seek ways to:

e) acknowledge multilinguality of students and society as something that is both normal and valued as an achievement;
f) activate students' existing knowledge of and in the languages that they know;
g) link new knowledge to that existing knowledge;

h) link language learning and literacy skill to existing knowledge of language and literacy in the full range of languages possessed by learners;
i) use a range of students' plurilingual resources and practices in the classroom to support learning through various means including interaction, individual tasks and resources;
j) build on students' plurilingual repertoires so that these repertoires expand and mature as the students do.

Teachers Taking up a "Plurilingual Stance"

In English-medium countries such as the United States, Canada, the United Kingdom and Australia, increased migration flows have resulted in English language learners (ELLs) enrolling in greater numbers than non-English language learners in some urban areas. Accordingly, a new focus has been placed upon the ways mainstream teachers are prepared to meet the language and literacy needs of ELLs. Existing research suggests that mainstream secondary school teachers feel inadequately prepared to cope with such learners (Gitlin, Buendia, Crosland & Doumbia, 2003; Reeves, 2006). Moreover, many mainstream teachers fail to identify with the practice of drawing upon students' home languages as a resource for language and literacy teaching. Much of this research has been conducted in the United States, and includes studies on teacher attitudes towards inclusion (Franson, 1999; Youngs & Youngs, 2001), curriculum changes (Reeves, 2006) and teacher training (Crandall & Christison, 2016; Hutchison & Hadjioannou, 2011). In Australia, research conducted by Hammond (2008) found that while teachers had predominantly favourable views on cultural and linguistic diversity, mainstream teachers had little confidence to incorporate multilingual pedagogies into their content teaching. To address this issue, Hammond (2014) calls for "more wide-ranging, theoretically robust accounts of teacher learning" to support EAL/D learners in particular (p. 530).

In a recent study into students' use of their plurilingual resources in an Australian high school, French (2015) interviewed teachers of a variety of school subjects on the place of students' home languages in school education. Many teachers were positively disposed towards students' plurilinguality as a resource for learning, but lacked strategies to engage this in the classroom. We include some of the teacher comments from the larger study to illustrate the complex influences and implications of a plurilingual stance.

The majority of teachers recognised the role of students' plurilingual repertoires as potential funds of knowledge. Mary (participants' names are pseudonyms), an IT teacher and member of school leadership, recognised home languages as a vehicle for recognising students' prior knowledge in the classroom. This is important to learning, because, she believed, "it's almost like an impossibility for anyone to learn without utilising what they already have". Likewise, Dennis, another IT teacher, saw home language as a useful tool in his classroom to remove barriers to learning. "It takes one barrier away and it makes them, gives them one less thing to worry about." Gerta, a teacher of Italian language, humanities and English, valued her students' plurilingual repertoires for learning: "Well really, we should be encouraging students to learn the best way that they can learn. So if that is the multilingual way, then that's what we should be encouraging." However, the counterpoint to this positive disposition was the lack of knowledge of how to support plurilingual repertoires in the classroom, also articulated by Gerta. "I think languages are so valuable but we don't, we don't use them as much as we should, so I don't know what the role should be." Comments such as these point us to the fact that, although teachers may take on a plurilingual stance, the curriculum they must work within, or the dominant practices of the institution, may not be set up to encourage or support such a stance.

At the same time as they espoused the value of students' plurilingual resources, teachers rued their inability to enact strategies to engage students' linguistic resources in the classroom. Mary showed a keen awareness of opportunities for students to draw on multilingual resources in her classroom, although she recognised implementing these strategies was not always as straightforward for other teachers as for herself. "Because I think a lot would just think it's too hard or I don't know how . . . I don't even know how, it's just trying to give that opportunity". With plurilingual teaching strategies outside of the expertise and experience of these teachers, some placed responsibility back onto the students. The difficulty for John, a physics and maths teacher and a speaker of Russian as his first language, was that he would not be able to assist his students if they chose to do this:

> I don't mind if one girl talks to another using a different language to help her understand. It's fine. It's perfectly fine and fine, but my problem is that it's like beyond my control. I cannot interfere or cannot influence this process. I don't mind if they do it, I am more than happy to accept this process. I don't say like, 'don't do it,' now, they can do this, fine. Well if they for example in addition to English physics book, they also read the same physics in Japanese to understand ideas better, then more than welcome. Problem is that I cannot do it myself.

In situations such as these, we might begin to think about the changing roles of teachers when students can draw on multiple resources to find the information they need. What is the job of the teacher in providing such resources, and how can the teacher assess the contribution of these resources to students' learning?

The questions of researchers in this field must mirror those of teachers. What is the role of students' home languages in the classroom? How can teachers engage these plurilingual resources? It is clear there is a place for more teacher education, knowledge, and support in helping teachers to think through what it means to take up certain positions in pedagogical terms (see also Ellis, 2013 on the need to acknowledge and value teachers' plurilingualism). Considering teachers are invariably dealing with learners from unequal social backgrounds, life trajectories and political circumstances, a 'critical' take, where explorations of assumptions, ideologies, values, authority, affect, and power that shape particular people in particular situations, needs to be at the center of teacher education. It is within this line of critical thinking that we take Kubota's (2014) following statement seriously into account.

The Problem with the Plurilingual Stance

While we are excited by the increasing studies on the trans-, multi-, poly-, and pluri-, as language teacher educators, we take heed of Kubota's (2014) critique of this 'multi/plural turn' where she argues that the multi/plural turn should not be embraced with unqualified optimism. She states:

> While notions such as hybridity, fluidity, and multiplicity are potentially liberating, they can obscure actual struggles and inequalities . . . Using the multi/plural frame of reference with insufficient critical reflection makes us complicit with a neoliberalism that exacerbates economic and educational gaps and with a neoliberal multiculturalism that evades racism and other injustices. (p. 17).

As we reflect on Kubota's comment in relation to language education and language teacher education, we are also reminded of examples from Cenoz's (2009) work in Basque multilingual education and other contexts involving minority languages that show translanguaging can be considered simultaneously as a threat to the survival of minority languages, or as an opportunity for their development. In the context of minority ethnic groups or groups with less social power, Wallace's (2013) argument that "the privileging of choice and freedom may not . . . work well for those who have not the cultural 'know-how' to play the system" (p. 232) is also an important factor to consider. This is illustrated in comments by teacher Gerta in French's study. She wondered:

> Would we be doing them a disservice by doing it in another language inside of the classroom? You know, if this is where they want to live and build a life, and that is the language that we speak, which is a downfall of Australia, that we only speak English, then are we doing them any justice by speaking another language there might not be any value in?

Key to the successful adoption of a plurilingual stance is understanding the complex socio-historical context in which students' language practices are formed and practiced. But we also must ask, do inevitable missteps due to gaps in teachers' understanding threaten the position of already vulnerable plurilingual students, or is it still more equitable for individual teachers to adopt such a stance even without full understanding of their linguistic setting?

As a language teacher educator, over the years I (Julie) have collected students' comments voiced in class while I observe my teachers in their teaching practicums. Adult learners have expressed that they appreciate teachers who allow them to use all of the resources they have available to them but, outside of their safe classrooms, they realise their resources are either not appreciated, accepted or not helping them to achieve their goals in crucial moments such as finding jobs. International students recognise there is a more welcoming attitude towards World English accents and pronunciations as they learn English in English medium countries. But they do not know how to deal with their own impatience with those they cannot understand nor what to do about the deeper desires that have been instilled in them that make them feel their pronunciation is shameful. Teachers who don't have much understanding of the politics behind certain dialects, varieties, registers and styles of particular languages and ways of dealing with sensitive cultural issues also run into trouble when asking their students to draw on words they know from their other languages to complete classroom tasks. I have seen heated classroom scenarios where students from Hong Kong, mainland China, Taiwan and who are Chinese residents of Korean descent, have had to work together while each of them disagreed passionately on the other's interpretation causing tension-filled silence and hostility in the classroom. In a high school setting, French and de Courcy (2016) note the implications of a curriculum and system that does not account for social and linguistic distinctions between users of Farsi, Dari and Hazaragi languages. The provision of 'home language' lessons in a single variety, Persian, is an example of educational policy that falsely homogenises the ethnic, linguistic, religious, academic and individual characteristics of students, advantaging some, but disadvantaging many. Blanket statements that usually have good intentions at their core, such as 'don't worry about XYZ' or 'be yourself', 'just be confident', or 'it doesn't matter if you get it wrong', ultimately cause more irritation and silence in learners, and are not always productive in helping learners to develop their 'whole self' in and outside of the classroom where real problems exist. Teachers' primary place of concern is understandably the context of classroom spaces. However, following Kubota, we believe "increased attention to places where real problems exist can make our professional activities more socially meaningful and transformative" (p. 18).

We are now asking questions such as, what do these explosions of terminologies and ideas in the 'multi/plural turn' mean in terms of pedagogy and teacher and learner practices in and out of spaces of language teaching and learning? To what extent can/should teachers take up a plurilingual stance? Is it all or nothing, or is a partial adoption still of value? What are the strengths and weaknesses, threats and opportunities, possibilities and constraints in taking up a plurilingual stance in teachers' local teaching spaces where politics, policies, curriculums, cultural discourses and practices, ideologies and desires differ? What alternative views, knowledge, and approaches might come to light if we pay more serious attention to, as Kubota suggests, "asymmetrical relations of power and inequalities that privilege or stigmatise individuals and groups due to their plurilingualism, cosmopolitanism, and hybridity on the one hand, or their monolingualism and monoculturalism on the other" (p. 17)? What new or different possibilities, constraints, or consequences emerge when we critically explore the unique *assemblages*, "the literal bringing together of a range of heterogeneous elements in different modalities to offer different perspectives on a phenomenon" (Denshire & Lee, 2013, p. 221), that constitute different spaces of language teaching and learning? And what might our findings tell us about the kinds of skills, knowledge, and understandings teachers need in continuing to teach in increasingly heterogeneous but unequal and uncertain times? Importantly, we are not only asking these questions, but by examining pockets of current plurilingual practices, we propose strategies that can be adopted by teachers.

About the Book

The chapters in this book provide teachers and teacher educators a close look into the possibilities and constraints in taking up a plurilingual stance within the unique dynamics that constitute particular spaces of teaching and learning (i.e. policies, histories, discourses, pedagogies, practices, linguistic and cultural repertoires, etc.). A range of contexts are addressed, with mainstream curriculum to specialised settings such as EAL, CLIL or community language classrooms; students ranging from early childhood to adult learners as well as pre-service teaching courses; groups with shared language backgrounds through to highly heterogeneous linguistic mixes; and settings where teachers have different relationships with policy, from highly regulated to subversive practice. Through a critical analysis of the context, each contributor will propose pedagogical possibilities s/he thinks is most appropriate for the setting. The chapters will end with recommendations on the kinds of skills, knowledge and understandings that are necessary for teachers in the respective learning area (e.g., language teaching, Literacy, CLIL).

The aim of the book is to help teachers to think more deeply, rigorously and critically about their orientations, beliefs, values and approaches to language teaching and learning. In drawing out the complex dynamics that assemble in particular teaching and learning settings, we believe teachers will gain clearer insight into the dynamics that flow in their teaching spaces so that they may "develop the knowledge and skill, attitude, and autonomy necessary to construct their own context-sensitive pedagogic knowledge" (Kumaravadivelu, 2001, p. 541). Trendy and new terms are moving at a rapid pace in multilingual studies. This book aims to provide a reflective punctuation point or pause in thinking through the ideas before translating them into practice.

The majority of the chapters will focus on English language learning in different contexts, but we also include studies where English is not the main focus but where English is used as a vehicle for teaching content. Most books on multilingualism overlook content focused contexts, neglecting the significant proportion of teachers whose daily work is being reshaped by increasing plurilinguality of students and the multilingual world for which teachers prepare them.

By showing readers (whom we assume will be mostly teachers and students interested in multilingual educational studies) how a rich and insightful analysis is done, teachers will gain direct insight into how to examine their own beliefs and practices, and will be able to explore what language ideologies sit at the heart of their contexts and practices.

Chapter Organisation

This edited volume comprises 12 chapters and casts a wide lens on plurilingual learning and teaching practices in diverse contexts. Among the authors are researchers who are well established in the field, as well as emerging scholars whose research is contemporary and topical. Collectively, the chapters examine key issues related to plurilingual approaches and resources in varied locations around the globe, ranging from highly urbanised to rural settings, from formal education to out of school contexts, and within policy environments that serve to either reinforce plurilingual approaches or to constrain them. The chapters are divided into four broad themes: 1) Plurilingual language-in-education policies 2) Plurilingual student repertoires 3) Plurilingual classroom practices and teacher perspectives and 4) Plurilingualism in higher education contexts.

Part 1 begins with predominant issues of language-in-education policies and the ways in which they address plurilingual teaching and learning. Joseph Lo Bianco begins the discussion with a helpful contextualisation of the ways in which globalisation and migration have forced language policies that have previously privileged official, dominant languages to "make space" for sub-national languages. He provides a taxonomy of categories of pluralism in language education, covering a broad range of international settings from North America, Europe, Australia, Pacific Island nationals and Southeast Asia, and makes a strong case for those involved in plurilingual teaching and learning to be viewed as legitimate shapers of language policy.

With Chapter 3, Priscilla Cruz and Ahmar Mahboob move the discussion to the Philippines, where they offer a critical analysis of the country's language policy shift towards mother-tongue based multilingual education (MTB-MLE). Drawing on the perspectives of a range of stakeholders, the chapter discusses the ways in which MTBL-MLE helps to develop and maintain the use of local languages in school settings, where teachers use them to address classroom content rather than merely for regulative and interpersonal purposes.

Rebecca Hetherington's Chapter 4 makes a valuable contribution to the literature on Australian language in education policy, which has a crucial role to play in the maintenance and revival of indigenous languages. In her analysis,

Hetherington draws on in-depth interviews with indigenous Australian community members, arguing that it is their views, needs and interests that should be foregrounded in the shaping of language policies that affect them and their communities.

Part 2 of the volume narrows the lens slightly from the broad-picture policy context to more situated contexts of plurilingual student repertoires, focusing on students' access to what Angel Lin (2015) refers to as "trans-semiotic" resources, including multiliteracies and digital technologies. The first study comes in Chapter 5, by Emi Otsuji and Alastair Pennycook, who explore the metrolingual practices of students at two tertiary institutions in Tokyo and Sydney. The authors provide accounts of both their out-of-class and in-class language use, arguing that focusing too narrowly on translingual educational practices may cause us to overlook the myriad, fluid and creative ways in which students access semiotic resources across multiple digital and face-to face contexts.

The second study, by Ofelia García, Laura Ascenzi-Moreno and Sara Vogel in Chapter 6, reinforces the semiotic potential of digital technologies by providing an account of how a sixth-grade student from China makes creative use of online tools to engage more meaningfully in a New York language arts classroom community. Their analysis of the student's fluid movement between English and Chinese, as well as between translation software, online search tools and spoken and written modes, makes a case for the ways in which "digital translanguaging" can enrich the ways in which students and teachers interact with one another.

Multimodal student repertoires are also the focus of Chapter 7, albeit in a far more rural setting. In this study, Brendan Rigby explores the potential of participatory visual research methodologies to research the literacy practices of children in northern Ghana who do not have access to mainstream schooling. Rigby suggests that the ways in which Ghanaian children document their myriad literacy practices through the lens of a camera, including embodiment, gesture and performance, provide valuable data on which to build culturally responsive literacy pedagogies and policies.

Part 3 directs our attention to classroom practices and the perspectives of teachers, providing another range of contexts from Australia, South Africa, Canada and New Zealand. Beginning with Chapter 8, Sue Ollerhead, Mastin Prinsloo and Lara-Stephanie Krause collaborate to compare the ways in which translingual innovation is taken up in two very different contexts: South African township schooling, where the majority of children speak languages other than English yet are taught and tested in English, and Australian urban schooling, where newly arrived students are immersed in English language instruction to prepare them rapidly for mainstream schooling. By carrying out a contrastive analysis between two very different sites, the authors make a case for plurilingual pedagogies to be viewed as "placed resources", and for teachers working in such sites to view their work as occurring within "contact zones", where cultures come together in social spaces characterised by unequal power relationships.

In Chapter 9, Enrico Piccardo and Angelica Galante move the focus on teacher perspectives to North America, where plurilingual approaches are embraced in theory, yet remain challenging to implement in school classrooms. In this chapter, the authors advocate for plurilingual pedagogies that appeal to authentic and personal learning experiences for students. As an example, they illustrate how the dramatic arts can facilitate learners' semiotic agency, through the use of meaningful language development through interactional and situational authenticity.

Teachers are also the focus of Brian Davy and Mei French's Chapter 10, which examines teachers' responses to student plurilingualism in two culturally and linguistically diverse schools, in New Zealand and Australia. Documenting a range of teacher responses to their students' plurilingual practices, Davy and French conclude that in order for teachers to harness their students' multilingual resources effectively, they need to be cognizant of the numerous and often contradictory factors students face in negotiating their plurilingualism.

Part 4 concludes this volume with a collection of perspectives related to plurilingualism in higher education contexts, including cases from Timor-Leste and South Africa. To begin with, Trent Newman explores in Chapter 11 the strategic ways in which Timorese university lecturers translate and explain key disciplinary terms to their students. Drawing upon research conducted in three Timorese higher education institutions, Newman shows how the plurilingual practices of lecturers are closely aligned with their conceptualisations of workplace language use.

In Chapter 12, Monica Hendricks and Ntombekhaya Fulani move the discussion to the higher education context of South Africa, in which the issue of language, specifically as the medium of instruction, has played a significant role in recent student protests calling for institutional and cultural reform at South African universities. In this study, the authors examine the ways in which university lecturers shift their language practices between English and isiXhosa in both oral and written modes in a teacher education program. In doing so, they illustrate how translanguaging can be both pedagogically and politically transformative: Not only does it serve to increase bilingual students' access to epistemic knowledge, but it also acts to disrupt the current hegemonic position of English in South African tertiary education.

Richard Fay, Jane Andrews and Ross White conclude the volume with Chapter 13, by examining the ways in which "linguistic preparation" and a "translingual mindset" can contribute to the field of researcher education. The authors make a strong case for foregrounding the role of language in researcher education and praxis across diverse disciplines, not only those that are language-oriented. They point to the potential of translanguaging and translingual insights to offer valuable insights into "researching multilingually" in linguistically diverse contexts, thereby informing and shaping all aspects of the research process, from design to literature review to fieldwork, analysis and presentation of results.

Across the diversity of contexts represented in these chapters, a common thread is the clear portrayal of plurilingualism as an individual's repertoire of connected linguistic resources. We see that learners apply these plurilingual resources strategically in engaging with education, whether language learning, content learning, or negotiating the structures of schooling. In engaging with these chapters, we hope that our readers, be they students, teachers, researchers (or perhaps all of the above) will make connections between the diverse contexts, plurilingual practices and responses presented therein, and their own practice. Readers may take a new perspective in considering ways in which plurilingualism shapes student experience, teacher practice, institutional approaches and policy across schooling and higher education. The data and analytical perspectives of these studies can guide and stimulate teachers to embrace the challenge of critically and creatively building on the plurilingual repertoires of their students. There are many possible layers of response to this challenge. Educators can seek out and acknowledge plurilingual identities and ways of learning in their students. Teachers and teacher educators can build on students' personal, social and electronic plurilingual practices in teaching practice, and from this develop pedagogies that engage plurilingual resources in responsive and enriching ways. The role of plurilingual learners and their teachers can yet come to the fore in shaping policy that elevates plurilingualism to both an end and a means of education. There is ambition in these goals, but they are very firmly grounded in the everyday, yet far from ordinary, experience of plurilingual learners.

References

August, D., & Hakuta, K. (Eds.). (1998). *Educating language-minority children*. Washington: National Research Council, Institute of Medicine, National Academy Press.

Ashworth, M. (2000). *Effective teachers, effective schools: Second-language teaching in Australia, Canada, England and the United States*. Toronto, ON: Pippin Publishers.

Bailey, B. (2012). Heteroglossia. In M. Martin-Jones, A. Blackledge & A. Creese (Eds.), *The Routledge handbook of multilingualism* (pp. 499–507). London, UK: Routledge.

Blackledge, A., & Creese, A. (2010). *Multilingualism: A critical perspective*. New York: Continuum.

Blommaert, J. (2005). *Discourse: A critical introduction*. Cambridge: University Press.

Canagarajah, S. (2011). Translanguaging in the classroom: Emerging issues for research and pedagogy. *Applied Linguistics Review, 2*, 1–28.

Canagarajah, S. (2013). *Translingual practice: Global Englishes and cosmopolitan relations*. New York: Routledge.

Cenoz, J. (2009). *Towards multilingual education: Basque educational research from an international perspective*. Bristol, UK: Multilingual Matters.

Coleman, J. (2012). The ESL teacher as productive pedagogical mentor. *TESOL in Context, Special Edition S3*. Retrieved from www.tesol.org.au/files/files/253_jackie_coleman.pdf

Collier, V. P. (1992). A synthesis of studies examining long-term language minority student data on academic achievement. *Bilingual Research Journal, 16*, 187–212.

Cope B., & Kalantzis, M. (Eds.). (2000). The 'what' of literacies: Literacies as multimodal designs for meaning. *Literacy learning and the design of school futures*, (pp. 171–321). London, UK: Routledge.

Cope, B., & Kalantzis, M. (2009). Multiliteracies: New literacies, new learning. *Pedagogies International Journal*, *4*, 164–195.

Crandall, J., & Christison, M. (2016). An overview of research in English language education and professional development. In J. Crandall & M. Christison (Eds.), *Teacher education and professional development in TESOL* (pp. 3–34). New York: Routledge.

Cross, R. (2011). Troubling literacy: Monolingual assumptions, multilingual contexts, and language teacher expertise. *Teachers and Teaching*, *17*(4), 467–478.

Cross, R. (2012). Creative in finding creativity in the curriculum: The CLIL second language classroom. *Australian Educational Researcher*, *39*(4), 431–445.

Cummins, J. (2000). *Language, Power and Pedagogy: Bilingual Children in the Crossfire*. Clevedon, UK: Multilingual Matters.

Cummins, J. (2006). Identity texts: The imaginative construction of self through multiliteracies pedagogy. In O. García, T. Skutnabb-Kangas & M. Toress-Guzman (Eds.), *Imagining multilingual schools: Languages in education and globalization* (pp. 51–68). Clevedon, UK: Multilingual Matters.

Cummins, J., & Early, M. (Eds.). (2011). *Identity texts: The collaborative creation of power in multilingual schools*. Stoke-on-Trent, UK: Trentham Books.

de Jong, E. (2011). *Foundations for multilingualism in education: From principles to practice*. Philadelphia, PA: Caslon.

de Jong, E., & Freeman Field, R. (2010). Bilingual approaches. In C. Leung & A. Creese (Eds.), *English as an additional language: A reader for teachers working with linguistic minority pupils* (pp. 108–122). London, UK: Sage.

Denshire, S., & Lee, A. (2013). Conceptualizing autoethnography as assemblage: Accounts of occupational therapy practice. *International Journal of Qualitative Methods*, *12*, 221–236.

Eisenchlas, S., Schalley, A., & Guillemin, D. (2015). Multilingualism and literacy: Attitudes and policies, *International Journal of Multilingualism*, *12*(2), 151–161.

Ellis, E. (2013). The ESL teacher as plurilingual: An Australian perspective. *TESOL Quarterly*, *47*(3), 446–471.

Franson, C. (1999). Mainstreaming learners of English as an additional language: The class teachers. *Language, Culture and Curriculum*, *12*(1), 59–71.

French, M. (2015). Students' multilingual resources and policy-in-action: An Australian case study. *Language and Education*, 298–316. doi: 10.1080/09500782.2015.1114628

French, M., & de Courcy, M. (2016). A place for students' multilingual resources in an Australian high school. In C. Snowden & S. Nichols (Eds.), *Languages and Literacies as Mobile and Placed Resources* (pp. 153–169). Oxford, UK: Routledge.

García, O. (2009). *Bilingual education in the 21st century: A global perspective*. Malden, MA: Blackwell.

García, O., Bartlett, L., & Kleifgen, J. A. (2007). From biliteracy to pluriliteracies. In P. Auer & W. Li (Eds.), *Handbook of applied linguistics & multilingualism* (pp. 207–228). Berlin: Mouton de Gruyter.

García, O., & Li Wei. (2014). *Translanguaging: Language, bilingualism and education*. New York: Palgrave Macmillan.

García, O., & Sylvan, C. (2011). Pedagogies and practices in multilingual classrooms: Singularities in Pluralities. *Modern Language Journal*, *95*(iii), 385–400.

Gitlin, A., Buendia, E., Crosland, L., & Doumbia, F. (2003). The production of margin and center: Welcoming-unwelcoming of immigrant students. *American Educational Research Journal*, *40*(1), 91–122.
González, N., Moll, L., & Amanti, C. (2005). *Funds of knowledge: Theorizing practices in households, communities and classrooms*. Mahwah, NJ: Erlbaum.
Hammond, J. (2008). Intellectual challenge and ESL students: Implications of quality teaching initiatives. *Australian Journal of Language and Literacy*, *31*(2), 128–154.
Hammond, J. (2014). An Australian perspective on standards-based education, teacher knowledge, and students of English as an additional language, *TESOL Quarterly*, *48*(3), 507–532.
Helot, C., & Young, A. (2002). Bilingualism and language education in French primary schools: Why and how should migrant languages be valued? *International Journal of Bilingual Education and Bilingualism*, 96–112.
Hornberger, N. H., & Link, H. (2012). Translanguaging in today's classrooms: A biliteracy lens. *Theory into Practice*, *51*, 239–247.
Hull, G., & Schultz, K. (2001). *School's out!: Bridging out-of-school literacies with classroom practice*. New York: Teachers College Press.
Hutchinson, M., & Hadjioannou, X. (2011). Better serving the needs of limited English proficient (LEP) students in the mainstream classroom: Examining the impact of inquiry-based hybrid professional development program. *Teachers and Teaching: Theory and Practice*, *17*(1), 91–113.
Jørgensen, J., Karrebæk, M., Madsen, L., & Møller, J. (2011). Polylanguaging in superdiversity. *Diversities*, *13*(2), 23–38.
Kubota, R. (2014). The multi/plural turn, postcolonial theory, and neoliberal multiculturalism: Complicities and implications for applied linguistics. *Applied Linguistics*, *37*(4), 474–494. doi: 10.1093/applin/amu045
Kumaravadivelu, B. (2001). Toward a post-method pedagogy. *TESOL Quarterly*, *35*, 537–560.
Li Wei. (2015, February). New Chinglish: Bad, uncivilised and ugly, or creatively subversive? *Babel: The Language Magazine*, *10*. Retrieved from www.babelzine.com/2016-09-21-12-15-29/issue-guide.html
Lin, A. (2013). Toward paradigmatic change in TESOL methodologies: Building plurilingual pedagogies from the ground up. *TESOL Quarterly*, *47*(3), 521–545.
Lin, A. (2015). Egalitarian bi/multilingualism and trans-semiotizing in a global world. In W. Wright, S. Boun & O. García (Eds.), *The handbook of bilingual and multilingual education* (pp. 17–37). doi: 10.1002/9781118533406.ch2
Lo Bianco, J. (2002). ESL in a time of literacy: A challenge for policy and teaching. *TESOL in Context*, *12*(1), 3–9.
Makoni, S., & Pennycook, A. (2007). *Disinventing and reconstituting languages*. Clevedon, UK: Multilingual Matters.
McKinney, C., & Norton, B. (2008). Identity in language and literacy education. In B. S. F. Hult (Ed.), *The handbook of educational linguistics* (pp. 192–205). London, UK: Blackwell.
Molyneux, P. (2009). Education for biliteracy: Maximising the linguistic potential of diverse learners in Australia's primary schools. *Australian Journal of Language and Literacy*, *32*(2), 97–117.
Moore, D. (2006). *Plurilinguismes et École*. Collection LAL (Langues et Apprentissage de Langues). Postface de Daniel Coste. Paris: Didier.

Moore, D., & Gajo, L. (2009). Introduction—French voices on plurilingualism and pluriculturalism: Theory, significance and perspectives. *International Journal of Multilingualism*, *6*, 137–153. doi: 10.1080/14790710902846707

Norton, B. (2000). *Identity and language learning: Gender, ethnicity and educational change*. Harlow, UK: Pearson Education.

Ntelioglou, B., Fannin, J., Montanera, M., & Cummins, J. (2014). A multilingual and multimodal approach to literacy teaching and learning in urban education: A collaborative inquiry project in an inner city elementary school. *Frontiers in Psychology*, *18*(5). doi:10.3389/fpsyg.2014.00533

Otsuji, E., & Pennycook, A. (2010). Metrolingualism: Fixity, fluidity and language in flux, *International Journal of Multilingualism*, *7*(3), 240–54.

Pahl, K., & Rowsell, J. (2012). *Literacy and Education*. London, UK: Sage.

Piccardo, E. (2013). Plurilingualism and curriculum design: towards a synergic vision. *TESOL Quarterly*, *47*, 600–614. doi: 10.1002/tesq.110

Reeves, J. (2006). Secondary teacher attitudes toward including English-language learners in mainstream classrooms. *Journal of Educational Research*, *99*, 131–142.

Thomas, W., & Collier, V. (1997). School effectiveness for language minority students. *NCBE Resource Collection Series*, *9*. Washington, DC: National Clearinghouse for Bilingual Education.

Toohey, K. (2000). *Learning English at school: Identity, social relations and classroom practice*. Clevedon, UK: Multilingual Matters.

Wallace, C. (2013). *Literacy and the bilingual learner: texts and practices in London schools*. London, UK: Palgrave Macmillan.

Youngs, C. S., & Youngs, G. A. (2001). Predictors of mainstream teachers' attitudes towards ESL students. *TESOL Quarterly*, *35*, 97–120.

PART I
Plurilingual Language-in-Education Policies

2
PROVISION, POLICY AND REASONING

The Pluralisation of the Language Education Endeavor

Joseph Lo Bianco

An (Academic) Turn?

In 2014, two prominent publishers issued edited volumes with near identical titles (*The Multilingual Turn*, edited by Stephen May for Routledge, and *The Multilingual Turn in Languages Education*, edited by Jean Conteh and Gabriela Meier for Multilingual Matters). In that same year, Ryuko Kubota (2014) also identified a turn, a "multi/plural" shift in applied linguistics linked to postcolonial theory and neoliberal multiculturalism. This turn, however, is not unidirectional, and in Kubota's depiction, neither is it singular.

Nevertheless, this phase of newly productive thinking about language diversity imposes new demands on the discipline of applied linguistics in general, since much of this new writing deliberately sets out to challenge the discipline in various ways. Because applied linguistics is acknowledged as an autonomous field of inquiry, investigating language issues based in 'real world' situations (Brumfit, 1997), all this is healthy for the growth and sophistication of applied language studies. This chapter poses questions about the relationship between language education and provision, policy and reasoning. Although my discussion focuses largely on Australian experiences, some links are made to global consequences of these new ways to conceive multilingual communication environments. A key question explored in the chapter is how teachers and researchers can productively connect the insights, new directions and concepts of new disciplinary thinking in practical language education contexts, especially language policy.

This challenge is substantial if we take into account how circumscribed understandings of multilingualism are in practical reality. In most societies, a multilingual demography is discussed as a threat or at least a challenge to social cohesion. This is increasingly true in Denmark, Thailand, Turkey, Myanmar, and even in societies with long and established traditions and public rhetoric of recognition of multiculturalism, such as Australia and Canada (see Horst; Joshee, Peck, Thompson, Chareka & Sears; Özsoy & Bilgi; Lo Bianco & Slaughter; Wang, Hong & Schapper; in Lo Bianco & Bal, 2016). In other societies such as Brazil and South Africa, race and cultural affiliation, rather than language diversity, are the central feature of national discussions about pluralism (see Chamlian & Kolwalewski; Soudien & McKinney; in Lo Bianco & Bal, 2016). The dominant way to think about multilingualism appears to be how political systems and institutions can "manage" it (Little, Leung, & Avermaet, 2014).

At the heart of most change that follows public debate and political agitation is a pattern of cycles, oscillating between 'centripetal and centrifugal forces' (Lo Bianco, 2010). The first tends towards convergence and the second towards divergence. These are relationally organised and interactive, as politico-discursive pressures that mutually constitute each other. Change brought about by political demands, new thinking, or via new social movements, rarely erases existing arrangements. Instead, prevailing over and changing an existing state of affairs tends to lead to temporary new practices and accommodations, the original remaining available to all actors as an alternative to the new.

Observing Australian language policy closely shows that even at times when one pattern of understanding languages, similar to Ruiz's (1984) Language as Resource orientation, appears to have prevailed, a shift to an alternative, even to the complete opposite, such as viewing multilingualism as a major social problem, can occur rapidly (Ruiz, 2010). Such radical shifts have characterised English literacy policy in schools (Schalley, Guillemin, & Eisenchlas, 2015), literacy policy and programming for adults (Wickert, 2001) and languages other than English, whether focused on indigenous, immigrant and international languages (Lo Bianco & Aliani, 2013).

Not the *Topic du Jour*

Commenting on the upsurge of academic interest in contemporary language studies Stephen May described multilingualism as a *"topic du jour"* (May, 2014, p. 1). Despite *"terminological proliferation"*, he notes that the situation is positive because of *"the increasing focus on superdiverse linguistic contexts"*. The study of superdiverse linguistic contexts has generated a range of compelling explanatory notions: Multivocality, plurilingualism, translanguaging, metrolingualism and polylanguaging. These all have resonance for pedagogy, programming, curriculum writing, and for how we understand the communicative choices and behaviours of individuals and groups, and should also impact on public policy formulation.

Unfortunately, language diversity of any kind, let alone as described and celebrated in the multilingual turn, is not any kind of '*topic du jour*' in policymaking circles. A brief survey shows instead strong moves towards limiting diversity, by foregrounding either monolingual or prestige biased choices.

Across Asia there is almost complete domination of standard 'inner circle' English as the first foreign language of instruction (Cha & Ham, 2008), even in societies with large domestic second languages, and always in preference to other Asian languages of neighbour societies. Globally, the first few decades of the 21st century have been marked by the largest attrition of indigenous languages in history, especially in North America and Australasia (Lo Bianco, 2014). This is despite important progress in declarations of and legal-academic theorisation about language rights (Skutnabb-Kangas & Phillipson, 2016). There are few settings in the world where violation of language rights is banned in law or contested in education and employment practices. In many immigrant-receiving nations education, employment, citizenship and public participation are marked by major language inequalities and prejudices (Piller, 2016).

The main focus of language education planning in many parts of the world is for cultural assimilation, with occasional weak acknowledgment of diversity. Most minority languages in societies that do gesture towards multilingual education remain positioned in intellectually inferior diglossic relationship with official languages, inevitable given that most minority language support tends to be limited in duration and delivered through transition pedagogies. Extreme limitations on mother tongue education are evident in Southeast Asia for indigenous and ethnic languages (Lo Bianco, 2016) and in colonial, post-colonial and globalised sub-Saharan Africa (Kamwangamalu, 2016). In these settings African languages continue to be minoritised in upper schooling, and in all economic domains, and therefore denied the chance to develop the social and economic prestige that might assure them intergenerational vitality, even in states that make liberal declarations favouring multilingualism (Kamwangamalu, 2016). In the Americas, researchers have noted many bright spots where progress and development have been achieved such as promising examples where new speakers of endangered languages are being identified and innovative projects of revitalisation are underway, yet the great majority of languages shed users and uses and remain intergenerationally endangered (Coronel-Molina & McCarty, 2016).

Perversely, as Schalley, Guillemin, and Eisenchlas (2015) show in a recent examination of 30 years of "government policies and prominent initiatives", a pattern of public restriction has coincided with academic expansion. These writers call this a "distinct negative correlation" (p. 162) so that "the more multilingual Australia has become, the more assimilationist the policies, and the more monolingual the orientation of the society" (p. 162). Ominously for future developments they cite a significant speech by Australian Minister for Social Services, Scott Morrison, delivered in London in January 2013, in which he argued for a "post multiculturalism agenda" premised on "the supremacy of Australian values, [and] the primacy of the English language" (cited in Schalley et al., 2015, p. 173).

In light of these restrictions and reversals what lessons can applied linguists and 'multilingual turn' researchers gain from the reflections and research of specialists who analyse policy production? One aim of the present volume is to illuminate some possibilities and constraints related to how particular ideas generated in research can be implanted in policy and practice. This will be the focus of my discussion here, although I will not address the pedagogy implications of 'new multilingualism studies', but focus instead on language education provision, policy and reasoning in superdiverse multilingual contexts. Provision, policy and reasoning can be seen as barometers of how the wider evaluation of multilingualism is faring in practice, at a time when diversity and pluralisation of language education in research, teaching and teacher education, are generating such a rich and powerful account of multiplicity and fluidity of language in society. The present discussion, therefore, addresses how we are to think about the task of influencing the decision-making, resource-dispersing, curriculum-formulating, and assessment-imposing political sphere. This space of power, resources and decision-making structures public education, and while teaching does provide a space of semi-autonomous activity, pedagogy is not immune from public policy.

Poor Performance

On 6 December 2016, Australia's multilingual public radio and television network, the Special Broadcasting Service, sent a program to air and online entitled: "Our languages, a national resource, in 'terminal decline' (SBS, 2016)." The by-line accompanying this sensational claim reads: "Australia is losing the riches of its many languages. Even school children from immigrant families are abandoning the study of their mother tongues. In the nation's most multicultural state, researchers claim students are being 'punished' with the scaling down of their HSC marks" (Feneley & Calixto, 2016).

These three sentences encapsulate recurring issues of administrative unresponsiveness, intergenerational attrition and policy crisis, collectively presented as an overall linguistic calamity. Ominously announced as ". . . the collapse of Australia's multi-lingual ambitions", the Special Report sets out "the grand failure of that vision for multicultural Australia" which is turning bilingual students into monolingual ones.

The SBS itself has a substantial investment in this vision. Beginning full time transmission in 1980 (McLean, 2014), it has long been the most visible element of national multicultural policy (Jupp, 2007), the 'meta-policy' on which the pluralisation of Australian language education commenced in the mid 1970s. The vitality of Australia's demographic multilingualism and its cultivation in formal education owes its origin to debates and experimentation with language rights, cultural diversity and ethnic participation in the era of the reformist Whitlam government (1972–1975), widely recognised as the most energetic phase in Australian language politics (Ozolins, 1993).

Reflecting this ethos, the SBS website (www.sbs.com.au/aboutus/our-story/) describes its mission that:

> ... regardless of geography, age, cultural background or language skills [all Australians] should have access to high quality, independent, culturally-relevant Australian media ... including the estimated three million Australians who speak a language other than English in their homes ... to share in the experiences of others, and participate in public life.

It is a sobering judgment when the premier mechanism of public dissemination of multilingual information and entertainment, direct heir of nation-changing cultural choices that refashioned public life through recognition of diversity, decides that multilingual communication is in 'terminal decline'. Key evidence supplied for this claim (Cruickshank & Wright, 2016) is on participation rates in school language programs, especially enrolments in languages in the pre-tertiary final school level (Year 12) in New South Wales, the most populous state, and the effects of the practice of 'scaling'. Statistical scaling is applied to assessment marks to produce an individual student's Australian Tertiary Admissions Rank, or ATAR, the composite final year score to determine entry into most Australian undergraduate university programs.

Reviewing 2015 Higher School Certificate (HSC), Year 12, results for before and after effects of ATAR scaling the Universities Admissions Centre shows that the average HSC score for "Chinese Background Speakers" of "43 out of 50" is reduced by the ATAR scaling algorithm to 23. A score of 42 in Turkish was converted to 24.6; a score of 39.1 in Vietnamese was scaled to 26.6; and an average mark of 45 in Ancient Greek became an ATAR rank score of 41.1. The 2015 German HSC mark of 40.3 was scaled to 33.9. These languages combine the prestige classical subject of Ancient Greek, non-prestige community/heritage languages (Turkish, "Chinese Background", Vietnamese) and prestige foreign languages (German). The differential effect of scaling on these subjects demonstrates the essential critique of scaling: That it advantages relatively prestige languages (Ancient Greek and German) and marks down community based spoken languages identified with the ethnic or national backgrounds of students from minority communities.

The SBS story also foregrounds two other features of Australian language debates: Tension between multicultural rationales versus Asian trade languages in subject selection, and a version of the cultural rivalry between the country's two largest cities, Melbourne and Sydney. These dynamics are as follows:

> [I]n 1992 in NSW, 42 per cent of students from a Greek background studied their language for the Higher School Certificate. By 2011, only 7 per cent took Greek for the HSC. In the same period, Arabic study has plummeted

from 21.7 per cent to 9 per cent of students of Arabic background. And as Australia embarks on the so-called Asian Century, only one in six NSW students who start school as bilingual will further develop their language skills. Just 8 per cent of the state's students study a language for their Higher School certificate, less than half the result achieved by Victoria.

Commenting on this data, Dr. Ken Cruikshank (Cruickshank & Wright, 2016) remarked that while Australia has "an international reputation for its development of language policy and programs", in reality "young people . . . spend less time studying languages than young people in all other OECD countries" (p. 73). He shows that language study in NSW is concentrated in Years 7 and 8, where 70 per cent of students are offered language programs, but that this falls dramatically in Year 9 with the onset of elective options of languages. By contrast, in the State of Victoria language learning opportunities are more extensive, though not always of greater depth or duration. In 2015, 92.4 per cent of Victorian government schools offered language programs, accounting for 63 per cent of all students, with further large enrolments in 'taster' programs, making a total of 354,326 students. Additionally, 16,956 students were taking languages through special provision arrangements of the Victorian School of Languages, bringing total language enrolments to 374,961 (DET, 2016; Table 1.1).

There has been recent improvement in Victoria so that 92.1 per cent of primary schools now offer languages, accounting for 77 per cent of government primary school students engaged in language learning. At the secondary level, 87.9 per cent of Victorian students have access to language learning. This figure declined at the Year 12 level when only 17.4 per cent of government school students completed a language, through various assessable official modes of provision, though this figure is far higher than for NSW.

The concrete problems revealed in this overview of design and delivery, persistence and performance, are classic issues for language provision policy. An unresolved sociological tension with direct policy consequences is how community-based and school-supported languages are connected, what choices are made by systems and by speakers, and what kinds of program design are implemented in practice. One upshot of the SBS report is that much more robust policy input is needed from applied linguistic research to design an adequate formal language-teaching regime that is appropriate for a hugely multilingual society, a design in which national priorities and community preferences are so badly misaligned.

The next section discusses interaction between the worlds of research and practice that could lead to this more substantive involvement of research knowledge in policy design, through conversations between applied linguistics researchers and policy makers, to build more socially responsive language education arrangements.

Policy Analysis Lessons

A major issue within studies of public policy has been the problem of agenda-setting, essentially how topics or areas of concern are selected for attention. Policy makers are faced with multiple claims from constituents, pressure groups and other interests for policy attention to be devoted to particular causes or topics. The responsiveness of elected decision makers to constituent pressure is dictated to some extent by the programs of their political organisations, and their interests and ideological inclinations. However, political programs are often only general sets of parameters or orientations derived from the underlying political philosophy of the party or individual, and most studies of how issues are taken up in practice in pressure group democracies reveal ample scope for citizen or expert input. As 'experts', applied linguists are positioned in policy conversations as suppliers of knowledge. To make progress in dialogue with policy makers, the purveyors of this knowledge need to be present in conversations on political programs. Effective presentation of research findings relies on the persuasive potential of research, its legibility within prevailing political discourse, and the extent to which a shared appreciation of problems and solutions can be negotiated between applied linguists' perspectives and those of decision makers.

During the 1970s, Australian governments conceded to demands from organised alliances of ethnic and indigenous organisations, supported by applied linguistics researchers, language educators and various civil society support groups, to overturn discriminatory language laws and to adopt officially supportive positions on multiculturalism (Ozolins, 1993). In retrospect, the policy rhetoric of the period appears more accepting of input from researchers than exists today, given that the climate was generally reformist and open to experimentation, and in fact produced sweeping educational transformations across many areas of public policy at the time (Clyne, 2005). A range of impressive new innovations were commenced to recognise the presence of multilingualism in health, legal, and educational settings, both symbolic and affirmative, but often pragmatic and institutionalised as well (Jupp, 2007). Provision and policy for indigenous and community language education was created, generating a distinctively Australian language planning experience, bolstered by a kind of citizenship/settlement reasoning that supported language maintenance for immigrant/community languages, a 'reconciliation' and social justice legitimation for indigenous language communities, and skills/competencies/intercultural reasoning for additional language acquisition throughout mainstream society (Clyne, 2005; Ozolins, 1993). All these innovations, in practice and in ideology, flowed from interaction between knowledge brokers and power holders. None of these policy positions was inevitable, alternative ones were possible and are regularly proposed, and the space in between can be seen as 'agitational potential'. This field of potential policy is studied by analysts and is of direct relevance to the question for applied linguistics that emerges from the multilingual turn.

Today Australian language policy has reverted to a more conventional preference for prestige foreign languages over language maintenance activities or language reclamation efforts (Liddicoat, 2010). There is a major gap therefore between the preoccupations of researchers and teachers with the sociolinguistic reality of multilingualism and apparent official indifference. How are these to be reconciled? This gap becomes a pronounced gulf when it comes to the political morality invested by academics in the new depictions of communication, and claims that new pluralisms open space for various kinds of emancipation or human rights. Does academic belief and evidence recognising superdiverse social realities open space for minority communities to gain traction in public policy? If it is accepted that recognition of pluralism is empowering, how can research knowledge be applied to policy production? Is it realistic to hope for impact and change on the basis of research knowledge? Does 'terminological proliferation' assist or hinder this process? What are the consequences of succeeding in persuasion of public officials?

To address the prospects for productive exchanges and develop an argument about how these might occur, I will trace some steps in thinking about research knowledge and policy action in general terms, informed by ideas from key policy analysts: Giandomenico Majone and Carol Weiss. I will draw on some of their early thinking in this area and then briefly outline a map of policy studies, the 'Multiple Streams Framework' (Weible and Sabatier, 2014), to look at points of intersection that are promising.

Policy as Argument and Persuasion

The intersection between research and policy derives from a long history of philosophical reflection on knowledge and ruling, from Plato through Machiavelli to modern scholars, and it is often termed the relationship between knowledge and power. Political decisions revolve around the grounds for action, what legitimations are sufficient for power holders to take action in knowledge-influenced fields, such as education.

Majone's (1989) analysis of the point of intersection between 'science' and public policy addresses what are shown to be incommensurable notions of rules of argumentation. Each domain, academic research and public decision-making, utilises and relies on different rationalities: Principles of falsifiability within science, evidentiary robustness in legal settings, and pragmatic achievability and public accountability in politics.

In Majone's terms these are typified by evidence, argument and persuasion. His work was one of the first in mainstream policy analysis to shift discussions away from technical and managerial operations towards the conversational rationalities inherent in the process of making policy decisions and disbursing resources. His writing has convinced many policy analysts that understanding how argument works is a necessary, legitimate, and acceptable supplement to the traditional focus on efficient technical procedures that policy analysis has utilised. The main way to do policy had traditionally been understood to be an exclusive activity between public servants and elected officials, the former supplying the latter with costed options, with the possible mediation of political advisers, and occasionally supplemented by technical demonstrations. Close analysis of real world actually occurring policy revealed instead that it contains many emotional, narrative-centred, interest based and other 'non-technical' elements, essentially politics infused with value judgements and political interests. Majone's project was to repudiate the technical/managerial paradigm and offer an argumentative/ persuasive alternative, injecting a specific focus on 'rhetorical skills' for intending policy analysts and practitioners, also relevant for those seeking to influence policy processes. Even explicitly evidence-based policy contains strong elements of rhetorical skill, because there is often contestation around what counts as evidence, how it is defined, collected and interpreted. In these ways, public discourse is central to effective policy processes.

In Majone's approach, policy analysis "has less to do with formal techniques of problem solving than with the process of argument" (1989, p. 7). His aim is to install persuasion and advocacy within the professional preparation of public officials, policy analysts and the general public, but also to extend the understanding of policy processes beyond cost and administrative efficiency operating through formal 'objective' procedures of evaluating options.

Carol Weiss, like Majone, was both a policy practitioner (adviser) and theoretician with a long focus of analysing major US and international policies to isolate the effects of and influence from 'knowledge', especially knowledge produced by researchers and research studies. Her work confirms the cultural hypothesis that policy makers and researchers inhabit different conceptual and reasoning domains, and that they often do not link well. During the 1960s Weiss evaluated the US "War on Poverty", expecting but not finding traction from her detailed, long term analysis (Dale, 2003). Reflecting on the failed 'take up' by government of expert advice her academic focus shifted to the role of evaluation, decision-making processes and politics, and especially the limits and impact of research on the essentially political processes of governmental calculations. According to Weiss, policy makers, community advocates and academic researchers all bring unique and often mis-aligned stocks of 'information', 'ideology' and 'interests' to their interactions (Weiss, 1983). Realistically, many researchers and most research can only expect to have indirect and therefore long-term impact on the social and political dynamic of public decision making. The marketplace of knowledge generation is crowded. A multitude of agencies, interest groups, think tanks, university based academics, management consultants, investigative journalists etc. produce and peddle knowledge to influence decision-making. Prospects for success must be assessed against the existing stocks of information that policy holders have, the persuasiveness and rhetorical skill of researchers and the power of their interests, and those of policy makers and the perceived, if undeclared interests of academics. Yet, there are some areas where research information is clearly the source of policy change and influence, such as the slow-acting origin of changed interpretational frameworks for difficult social problems. Studies of how research knowledge is used have shown its relevance to exposing myths, but only after the long percolating effects of introducing new knowledge into societies play out. New knowledge also builds policy maker capacity, such as Majone's stress on teaching public officials rhetorical skill, and new knowledge is tracked as the source for disconfirming long held assumptions, setting new agendas. In these ways, research and knowledge generally contribute to policy 'enlightenment' (Weiss, 1977).

There are many insights here of relevance to multilingualism research, such as how new ways to name and group the phenomenon of language in super-diverse societies that suggest long term traction for the 'turn' are possible. The flow of new notions percolating into conversations beyond researchers and multilingual communities can be tracked. In recent work, I reflected on the related 'turn' in English studies, especially the efforts of teachers and researchers working in the paradigm of English as a Lingua Franca who want to influence publishers, education systems and assessment agencies to dismantle the privilege bias accorded to 'inner circle' Englishes (Lo Bianco, 2014).

In more recent work, policy analysts are building on these foundations of Majone and Weiss, producing frameworks to account for radically different policy practices in different societies and in the same societies over time and under different political regimes. As a result, current frameworks attempt to incorporate multiple influences on policy, the ambiguity and contradictions of the process and the roles of information, as knowledge, research, data or wisdom, at different stages of agenda-setting, decision-making, and the carrying out of decided policies into action (Weible & Sabatier, 2014).

Three streams of influence, the events and ideas circulating around the topic, are strong and invariably struggled over in what becomes enacted as policy: *The problems stream* (focusing on the names of problems, their representation and how they come to the attention of policy makers); *the politics stream* (which addresses both the formal political process and pressure, persuasion, media and other ways to enter the formal political stream); and *a policies stream* (the existing policy settings, the evaluations and critiques of these, past policy attempts and related ideas linked to the 'values acceptability' of new proposals and their 'technical feasibility and cost').

Individuals or groups might exploit a propitious position they hold, whether crafted by them through skill, rhetorical mastery or because of good fortune, and become 'policy entrepreneurs', exploiting a 'policy window' (Kingdon, 1995). The flow of ideas, events and discourse varies greatly according to the traction that policy entrepreneurs are able to gain on different issues, or if there is mediation from think tanks, media promotion, strategically well placed individual champions, civil society groups or political alliances of citizens making collective demands and achieving political traction. The Multiple Streams Framework is able to accommodate knowledge processes and new ideas, such as the new terminology and concepts generated by research making multilingualism normal rather than exceptional. Multilingual studies can generate a new rationality of policy analysis and action, for single actors and ethnic groups or professional associations, or discipline groupings, but what is currently missing is effort from applied linguistics associations, journals or conferences, to develop convincing or persuasive representations of social problems in language, in interaction with policy makers, public officials or opinion-influencing media.

The question arises, to what extent do applied linguists, researchers and practitioners desire such interactions? What mechanisms are there to facilitate interaction with policy? What will be the costs and rewards, consequences and repercussions, of such engagement?

Reflection on Policy Engagements: Adult Literacy and Asian Languages

The Ordeal of Success 1) Adult Literacy

One of the most compelling accounts of such interaction is by Rosie Wickert (2001), writing as a researcher who was also a policy actor, on behalf of increased provision, better policy and acceptance of a permanent social justice oriented Australian practice of adult literacy education. Wickert's analysis is a story of policy influence, initially through a door-opening statistical study of the incidence of literacy difficulties among adults, extending to narratives about the explanation of the statistics and the policy and programming responses. The original study, No Single Measure, consisted of the results of a sample of adults on information processing and literacy tasks during the late 1980s and persisted through the early 1990s into full-blown policy adoption. The account combines insider reflection, honest appraisal of outcomes, and a theorised account of the process.

The wider socio-political and ideological context is critical. During the late 1980s and early 1990s, international attention to the problem of adult literacy shifted from a human rights perspective under the aegis of UNESCO to a human capital perspective under the influence of the OECD. This macro and major political/economic shift presented professional organisations, researchers and teachers with a major challenge and opportunity. The field repositioned itself to take advantage of the policy opening in which Australian Federal government authorities who had in 1990, International Literacy Year, imagined that the issue of adult literacy was only relevant as an item of provision of foreign aid to Pacific Island developing countries, to a rapid and radical shift, only 4 years later, in which the role of domestic adult literacy problems was acknowledged, and re-conceived as hampering micro-economic reform. This reform agenda emphasised the role of human capital skills in facilitating economic competitiveness, international exposure, and capital-intensive enterprises.

Wickert's analysis traces the role of statistically presented information, her own national assessment of the incidence, distribution and characteristics of English language literacy difficulties among adults in this context of intense public attention to a field previously dismissed as marginal to policy and primarily the responsibility of welfare or charity-oriented private tutoring. As a key researcher, transformed into a policy entrepreneur, unanticipated complications emerged, such as the relationship with immigrant and Aboriginal people receiving ESL education and the preferences and politics of the field. Engagement in policy production, described by some academics as 'getting your hands dirty', proved to be successful, yet also risky, demanding and problematical. The key professional associations became enmeshed with a major expansion of adult literacy provision, provoking both celebration and concern. While significant resource increases achieved greater provision of adult literacy programs and research, and other progress, new administration imposed tight and intrusive accountability requirements, diverted attention from and even silenced critical voices and led to prioritisation and curriculum models that proved problematical for many practitioners and researchers. Some groups of past client groups, those not directly linked to the labour market, saw provision weaken and worsen, and radical changes to the nature of the field resulted.

Wickert and other scholars[1] report on the coalition building, policy struggles and terminological changes implicated in this repositioning of adult literacy away from welfarist charity towards a second chance education right, documenting the many unforeseen effects among the success and later reversals. Lamented by some was a generalised loss of professional autonomy, compromise of position and radical intrusion of bureaucracy into measurement, curriculum, and student selection, in a process Wickert labels 'appropriation'.

The Ordeal of Success 2) Asian (Trade) Languages

Different in content but similar in its relations between research and policy is recent history of Asian language teaching. Australia's geo-political enmeshment with Asia has grown from economic and security concerns to become a staple of public policy, a 'national project' (Lo Bianco and Slaughter, 2016), shared by all major political interests and invested with nation-saving crisis talks for decades (Dawkins, 1988). A recurring aspect of Asia-centering discussions in policy documents is to rebuke the nation's education for its lack of preparation for the "Asia literate" citizens and workers required in future decades. As a result, and like the adult literacy example above, a field of relatively marginal educational activity, the teaching of Asian languages in schools and universities, has been appropriated to a central role in national discourses of economic restructuring. Consequently, student language skills, their cultural capabilities and stocks of knowledge about Asian societies, now feature in public debate about core and mainstream national skills for economic reconstruction and even for national survival (Dawkins, 1988). Unlike the marginalisation of Indigenous language education problems and challenges, and immigrant language maintenance efforts, or the educational claims of world languages other than Asian ones, or Asian languages other than trade-linked ones, the study of select Asian trade and security connected languages has been granted substantial policy attention, public financing and promotion.

In 2012, Prime Minister Julia Gillard issued the most recent of a series of White Papers on Asian engagement, an all-of-government scrutiny of national preparedness. The *Australia in the Asian Century* (Commonwealth of Australia, 2012) report was released with high-level endorsement from business and major mainstream media focus.

The report endorsed the small number of languages selected in 1994 for priority status according to external trade and geo-political proximity, not according to criteria linked with speaker populations in Australia or other educational or intellectual rationales, but trade volume statistics. The multilingualism imagined in this, and all related documents, was strictly of the foreign kind, distanced in time and geographic space from speakers, classrooms and communities. Yet, as evidenced in the SBS report, public discussion about Asian language teaching, referring to trade foreign languages, tends to be crisis driven, whether related to declining enrolments (Sturak & Naughten, 2010), poor student interest, or low assessed proficiency gains from participation in school programs (Scarino & Elder, 2012).

Unlike the policy entrepreneurship evident in Wickert's (2001) discussion of adult literacy, the promotion and priority for key Asian languages has been the result of policy processes that recruit academics, teachers and community members to support and legitimise rather than influence and shape policy, pedagogy and reasoning.

In Singh's (2001) estimation a considerable part of the project of Asian engagement recycles orientalist notions of bounded, distant enclosures of foreign languages, and in any event has little affinity with any of the assumptions, findings, and concerns of the multilingual turn with its focus on superdiverse societies. Recent focus on diaspora populations and their possible contribution to the 'engagement effort' (Rizvi, Louie, & Evans, 2016) suggest efforts to overcome this legacy and risk of representing Asian societies as increasingly powerful foreign 'others', inhabiting bounded distant spaces.

Conclusion

The Australian language education enterprise today is beset by a crisis of underperformance in provision, weakness in policy conception and reasoning bound to obsolete notions of languages linked to relatively homogenous bounded nations. Linguistic human rights are largely denied, unrecognised and denigrated, and the general reasoning of contemporary policy has lost its decades old commitment to a sustaining national principle of cultural diversity as an inevitable, enriching and productive resource.

These negative characteristics can be traced to the appropriation of public policy on languages into the exclusive hands of officials removed from the demographic realities of the wider society. Policy analysts sensitive to the role of discourse, rhetoric and discussion in their power to reconstitute assumptions and reorganise knowledge have linked such changes to the presence in policy debates of academics and community organisations. In other words, when policy draws on multiple sources of knowledge, information and experience its content and direction become more attuned to the realities of the community it is ultimately intended to serve.

For the multilingual turn to impact more deeply on the educational settings of contemporary society will require extensive interaction between applied linguistics researchers, teachers and other educators with policy making officials, in conversations designed to produce shared and new conceptual understandings of the role of languages and the characteristics of multilingual communication in contemporary society. Only through knowledge exchange, reciprocity and mutual encounter, could Australia transform its essentially 'neoliberal multiculturalism' (Kubota, 2014) into a more productive and enriching communication order.

Note

1 In the same volume as Wickert's article analysis by Moore; Taylor; Castleton; McHugh, Nevard and Taylor; Falk; McKay; Kell; Childs; and others reinforce and deepen this documentation of academic participation in activist applied linguistics on adult literacy and ESL.

References

Brumfit, C. (1997). Theoretical practice: Applied linguistics as pure and practical science. In A. Mauranen & K. Sajavaara (Eds.), *Applied linguistics across disciplines* (pp. 18–30). Milton Keynes: Catchline.

Cha, Y. K., & Ham, S. H. (2008). The impact of English on the school curriculum. In B. Spolsky & F. Hult (Eds.), *The Handbook of Educational Linguistics* (pp. 313–328). London, UK: Blackwell.

Clyne, M. G. (2005). *Australia's language potential.* Sydney: University of New South Wales Press.

Commonwealth of Australia (2012). *Australia in the Asian Century: White paper.* Canberra: Australia in the Asian Century Task Force.

Conteh, J., & Meier, G. (2014). *The multilingual turn in languages education: Opportunities and challenges.* Bristol, UK: Multilingual Matters.

Coronel-Molina, S. M., & McCarty, T. L. (Eds.). (2016). *Indigenous language revitalization in the Americas.* New York: Routledge.

Cruikshank, K., & Wright, J. (2016). A tale of two cities: What the Dickens happened to languages in NSW? *Australian Review of Applied Linguistics, 39*(1), 72–94.

Dale, S. (2003). In conversation: Carol Weiss and Evert Lindquist on policymaking and research. IDRC Digital Library (IDL). Retrieved from https://protect-au.mimecast.com/s/Rv1YBmtMKpNQF4?domain=idl-bnc.idrc.ca.

Dawkins, J. (1988). Australia Day statement 1988. In E. M. McKay (Ed.), *Challenges and opportunities: Our future in Asia* (pp 13–21). Parkville, Vic: Asian Studies Association of Australia.

DET. (2016). *Languages provision in Victorian government schools, 2015*. Melbourne: Department of Education and Training.

Feneley, R., & Calixto, J. (2016). Our languages, a national resource, in 'terminal decline.' SBS Australia. Retrieved from www.sbs.com.au/news/article/2016/11/23/our-languages-national-resource-terminal-decline.

Jupp, J. (2007). *From white Australia to Woomera*. Cambridge: University Press.

Kamwangamalu, N. (2016). *Language policy and economics: The language question in Africa*. Palgrave Macmillan.

Kingdon, J. W. (1995). *Agendas, alternatives and public policies* (2nd ed.). New York: Longman.

Kubota, R. (2014). The multi/plural turn, postcolonial theory, and neoliberal multiculturalism: Complicities and implications for applied linguistics. *Applied Linguistics, 37*(4), 474–494.

Liddicoat, A. J. (2010). Policy change and educational inertia: Language policy and language education in Australian schooling. In A. J. Liddicoat & A. Scarino (Eds.), *Language in Australian education: Problems, prospects and future directions* (pp. 11–24). Newcastle: Cambridge Scholars.

Little, D., Leung, C., & Avermaet, P. V. (2014). *Managing diversity in education, languages, policies, pedagogies*. Bristol, UK: Multilingual Matters.

Lo Bianco, J. (2010). The struggle to retain diversity in language education. In A. J. Liddicoat & A. Scarino (Eds.), *Languages in Australian education: Problems, prospects and future directions*. Newcastle: Cambridge Scholars.

Lo Bianco, J. (2014). Dialogue between ELF and the field of language policy and planning. *Journal of English as Lingua Franca, 3*(1), 197–213.

Lo Bianco, J. (2016). *Synthesis report: Malaysia, Myanmar and Thailand: Language, education and social cohesion initiative*. Bangkok: UNICEF East Asia and Pacific Regional Office (EAPRO).

Lo Bianco, J., & Aliani, R. (2013). *Language planning and student experiences: Intention, rhetoric and implementation*. Clevedon, UK: Multilingual Matters.Lo Bianco, J., & Bal, A. (2016). *Learning from difference: Comparative accounts of multicultural education*. Dordrecht: Springer International.

Lo Bianco, J., & Slaughter, Y. (2016). The Australian Asia project. In G. Leitner, A. Hashim & H.-G. Wolf (Eds.), *Communicating with Asia: The future of English as a global language* (pp. 282–295). Cambridge: University Press.

McLean, G. (2014). National communication and diversity: The story of SBS. In A. Jakubowicz & C. Ho (Eds.), *'For those who've come across the seas . . .': Australian multicultural theory, policy and practice* (pp. 45–56). New York: Anthem Press.

Majone, G. (1989). *Evidence, argument, and persuasion in the policy process*. Yale: University Press.

May, S. (2014). *The multilingual turn: Implications for SLA, TESOL and bilingual education*. New York: Routledge.

Ozolins, U. (1993). *The politics of language in Australia*. Cambridge: University Press.

Piller, I. (2016). *Linguistic diversity and social justice*. Oxford: University Press.

Rizvi, F., Louie, K., & Evans, J. (2016). Australia's diaspora advantage: Realising the potential for building transnational business networks with Asia. Australian Council of Learned Academies. Retrieved from www.acola.org.au.

Ruiz, R. (1984). Orientations in language planning. *NABE Journal, 8*(2), 15–34.

Ruiz, R. (2010). Reorienting language-as-resource. In J. Petrovic (Ed.), *International perspectives on bilingual education: Policy, practice, and controversy* (pp. 155–172). Charlotte, N.C.: Information Age Publishing.

Skutnabb-Kangas, T., & Phillipson, R. (Eds.). (2016). *Language rights*. London, UK: Routledge.

Scarino, A., & Elder, C. (Eds.). (2012). Describing school achievement in Asian languages for diverse learner groups [Special issue]. *Australian Review of Applied Linguistics, 35*(3), 225–230.

Schalley, A. C., Guillemin, D., & Eisenchlas, S. A. (2015). Multilingualism and assimilationism in Australia's literacy-related educational policies. *International Journal of Multilingualism, 12*(2), 162–177.

Singh, M. G. (2001). Advocating the sustainability of linguistic diversity. In J. Lo Bianco & R. Wickert (Eds.), *Australian policy activism in language and literacy* (pp. 123–148). Melbourne: Language Australia.

Sturak, K., & Naughten, Z. (2010). *The current state of Chinese, Indonesian, Japanese and Korean language education in Australian schools*. DEEWR. Retrieved from www.deewr.gov.au/Schooling/NALSSP/Documents/CurrentStateAsianLanguageEducationOverarchingReport.pdf.

Weible, C., & Sabatier, P. (2014). *Theories of the policy process*. Boulder: Westview Press.

Weiss, C. H. (1977). Research for policy's sake: The enlightenment function of social research. *Policy Analysis, 3*(4), 531–545.

Weiss, C. H. (1983). Ideology, interests, and information. The basis of policy positions. In B. Callahan & B. Jennings (Eds.), *Ethics, the social sciences and policy analysis* (pp. 213–246). New York: Plenum Press.

Wickert, R. (2001). Policy, activism, and processes of policy production: Adult literacy in Australia. In J. Lo Bianco & R. Wickert (Eds.), *Australian policy activism in language and literacy* (pp. 75 93). Melbourne: Language Australia.

3

MOTHER-TONGUE-BASED MULTILINGUAL EDUCATION IN THE PHILIPPINES

Perceptions, Problems and Possibilities

Priscilla Angela T. Cruz and Ahmar Mahboob

Introduction

With the rise of English as "the" international language and the rise of national (e.g., Filipino) or large regional (e.g., Kiswahili) languages as "the" languages of wider communication within a country/region, non-dominant and minority languages are struggling to maintain a sustained population that continues to use and develop the language. One attempt to redress this problem is through mother-tongue based multilingual education (MTB-MLE), which involves using the students' first language (L1) as a medium of instruction for all classes, including second language (L2) classes, in school (Walter et al., 2010). These recent developments involving MTB-MLE policies may help to counter and perhaps even reverse the process of language loss and language shift. However, in order for this to happen, we need to understand people's attitudes towards such policies, the sociolinguistic distribution of (variations of) languages, and how people generally perceive the way local languages are used (or useful) in education. At the same time, we need to develop appropriate pedagogical models and approaches for using local languages in the classroom. This chapter looks into these questions with a focus on MTB-MLE in the Philippines.

The Philippines, with the introduction of new curricula for elementary and secondary school, has recently shifted its educational policy away from one that is English and Filipino dominant into that which makes space for mother tongues. Lorente (2013) writes that this move "acknowledg[es] the role of local communities and how local knowledge can be valued in the classroom with the use of the mother tongues" (p. 197). So far, there has been a positive response to this program. Teachers in government schools, for instance, have noted that

MTB-MLE has led to greater student engagement in classroom work and generally, better overall performance (Amarles, 2016). While this and other such studies claim that MTB-MLE is successful, there is an absence of research based on classroom discourse. In reviewing the current research on MTB-MLE in the Philippines, we note that despite some studies that show positive outcomes (Amarles, 2016; Dekker, 2010), there are a number of problematic areas that need to be addressed. Some of these problem areas will be explored in this chapter, such as the tendency to use these languages for mostly interpersonal or regulative purposes rather than content instruction. Furthermore, we also discuss why MTB-MLE should be implemented in conjunction with developing mother languages so that these languages can express all the registers necessary for imparting the needed content in the various subject areas of school. We argue that without developing local languages, MTB-MLE policies may not be as successful. In order to address these problems, we provide some suggestions on how these languages can be used more productively in classrooms.

An Overview of Some of the Core Language Issues in the Philippines

In this section, we briefly discuss some core language issues in the Philippines that may impact on mother tongue-based policies in education. These are sociolinguistic conditions, social aspiration, and attitudes toward language.

The Philippines is highly multilingual and culturally diverse. The country is composed of over 7,000 islands and over 100 languages. McFarland (2008) has written that "[t]hese are languages, not dialects, which is to say that these variations are so different one from the other that the (monolingual) speaker of one language does not understand communication in one of the other languages" (p. 132). However, two languages enjoy a privileged position in the Philippines. These are English and Filipino. English was introduced through American colonisation and, for over a century, the country has been in the "grip of English" (Lorente, 2013, p. 187) because of its promises of social mobility and American/Western values of democracy and liberty. Filipino, on the other hand, is a national language imposed by government policies. *Filipino* is actually Tagalog, which is the language of the country's dominant ethnic group. It was renamed Filipino in the 1987 constitution in an attempt to "de-ethnicize" the language (Tupas, 2015, p. 591). Both English and Filipino have enjoyed being the primary languages of schooling. In the past, bilingual education policies have stipulated the use of Filipino for subjects like social studies and practical arts while English has been reserved for the sciences and more specialised fields.

The divide between English for more specialised fields and Filipino for local ones easily reflects the aspirational dimension of English. Gonzalez's (2004) research has pointed out that English is used for upward mobility, specifically in the powerful domains of business, law, and politics while Filipino is used for more local domains such as the mass media. In this country, language is valued social capital where those who speak English and Filipino to some extent have a greater potential for finding lucrative jobs. Because the country is a noted provider of contact service employees, those who speak English can work in the many call centers of the country. English is aspirational because it offers the potential for employment.

When it comes to aspirations related to language, it is useful to consider the differences between language allocation and affiliation (Mahboob, 2017). Individuals all receive allocated languages. These are the languages of home and one's immediate social group. Mother tongue policies assume that students learn best in the languages allocated to them. This is not surprising as students who have to learn in a language other than those allocated to them have the double problem of learning a new language (the language of schooling) and learning new content (such as Math) in that new language. However, there are also the languages of affiliation. These are the languages that are associated with communities that individuals want to access. Because of affiliation, languages in the Philippines are not perceived as equal in status. The desire to affiliate with a language, such as English, is a very important element in why individuals may or may not support a mother tongue policy, as our previous research has suggested.

In a previous study, we discussed the results of a survey that showed negative attitudes toward mother tongues in the Philippines (Mahboob & Cruz, 2013). Respondents were asked what languages they perceived to be more important in schooling. Most of the results indicated an unfavorable attitude toward mother tongues in school, where English is still largely perceived as the ideal medium of instruction. Filipino and other local languages were considered to be valuable in primary or elementary education but not in higher education. In this study, about 50 per cent of the respondents felt that English should be the medium of instruction in primary education, over 80 per cent felt it was ideal for secondary school, and close to 95 per cent preferred it to be the language of higher education. On the other hand, only about 20 per cent felt that Filipino and other local languages could be used as a medium of instruction in primary school. This number dwindled to just under 2 per cent in higher education. Furthermore, respondents also indicated that other foreign languages were perceived to be even more useful than these local languages in schooling. To the question on which languages should be taught in school, over 80 per cent responded with English while only 50 per cent answered with Filipino. Other local languages were only supported by close to 15 per cent while foreign languages (like Chinese, Spanish, Japanese, and French) got close to 23 per cent. These results indicate that attitudes to English and other languages need to be considered in implementing a mother tongue-based system, which it seems the country sorely needs.

The Need for MTB-MLE

While English has arguably become the language of prestige and socio-economic mobility in the Philippines, the effects of English have been disastrous for education (Azurin, 2010; Dekker, 2010). One effect of the privileged position of the language is its long-term use as a medium of instruction (MOI) in schools. Azurin (2010) has written about the debilitating effects of this policy: "[teachers have] realised that faulty communication in the classroom has mostly led to poor comprehension of the concepts and skills to be implanted" (p. 4). Aside from students not understanding (and hence, not learning), important concepts and skills, the use of English in schools has caused a break between the students' local world and their school world. This break has been considered as leading to an interruption in the development of critical thinking. Dekker (2010) reminds us that even before children start school, they can already process concepts in their mother languages. This ability to think in their mother tongues is something that is not exploited or developed in an English medium of instruction system. A mother-tongue based system, on the other hand, "enables participatory classroom activities where learners are actively involved in learning with understanding from the first day" (Dekker, 2010, p. 25).

The positive effects of MTB-MLE have been studied and documented by Dekker and her colleagues who, for over a decade now, have piloted an MTB-MLE program in Lubuagan, a small town in the northern part of the Philippines (Nolasco, 2008; Walter et al., 2010). The results of the project are overwhelmingly positive, with students who were taught in their mother tongues scoring more than 20 per cent higher in exams than their peers who were taught in English (Walter et al., 2010). Students who were taught only in the mother tongue scored higher not just in "content courses" such as Math but also in the language classes of English, Filipino, and Reading. In this program, the students' L1 was used to teach them English. Dekker's team attests that:

> Beginning with the first language first, and providing well planned second language learning supports learners more effectively than immersion, or submersion, in a second language. Research shows that when the first language is used in education for up to six or more years, learners exceed the achievement of monolingual learners, enabling parity in higher education and the world of work.
>
> (Walter et al., 2010, p. 41)

This study is only one among other studies conducted both in the Philippines and around the world that provide convincing evidence for the use of mother tongues in the classroom. However, there is also a need to be critical of some problematic areas in MTB-MLE. In the next section, we frame MTB-MLE within discussions of language and knowledge-building and what roles variations within languages can play where building knowledge is concerned.

MTB-MLE and Forms of Knowledge

It is necessary to differentiate the knowledge children go to school for from the knowledge learned at home and within their immediate social group. Bernstein (1975) has drawn up the useful distinction between *commonsense* and *uncommonsense* knowledge. He argues that commonsense knowledge is "everyday community knowledge" (p. 90), learned through interactions with family and immediate peer groups. Uncommonsense knowledge, however, is "freed from the particular, the local" (p. 90) and is represented by the specialised or technicalised discourses of the sciences and the arts. Martin (1993) describes the differences between the language of commonsense and uncommonsense. He writes that commonsense is discursively designed to negotiate feelings and community with family and friends. Uncommonsense, on the other hand, can be represented by scientific discourse which is characterised by "meanings that are not readily available in spoken form" (p. 95). Scientific discourse, after all, can be noted to show lexical items which are not commonly used and can only be understood by those who have access to the same uncommonsense knowledge. So, one important consideration for deciding upon what language/s to use in school is to gauge to what extent these language/s can express the discourses of uncommonsense knowledge.

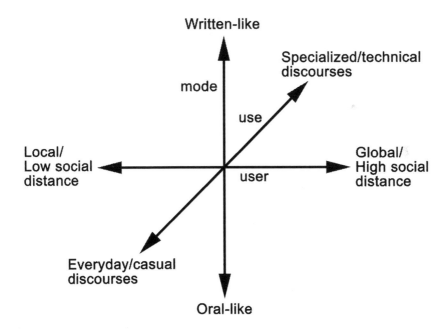

FIGURE 3.1 Language variation framework (Mahboob, 2017, p. 18)

It is useful to consider, at this point, Mahboob's three-dimensional framework for examining language variation. In this framework, Mahboob (2017) illustrates how a language can vary internally to express the meanings of both common and uncommonsense.

In this framework, the difference between commonsense and uncommonsense can be traced along the intersecting clines of users, uses, and modes. Commonsense discourses tend to be everyday discourses between individuals with low social distance such as friends, family, or people of the same neighborhood. Uncommonsense discourses tend to be specialised and are exchanged between individuals of relatively high social distance. A highly developed language such as English can express the meanings of both commonsense and uncommonsense. Schooling opens the opportunity for ontogenetic (Martin, 1997) development, or one that involves widening the ability of a child to access and construe the different language variations that will be necessary throughout his or her life.

Halliday's arguments on language development should also be discussed. He argues that language development is composed of three aspects, which are "learning language, learning through language, and learning about language" (Halliday, 2004, p. 308). To Halliday, "learning language" is about the largely unconscious process involved when children manage to talk to and interact with the people around them. "Learning through language" is about "how we use language to build up a picture of the world in which we live" (Halliday, 2004, p. 317). Through this perspective, we recognise that it is through language that we perceive and structure our experiences of the world. A child might learn the wording *good girl* and, in so doing, also learn how the world is structured around *good* and *bad*, *girl* and *boy*.

"Learning about language," on the other hand, is quite different. This refers to how individuals "come to understand the nature and functions of language itself" (Halliday, 2004, p. 322). When we learn language, much of what we know remains unconscious knowledge or "knowledge stored in the gut" (p. 322). This is developed in childhood when children learn the "right" ways to say things, such as the difference between *give me that* and *please give me that*. However, as a child starts to deal with the uncommonsense knowledges of adulthood in school, then an understanding of language itself becomes necessary. In this sense, knowledge about language is a form of uncommonsense knowledge. Through this type of knowledge, students can learn the patterns of discourse that will allow them to adjust their uses of speech or writing to express both commonsense and uncommonsense across variations in users, uses, and modes. So, uncommonsense knowledge of language leads to the ability to learn and talk about both the commonsense knowledge of community and the uncommonsense knowledge of all the fields of schooling, whether they involve the sciences, social sciences, economics, or culture and the arts.

Forms of knowledge, language variation, and the three aspects of language development have implications for MTB-MLE. First, it is necessary to consider to what extent any language chosen as a medium of instruction can construe uncommonsense. This means that the language has been developed enough to express the specialised discourses of all the subjects necessary for schooling. But, it is also necessary to perceive this language as *meta-knowledge* that is expressed as a *meta-language* that students need in order to understand, express, and critique uncommonsense on their own. Furthermore, although learning about language can be an unconscious process, the language used as a medium of instruction has also got to be learned consciously so students can clearly learn to navigate the discursive differences between commonsense and uncommonsense. When languages, such as the local languages of the Philippines, remain marginalised as languages of local purposes and identities, then they may not have developed the registers needed for the specialised discourses of high social distance and largely technical fields. It is from this perspective that we caution against simply imposing MTB-MLE without considering the need to develop these local languages. The more these languages are developed, the less people will perceive them as less useful than English.

Furthermore, another issue that has to be considered is what MTB-MLE will mean for *how* local languages are used in the classroom. It can be observed that prior to MTB-MLE, local languages had already been used in the classroom, as this sample will suggest:

> *Ba't dala mo pa yung bag mo?* [Why did you bring your bag with you?] {The boy does not reply and pastes the tag *circumference* on the Manila paper.} *Ano ba ang problema mo?* [What is your problem?] Okay. So again, everybody, read.
>
> (Canilao, 2015)

In this excerpt, the teacher is managing a classroom. A student (a boy) has gone up to the board to stick a tag (*circumference*) on Manila paper. The boy, for some reason, is carrying his bag so the teacher asks him, in the local language, why he has his bag with him. Here, we can observe that the local language is used for the regulative purpose (Christie, 1999) of managing behavior. However, for MTB-MLE policies to be effective, local languages should be used for both regulative and instructional (Christie, 1999) purposes. Instructional purposes would involve skills and knowledge building. To allow for local languages to function in instructional discourses would mean using them in a planned manner in order to build knowledge and skills. If they are used only in unplanned ways for regulative or interpersonal purposes, then they may lose the potential to support students in the process of learning uncommonsense in the target language. They may also remain underdeveloped as they are only called to construe some meanings and not others.

Building Uncommonsense About the English Language Through Local Languages: Focus on the Classroom

In this section, we suggest means by which to structure lessons around the uses of local languages to construe and unlock various meanings in the English language learning classroom. We will briefly model a lesson involving the shift between the target language (English) and a local language (Filipino) in order to demonstrate how the use of a local language can build skills and knowledge in English. This lesson builds reading skills and focuses on knowledge about nominal or noun groups. In our presentation of this lesson, we draw from Halliday's work (in Halliday & Hasan, 1985) on the metafunctional organisation of language and Rose and Martin's (2012) work on curriculum genres.

Halliday (in Halliday & Hasan, 1985) has written that any communicative situation involves the three variables of field, tenor, and mode. *Field* involves *what is happening,* tenor involves *who are taking part*, and *mode* refers to *what part language is playing*. These three variables are expressed through the three metafunctions of language. These are the ideational (field), interpersonal (tenor), and textual (mode) metafunctions. Any use of language construes a configuration of these three types of meanings. Ideational meanings are those of experience and involve people or things, events, and the various circumstances that impact on events (such as time and place). Interpersonal meanings construe social relations. In the sample above, the local language was used for the interpersonal purpose of managing behavior and identity. Textual meanings, on the other hand, organise ideational and interpersonal ones into written, spoken, or multimodal texts. This organising metafunction allows receivers to "take in" ideational and interpersonal meanings in relatively clear and structured ways. Ideational, interpersonal, and textual meanings are all construed through specific patterns of grammar, vocabulary, discourse, and various multimodal expressions.

In their paper "Using local languages in English language classrooms," Mahboob and Lin (in press) argue that local languages can be used to construe all three types of meaning in order to scaffold learning *the* target language and learning *in* the target language. Where ideational meanings or field information are concerned, for instance, technical terms can be presented in the target language but explained in the local one so students can "relate" to the definitions. Local languages can be further used interpersonally to negotiate, discuss, and critique community values. Textual meanings can be expressed through local vocabulary in terms of calling students' attention to, for example, topic shifts in a text. From a metafunctional perspective, what is important is the consciousness of using local languages for very specific functions in the classroom. This systematic use of local languages will be further discussed through Rose and Martin's (2012) work on curriculum genres.

Rose and Martin (2012) have observed that the learning activity has five phases. These are Prepare, Focus, Task, Evaluate, and Elaborate. In the Prepare phase, the learners are "prepared" for the coming learning task, whether by "introducing" the task or telling them what they might have to do or look for. In the Focus phase, learners are explicitly told to pay attention to a feature in the text that is central to the learning activity. They could also be asked a question whose response constitutes the Task phase. In the Evaluate phase, the teacher affirms (or does not) the student's fulfillment of the task. The Elaborate phase, on the other hand, allows the teacher to add to the information currently being discussed. We argue that local languages can be purposefully deployed across all five phases to scaffold learning. We model this in a sample lesson on reading.

The text to be read is in English so local languages have to be used to scaffold students' understanding. This text is an excerpt from a magazine article on Manila (permission was granted by the author). Specifically, it describes the Chinatown district:

> The massive throngs of people and snarling jeepneys (a hybrid jeep and van) shouldn't dissuade you from hotfooting it to the world's oldest living, breathing Chinatown, which is currently on its fourth century. Binondo and Ongpin Streets serve as the main lifelines for this tightly packed community of local Chinese who can trace their ancestry by as many as ten generations. Both streets are a foodie's treasure trove of delights—tea eggs, fried siopao (a rice flour steam bun stuffed with meat), crunchy lumpia (eggrolls with veggies), hand-pulled empress hair noodles with slivers of beef, Macao-style custard egg tarts and hopia (sweet cakes fried in lard), for starters. This area isn't just about Chinoy chow, there are also odd items to be had, such as dusty sheet music stores and natural medicine apothecaries smelling of ancient herbs. Turn a corner and you'll find Chinese gold, mah-jongg sets, vermillion lanterns and lion dogs side-by-side with the latest Canto-pop CD collections and Taiwanese daytime dramas.
>
> (Cruz, 2012)

To successfully read this text, students have to process ideational, interpersonal, and textual meanings all at the same time. From an ideational perspective, they have to pick up on information on people, things, and various goings-on. From an interpersonal perspective, they need to unlock meanings that appraise or offer opinions on the ideational meanings. From a textual perspective, students need to understand how information "flows" from one point of the text to the next. In our lesson plan, we show how the five phases can be used as a framework to help students unlock all meanings through the combination of Filipino and English. Furthermore, we will also show how students can learn English through the ideational, interpersonal, and textual scaffolding of the local language.

The Prepare phase should involve "introducing" the students to the text so the local language is appropriate here. Here is a sample of a possible preparation in Filipino (English translation provided):

Magbabasa tayo ngayon ng isang maikling *paragraph* tungkol sa Chinatown, isang lugar sa Maynila kung saan nakatira ang mga kapatid nating lahing Filipino-Chinese. Kay dami niyang tao at maraming mabibili rito kagaya ng Chinese food, iba't ibang Chinese products, at mga Chinese herbs na ginagamit panggamot.

(Today, we will read a short paragraph on Chinatown, a place in Manila where our Filipino-Chinese brothers and sisters live. It is full of people and has many things to buy, from Chinese food to different Chinese products, including Chinese herbs which are used for medicinal purposes.)

Notice that the Prepare phase that introduces the reading is a summary of the entire text. Through the local language, students' expectations are built up in terms of what meanings they will have to process. This text uses high-level vocabulary so a detailed lesson plan should guide students toward reading and understanding this vocabulary. The detailed lesson plans that follow show how one part of the reading is taught in both the local and the target language. The right-hand column explains and expounds on the use and purposes of the local language at that point in the lesson. In the Philippines, a mix of Filipino and English, or *Taglish*, is often used, as will be seen in the Lesson 1.

In this lesson cycle, a definition was unlocked. Filipino is dominant here because uncommonsense knowledge is made more commonsense by linking new knowledge with the old. An expanding vocabulary is a key toward learning uncommonsense meanings. *Massive*, for example, can also be used in the sciences, as in "The planet Jupiter is massive next to the Earth." The definition is further elaborated on in Lesson 2.

In these lesson cycles, English is used to extend the definition of the new word while the local language is used to shift the uncommonsense new vocabulary to the commonsense of student experience. Ideational meaning is built up by discussing participants (people versus animals) and interpersonal meaning is built by defining *massive* and soliciting feelings ("feels tight"). In this next cycle (Lesson 3), an introduction to the structure of nominal groups is taught using another part of the text.

In these lesson cycles, Filipino and English are both used to build knowledge about English. Filipino is used to minimise the semiotic load (Rose & Martin, 2012; Kartika-Ningsih, 2016) of learning a new concept in English, which bridges commonsense and uncommonsense. In these multilingual lesson cycles, both languages work together to achieve the targeted lesson.

★

LESSON 1

Prepare	Basahin natin yung umpisa. (Let's read the start.) *The massive throngs of people and snarling jeepneys (a hybrid jeep and van) shouldn't dissuade you from hotfooting it to the world's oldest living, breathing Chinatown, which is currently on its fourth century.* Tignan natin yung salitang *massive*. Ang ibig sabihin nito dito ay "madaming-madami." (Let's look at the word *massive*. Here, this means "a lot.")	The local language is used interpersonally to give instructions. A key vocabulary item is identified and defined. Filipino is used here to build interpersonal meaning. *Massive* expresses an opinion which makes it a feature of the interpersonal metafunction.
Focus	Ano yung salita na nagsasabi kung gaano kadami ang tao sa Chinatown? (What word is telling us about the number of people in Chinatown?)	Further draws students' attention to the vocabulary item. Filipino is used interpersonally to solicit participation through a question.
Task	Massive!	
Evaluate	Very good!	English is used to affirm, which may give a positive view of the target language (Kartika-Ningsih, 2016).
Elaborate	Maari rin nating gamitin ang *massive* para i-*describe* kung gaano kalaki ang isang bagay. Puwedeng *massive* ang isang tao—napakalaki niya—or *massive* ang bagay kagaya ng *truck*. (We can also use *massive* to describe how large something is. A person can be *massive*—a very big person—or an object can be *massive* like a truck.)	Filipino is used to Elaborate because this phase extends the uncommonsense knowledge (new word) to students' commonsense experience. The elaboration combines interpersonal meaning (*massive*) with ideational meanings (people and trucks) to show how the combination of these two meanings expresses a new meaning.

LESSON 2

Focus	Ano yung salitang sumunod sa *massive*? (What word follows *massive*?)	This phase is targeted so even "weak" students can find the word and be affirmed.
Task	Throngs!	
Evaluate	Very good!	
Elaborate	Ang *massive throng* ay isang malaking-malaking grupo ng tao o hayop. Ang *throng* ay kapareho ng "crowd of people or animals." (A *massive throng* is a huge group of people or animals. A *throng* means the same as "a crowd of people or animals.")	As a new vocabulary item is added, English is used so new knowledge of the target language is gained.
Focus	Are there *people or animals* in Chinatown? Tignan niyo yung sumusunod. (Look at what follows.)	A new Focus calls attention to another language feature. English is used to introduce the Focus because the definition in the prior phase was in English. Students are then asked to identify an ideational meaning while an interpersonal meaning is used to give commands.
Task	People!	
Evaluate	Very good!	
Elaborate	*Massive throngs* of people refer to "a lot of huge crowds."	The target language is now used to build new vocabulary. The combination of interpersonal and ideational meaning (*a lot of huge + crowds*) models an English structure that is similar to *massive throngs of people*.
Focus	Alam niyo kung ano ang isang *crowd*? Kagaya sa *basketball game* o *concert*? (You know what a crowd is? Like in a basketball game or concert?)	A new Focus extends the vocabulary to the field of student experience. Filipino is once again used to bridge commonsense and uncommonsense.
Task	Yes!	
Evaluate	Of course!	
Focus	Ano ang feeling pag nasa *crowd* ka? (What does it feel like to be in a crowd?)	Uncommonsense is extended to commonsense.
Task	Mainit! (Hot!)	
Evaluate	Tama! (Correct!)	
Elaborate	It's very hot in a crowd.	The target language is used as interpersonal meaning

continued . . .

LESSON 2 Continued

Focus	Ano ang feeling pag nasa *massive throngs of people*? (What does being in massive throngs of people feel like?)	(*hot*) is added to the learning. Focus taps into experience but uses the new vocabulary and structure.
Task	Masikip! (Tight!)	
Evaluate	Correct!	
Elaborate	It feels tight.	Brings in a grammar structure in English that can be learned, discussed, or practiced.

LESSON 3

Prepare	Pag-usapan natin ngayon ang makakain sa Chinatown kagaya ng mga itlog o *eggs*, siopao, lumpia, *noodles*, *tarts*, hopia. (Now, we talk about what we can eat in Chinatown like eggs, siopao, lumpia, noodles, tarts, hopia.)	Filipino is used to introduce the next lesson which feels less threatening because key meanings are identified. Ideational meanings are in English. *Ngayon* is used textually to start a new lesson.
Direct*	Paki-*underline* nga sila. Nahanap niyo? (Underline them. Did you find them?)	*This new phase is inserted to ask the students to perform an action. Filipino is used interpersonally to give instructions.
Focus	Ano ang kasama ng salitang *eggs* o itlog? (What word comes with the word *eggs*?)	Filipino is used to focus students' attention. A translation of the lexis is given.
Task	Tea!	
Evaluate	Very good!	
Elaborate	*Tea eggs*. Ang *tea* ay tsaa sa Tagalog. Ang *tea eggs* ay mga pinakuluang itlog na binabad sa *tea* para lalo silang sumarap. Pang merienda ito. (The Tagalog for *tea* is "tsaa." *Tea eggs* are boiled eggs that were marinated in tea to make them delicious. These are a form of snack food.)	Filipino is used to elaborate but the English structure is retained.
Focus	Paano pa puwedeng lutuin ang mga itlog? (How else can eggs be cooked?)	The teacher is leading the students to produce the same grammatical structure as *tea eggs*.

continued . . .

LESSON 3 Continued

Task	Scrambled! Fried! Pinakuluan (Boiled)!	
Evaluate	Tama! (Correct!)	
Elaborate	*Scrambled eggs, boiled eggs, fried eggs.* Meron rin *soft-boiled eggs* o *poached eggs.* (We also have *soft-boiled eggs* or *poached eggs.*)	The response does not trigger the use of the structure, so the teacher models the structure in the next phase.
Prepare	Ngayon, tignan natin ang iba pang pagkain. (Now, let's look at the other types of food.)	A new phase of the lesson is introduced.
Focus	Ano pa ang ibang pagkain na mahahanap sa Chinatown? (What are the other foods that can be found in Chinatown?)	
Task	[Students read out the answers: Fried siopao, crunchy lumpia, etc.]	
Evaluate	Excellent!	
Elaborate	*Eggs*, siopao, lumpia—ang mga salitang ito ay mga *nouns.* Ang *noun* ay pangalan ng tao o bagay. Ginagamit ang mga *noun* para pag-usapan ang mga tao at bagay na nakikita natin. Ang mga *noun* ay puwede ring lagyan ng impormasyon para mas alam natin kung anong tao o bagay ang pinag-uusapan, kagaya ng salitang *tea eggs.* Maraming iba't ibang uri ng pagluto ng itlog. Pag nilagay yung salitang *tea*, nagiging klaro kung anong klaseng itlog ang pinag-uusapan. (Eggs, siopao, lumpia—these words are *nouns.* A *noun* is the name of a person or thing. We need *nouns* to talk about the people and things we see. But information can be added to nouns so we know better what or who we are talking about, like *tea eggs.* There are many ways of cooking eggs. If we add *tea*, then it's clear what type of egg is referred to.)	Filipino is used to define a technical term (*noun*) but the term itself is not translated. However, additional knowledge is expressed in Filipino.
Prepare	Balik tayo sa mga pagkain na mabibili sa Chinatown. (Let's go back to the food.)	
Direct	Isulat natin sa blackboard yung mga buong pangalan ng mga pagkain. (Let's write on the board the full names of the foods.)	
Task	[Students write.]	
Evaluate	Great!	

continued . . .

LESSON 3 Continued

Elaborate	Itong kombinasyon ng *noun* at iba't ibang salita na nagbibigay impormasyon tungkol sa kanila ay tinatawag na *nominal group*. The nominal group is a "group of words about a noun." (This combination of a *noun* and other words that give information about the *noun* is called the *nominal group*.)	Filipino is used to define uncommonsense. But, the more formal definition is given in English.
Prepare	Ngayon, mag-practice tayo. (Now, let's practice.)	
Focus	Look at the nominal groups on the board. Choose one noun and change the word that comes before it. Kunyari, *crunchy lumpia*. *Lumpia* yung noun, *crunchy* ang Describer niya. Palitan natin ang *crunchy*. (For example, *crunchy lumpia*. *Lumpia* is the noun, *crunchy* is its Describer. Let's change *crunchy*.)	Uncommonsense definitions have been established so English is used. But, the example is given in Filipino to connect commonsense and uncommonsense.
Task	Crispy lumpia!	
Evaluate	Tama! (Correct!)	
Elaborate	*Crispy* is a Describer. Ang Describer ay nagbibigay impormasyon tungkol sa kalidad ng isang tao o bagay. Kunyari, ang lumpia ay *crispy* imbis na *stale*. Pag ang isang pagkain ay *stale*, ito ay luma o makunat. (A Describer gives information on the quality of a person or thing. For example, the lumpia is *crispy* as opposed to *stale*. When food is *stale*, it is old or tough.)	The technical, ideational meaning is given in English but the definition is in Filipino. New vocabulary in English (*stale*) is built too.
Prepare	Lagyan natin ng mga Describer yung mga ibang pagkain. (Let's add Describers to the other foods.)	Filipino is used interpersonally.
Focus	Listahan ito ng iba't ibang Describer. Tignan niyo kung ano ang puwedeng gamitin sa iba't ibang pagkain. (Here's a list of different Describers. Try to see which ones can be used for the different foods.)	
Task	[Students do the task.]	
Evaluate	Very good!	
Elaborate	Nominal groups have a part called a Describer.	English is now used to summarise the lesson.

Conclusion

The move to integrate MTB-MLE into mainstream education is arguably a positive one and can help protect and promote minority/local languages. However, as this paper has argued, it is not sufficient to simply legislate this policy. For MTB-MLE to succeed, we need to advocate for, support, and develop local languages so that people see value in them and teachers use them for more than just regulative and interpersonal purposes. This chapter elaborates on what some of the current challenges with MTB-MLE are and also proposes ways in which local languages can be used more effectively in classrooms. We have outlined how local languages can be used in each of the five phases of a lesson cycle so that they are used for both instructional and regulative purposes.

To conclude, we firmly believe that local languages should be used in educational contexts and that this should be done conscientiously and with an understanding of what language is, how it creates meanings, and how it varies to create the right meaning in the right context. We hope that this chapter encourages further research into this area: Research that does not only analyse people's beliefs and attitudes, but research that analyses and informs MTB-MLE classroom discourse and practices.

References

Amarles, A. M. (2016). Multilingualism, multilingual education, and the English language: Voices of public school teachers. *Philippine Journal of Linguistics, 47*, 93–108.

Azurin, A. M. (2010). Re-inventing basic education: The shift to mother tongue-based instruction. In R. Nolasco, F. Datar & A. Azurin (Eds.), *Starting where the children are: A collection of essays on mother tongue-based multilingual education and language issues in the Philippines* (pp. 1–7). Quezon City: Talaytayan.

Bernstein, B. (1975). *Class, codes, and control: Towards a theory of educational transmission (Vol. 3)*. London, UK: Routledge.

Canilao, M. L. E. N. (2015). Examining the place of English in the teaching of Mathematics in an urban public elementary school in the Philippines. (Unpublished doctoral dissertation). Ateneo de Manila University, Philippines: Quezon City.

Christie, F. (1999). The pedagogic device and the teaching of English. In F. Christie (Ed.), *Pedagogy and the shaping of consciousness: Linguistic and social processes* (pp. 156–184). London, UK: Continuum.

Cruz, C. (2012). Rediscover Manila: 10 things I like about you. (Unpublished magazine article).

Dekker, D. (2010). What is mother tongue-based multilingual education? In R. Nolasco, F. Datar & A. Azurin (Eds.), *Starting where the children are: A collection of essays on mother tongue-based multilingual education and language issues in the Philippines* (pp. 23–25). Quezon City: Talaytayan.

Gonzalez, A. (2004). The social dimensions of Philippine English. *World Englishes, (23)*1, 7–16.

Halliday, M. A. K., & Hasan, R. (1985). *Language, context, and text: Aspects of language in a social semiotic perspective*. Oxford: University Press.

Halliday, M. A. K. (2004). *The language of early childhood*. J. Webster (Ed.). London, UK: Continuum.

Kartika-Ningsih, H. (2016). *Multilingual re-instantiation: Genre pedagogy in Indonesian classrooms* (Unpublished doctoral thesis). Australia: University of Sydney.

Lorente, B. (2013). The grip of English and Philippine language policy. In L. Wee, R. B. H. Goh & L. Lim (Eds.), *The politics of English: South Asia, Southeast Asia, and the Asia Pacific* (pp. 187–203). Amsterdam: John Benjamins Publishing Company.

Mahboob, A. (2017). Understanding language variation: Implications of the NNEST lens for TESOL teacher education programs. In J. D. Martínez Agudo (Ed.), *Native and non-native speakers in English language-teaching: Implications and challenges for teacher education* (pp. 13–32). Boston: De Gruyter Mouton. doi: 10.1515/9781501504143-002

Mahboob, A., & Cruz, P. (2013). English and mother-tongue-based multilingual education: Language attitudes in the Philippines. *Asian Journal of English Language Studies: The Official Journal of the UST Department of English*, *1*, 1–19.

Mahboob, A., & Lin, A. (2017). Using Local Languages in English Language Classrooms. In H. Widodo & W. Renandya (Eds.), *English language teaching today: Building a closer link between theory and practice*. New York: Springer International.

Martin, J. R. (1993). Technology, bureaucracy, and schooling: Discursive resources and control. *Cultural Dynamics*, *6*, 84–130. doi: 10.1177/092137409300600104

Martin, J. R. (1997). Analyzing genre: Functional parameters. In F. Christie & J.R. Martin (Eds.), *Genre and institutions: Social processes in the workplace and school* (pp. 3–39). London, UK: Continuum.

McFarland, C. (2008). Linguistic diversity and English in the Philippines. In L. Bautista & K. Bolton (Eds.), *Philippine English: Linguistic and literary perspectives* (pp. 131–156). Hong Kong: University Press.

Nolasco, R. (2008, July). *The prospects of multilingual education and literacy in the Philippines.* Paper presented at the Conference on Language Development, Language Revitalization and Multilingual Education in Ethnolinguistic Communities, Thailand: Bangkok.

Rose, D., & Martin, J. R. (2012). *Learning to write, reading to learn: Genre, knowledge, and pedagogy in the Sydney school*. South Yorkshire: Equinox.

Tupas, R. (2015). The politics of 'p' and 'f': A linguistic history of nation-building in the Philippines. *Journal of Multilingual and Multicultural Development*, *36*(6), 587–597. doi: 10.1080/01434632.2014.979831

Walter, S., Dekker, D., Dekker, G., Duguiang, N., Bawer, A., Bulawit, C., . . . Wansi, B. (2010). Initial results of the Lubuagan MTBMLE program. In R. Nolasco, F. Datar & A. Azurin (Eds.), *Starting where the children are: A collection of essays on mother tongue-based multilingual education and language issues in the Philippines* (pp. 38–43). Quezon City: Talaytayan.

4

BYPASSING UNREPRESENTATIVE POLICIES

What do Indigenous Australians Say About Language Education?

Rebecca Hetherington

Introduction

Language education policy must contend with issues such as who is to be taught which language forms and when, and how this teaching will occur, all of which depend on financial, political and community support. In addition, in many places colonial histories have combined with the formation of nation states to promote and perpetuate one or more national languages, often at the expense of indigenous languages. Indigenous language speakers have frequently been encouraged to move away from traditional modes of being and speaking, and toward assimilation with more recently dominant societal groups.

Despite this familiar scenario, speakers of indigenous languages have had some success in asserting their rights to heritage languages and cultures, partly in order to gain a greater degree of control over their education. Indigenous language education has therefore begun to appear in government language education policies. The existence of such policies is crucial, because they have the potential to ensure language maintenance and revival in indigenous communities; to validate language use and the cultural information it encodes; and to contribute to the equitable participation of indigenous communities in schooling and society.

The roles of both governments and communities are important to the pursuit of equitable participation in education. While Francis and Reyhner (2002, p. 18) argue that "only the indigenous community can put into motion the critical resources" to reverse language shift, Nakata (1999) and Hornberger (2008) agree that schools and governments must work *in concert* to achieve social justice, which is an important aim of indigenous language education. It is this juxtaposition of policy and the classroom that this chapter examines:

> ... on the one hand, ideological spaces opened up by policies or discourses may carve out implementational spaces; and on the other, implementational spaces at classroom, school, and community levels may serve as wedges to pry open ideological spaces that are closed or closing ...
>
> (Hornberger, 2008, p. 3)

In the Australian context, the effects of the colonial past continue into the present and have dramatic consequences for the relationship between the government and Aboriginal and Torres Strait Islander communities on the subject of language teaching and policy. While Indigenous[1] education and Indigenous language teaching are part of education policies around Australia, the views, needs and interests of Indigenous peoples have long been underrepresented or underplayed (Moran, 2016). Furthermore, Australia's highly diverse Indigenous population suffers from significantly higher mortality and incarceration rates than the population overall, as well as underrepresentation in schooling, so language education policy that engages and empowers students is particularly important. But despite the ongoing presence of a range of Indigenous language education measures (Lewthwaite et al., 2015, pp. 132–133) in Australian policy, as well as recent advances in the recognition of Indigenous contact languages (Queensland Department of Education, Training and Employment, 2013), these policy endeavours have largely failed to achieve substantial change in educational outcomes for Indigenous Australians (Department of Prime Minister and Cabinet, 2017; Pearson, 2009).

Instead of examining policies, this chapter therefore focuses upon the perspectives of Indigenous Australians on language education. The data come from interviews with four Aboriginal people, each of whom are involved, or have been involved, in language education. The interviews were conducted in the first half of 2015 as part of a larger, ongoing research project into policy representation, and were analysed using an iterative, inductive form of content analysis. The themes that emerged within the larger category of education were then compared with the principles of translanguaging, and the key points of agreement and disagreement are presented here. In this way, the interviews offer an opportunity to explore the application of translanguaging pedagogies in the context of Aboriginal and Torres Strait Islander education. Translanguaging pedagogies, outlined below, have the potential to support social justice for indigenous communities, and so may be able to substantially improve Indigenous language education and policy.

Translanguaging Theory

Scholars in the field of language education increasingly recognise problems associated with artificially dividing languages from one another both linguistically (Makoni & Pennycook, 2007) and within the individual learner, and theories of plurilingualism and translanguaging have sprung up to address these problems (Kubota, 2014). In broad terms, such theories argue that plurilingual speakers draw on one underlying repertoire of language features, rather than having separate repertoires for each language. Speakers choose the appropriate language features for each interlocutor, whether at the level of vocabulary or of prosodic or discursive techniques. Individuals are therefore *trans*-languaging; able to draw on and move between a range of features to be both creative (flouting or following norms of language use) and critical (using evidence to question, problematise or express views) (García & Wei, 2014, p. 24).

Adopting translanguaging pedagogy in the classroom allows students to draw on their existing linguistic resources in creative ways, thereby overcoming disadvantages experienced by students who are prevented from using their home or other languages in the classroom, and disassociating content knowledge from linguistic expertise. While many authors (Cenoz, 2009; Francis & Reyhner, 2002; Lewthwaite et al., 2015; Sellwood & Angelo, 2013) recommend the principles of a translanguaging approach (though not all use the term 'translanguaging'), this chapter draws most heavily on García and Wei (2014) and García and Kleyn (2016). This is primarily because of their focus on the transformative socio-political and ideological power that translanguaging pedagogies can offer. As García and Wei (2014, p. 37) explain:

> Translanguaging for us, however, is part of a moral and political act that links the production of alternative meanings to transformative social action. As such, translanguaging contributes to the social justice agenda. This in itself distinguishes our concept from many others . . .

This transformative social action takes place in part by granting legitimacy to the practices of multilingual speakers, increasing their confidence and enabling them to take a more active part in their education. This disrupts existing societal hierarchies, because multilingual students or learners of the dominant language are typically minoritised, and improving the education of minoritised students contributes to a more equitable society (García & Kleyn, 2016). Translanguaging theory may therefore offer a school-based contribution to better language policy.

The second reason to draw primarily on García and Kleyn (2016) and García and Wei (2014) is that they have provided detailed models of translanguaging pedagogy and how it can be (and is) enacted in classrooms. For teachers, in addition to taking a student-centred translanguaging stance, these authors promote the use of collaborative teaching structures and multimodal and multilingual resources. Some of these pedagogical tools are discussed in the context of Aboriginal and Torres Strait Islander language teaching below, but a full examination of translanguaging pedagogies is offered by García and Wei (2014).

Translanguaging in Aboriginal and Torres Strait Islander Contexts

The Indigenous Australian context has several distinguishing features that provide challenges and opportunities in language education and for the pursuit of social justice. While there were over 250 Indigenous Australian language groups at the time of colonisation in 1788, it is currently estimated that only around 120 of those languages are still spoken (AIATSIS, n.d.). Zuckermann, Shakuto-Neoh and Quer (2014, p. 56) estimate that only 13 of these are still spoken as native languages by children, although it is unclear whether this number includes Indigenous contact languages, which in Australia refers to English-lexified creoles.[2] Examples are Aboriginal English, Yumplatok (formerly Torres Strait Islander Creole) and Gurindji Kriol, which are each documented by linguists as established, mixed languages with thousands of native speakers, but which have only recently begun to be recognised in language policy (Queensland Department of Education, Training and Employment, 2013; Sellwood & Angelo, 2013). Of these contact languages, Aboriginal English receives additional acknowledgement in the Australian Curriculum (Australian Curriculum, Assessment and Reporting Authority, 2014), which increasingly refers to EAL/D (English as an Additional Language/Dialect) as a way of recognising that Aboriginal English and other Indigenous contact languages are legitimate languages that are separate from English, and whose speakers cannot be productively treated as speakers of (Standard Australian) English in school settings.

Some Indigenous languages and language varieties are taught in schools, in TAFEs (tertiary colleges of Technical and Further Education) and in universities, while some communities and organisations run language nests or local language classes. For others, there may be little or no organisational support beyond general policy statements, and limited or no language materials or funding. Bilingual education for Indigenous students, which was promoted in the 1970s in particular (Oldfield, 2016; Simpson, Caffery & McConvell, 2009), was partly dismantled by then Prime Minister John Howard in the late 1990s, following the increased focus on standardised testing in English literacy (Beazley, 1997; Moore, 1995). In the Northern Territory, which has a high percentage of Indigenous people, bilingual education was almost completely removed by the introduction of what has been termed the "First Four Hours Policy", which required that the first four hours of school be conducted in English (Dickson, 2012; Oldfield, 2016; Simpson et al., 2009). It is worth noting that the status of the Northern Territory as a territory rather than a state complicates Indigenous language teaching, because territories do not have as much power as states to resist federal government decisions (Martin, 2015).

Part of the challenge facing teachers of Indigenous languages in Australia is to raise the profile and status of these languages and the cultures they encode, particularly in the case of contact languages, which are frequently seen as 'bad English' rather than complete and complex linguistic systems (Sellwood &

Angelo, 2013). Recent education policy has begun to address this (Queensland Department of Education, Training and Employment, 2013, p. 7), but Indigenous educational markers have not improved (Department of Prime Minister and Cabinet, 2017). Raising language profiles, which may be done in Indigenous language classrooms and in other school contexts, can have a substantial impact upon many aspects of society, including government policy.

This awareness-raising is particularly challenging in the context of Aboriginal and Torres Strait Islander languages because of the reluctance of many Australians to recognise the uglier aspects of Australia's colonial history, which include genocide, dispossession, sexual exploitation, and the forced removal of children (Barta, 2008; Harris, 2003). This combines with neoliberal individualism to create a scenario in which Indigenous communities often have to struggle for recognition of the legitimacy of their views, let alone equitable educational treatment. In being subject to systems which purport to protect everybody from racism or bigotry, and to give everybody the opportunity to succeed, individuals may be blamed if they fail to take advantage of these opportunities, concealing existing systems of racial bias (Gomberg, 2007).

Such issues are perpetuated by a policy system that attempts to address 'problems', but which defines many problems in terms of individual motivation or capacity rather than systemic societal inequities (Bacchi, 2009). This is why examining what communities are actually doing and saying is crucial. Although the impetus for change ought not to be on small communities, which can only legitimately contest existing structures by positioning themselves within them, it has been shown that in the realm of Australian language policy, community action speaks louder than decades of words. These inequities highlight the importance of considering context in any classroom that attempts to contribute to social justice through education. Cultural learning must include recognition of Australia's colonial past, and in this case it has the potential to partly counteract dominant discourses and recognise the importance of alternative community action.

Linguistic Suitability for Translanguaging Pedagogies

Despite these challenges, on linguistic grounds the Aboriginal and Torres Strait Islander languages spoken in Australia may be peculiarly well suited to translanguaging pedagogies in the classroom. Many of these languages already demonstrate features that disrupt the expectation of languages as natural, separate entities that is increasingly critiqued in the field of applied linguistics (García & Kleyn, 2016; Makoni & Pennycook, 2007). One example is the aforementioned existence of Indigenous contact languages, which draw on a combination of Australian English and other languages and therefore fail to conform to separatist views of language.

Additionally, some Indigenous languages use the technique of trading language elements to follow conventions around taboo words, while others have been reconstructed using linguistic features from different but related languages. These techniques for language revival and maintenance were specifically raised by two interview participants. The first is Davina Woods, a Kuku-Yalanji/Kuku-Djungan woman currently an academic at Victoria University, and who was Federal Aboriginal Education Officer with the Australian Education Union in the 1990s. The second is an Indigenous community leader who asked to remain anonymous, and who has worked with schools to teach her local language within classrooms, as well as occasionally running additional language and culture classes. These participants spoke about language trading in the context of revival and education:

> [There's] evidence of languages being traded from Northeastern Australia to Southwestern Australia, there's the whole issue about those communities that won't speak the name of the dead and their names may be also the name of something that the community might use, so another name has to be found for that individual who might share that name, or that item that might share that name.
>
> (Davina Woods)

> ... as I got older I found out there was a lot of other language words involved. But even though they came from a different dialect, they were still part of the [language] group. So I looked into all these different languages, and now I—all the different dialects. So now I speak a mixture of all the different dialects instead of just the one, yeah.
>
> (Anonymous Community Leader)

These techniques demonstrate that some Indigenous peoples are already drawing on practices that promote linguistic fluidity, which is a feature of translanguaging theory. There are also Indigenous sign languages accompanying or replacing spoken language (NT Language Support Program, n.d.). As a result, there is already an understanding present in some communities and by some linguists and politicians (House of Representatives Standing Committee on Aboriginal and Torres Strait Islander Affairs, 2012) that language boundaries may be fluid or blurred. This suggests that some of the groundwork for a shift in social discourses and expectations around language and culture may already be in place, better enabling a shift to translanguaging pedagogies.

Educational Suitability for Translanguaging Pedagogies

In addition to the apparent suitability of Aboriginal and Torres Strait Islander languages to the adoption of translanguaging models, interview participants spoke about their teaching methods in the classroom, many of which already align with a translanguaging pedagogy. For example, because teachers of many languages in the process of revitalisation cannot access textbooks, stories or videos that use their language, they adopt the translanguaging pedagogy's multimodal approach (Cope & Kalantzis, 2009; García & Kleyn, 2016), which in this context can be adopted in two main ways. The first is to use land-based resources to learn about cultural practices and associated language. This is already happening in some communities—the anonymous community leader reflected on the value of a trip onto country:

> It was a program that—where we were able to take our kids out on sea and country. We were able to get a boat taken out to sea and do country and teaching them culture and language, and that was really good.
> (Anonymous Community Leader)

A second avenue for drawing on multimodalities available to teachers of Indigenous languages is to invite local community members into the classroom. Already, young children in some communities are able to attend language nests, while the anonymous community leader interviewed here had been working as a contractor in different schools for several years.

Translanguaging pedagogies also represent a key method of combining language and cultural awareness to address problems with the translation of Aboriginal and Torres Strait Islander concepts. Davina Woods stated that the English translations for many Aboriginal and Torres Strait Islander concepts are wholly inadequate for conveying the true meanings of the original concepts and that, in addition, people are unaware of this inadequacy:

> ... there needs to be a greater understanding of the fact that words that were applied at the time of first contact, between not only the colonisers but also later anthropologists such as Stenner [...] the translations into English of specific concepts is fraught with difficulties. [...] there has never been a true understanding of a lot of concepts from Aboriginal traditional cultural ways because there is no English equivalent.
> (Davina Woods)

The example given by Woods was *The Dreaming*, or *Dreamtime*, which she believes conjures up for most Australians the image of dreaming while being asleep. Instead, this concept is closely connected to the tradition and power of stories that are passed on through generations, and therefore the power of the word; Woods drew parallels with similar aspects of Christianity. The adoption of a translanguaging pedagogy would encourage the use of the original words in the local language, bypassing the widely-acknowledged issues of translation (Eco, 2003; Bassnett, 2002) and thereby enabling a deeper understanding and appreciation of Indigenous languages and cultures. Educationally, then, the interview data reveal several possible advantages to adopting a translanguaging pedagogy, aspects of which are already drawn on in language classrooms.

Public Awareness and Indigenous Identity

The interview participants believed that cultural awareness is crucial to shift the place of Indigenous communities in policy, schooling and society more broadly. However, there are several different perspectives on including *non-Indigenous* Australians in Indigenous language practices, cultures and traditions. For some it has the potential to raise awareness and legitimate Aboriginal and Torres Strait Islander perspectives, while others believe that there can only be a limited place for non-Indigenous engagement with Indigenous language and culture. It has also been suggested that the focus on Indigeneity could be harming the push for recognition in some contexts (Nakata, 1999).

The first of these perspectives is evident in the interview data. David Newry is part of the Miriwoong language group, from the Kimberley region. He helped to establish and run Mirima Council, and played a crucial role in developing the Kimberley Interpreting Service. He is currently engaged by the Mirima Dawang Woorlab-gerring Language and Culture Centre as Senior Language and Culture Consultant. Newry runs cultural awareness courses for local, non-Indigenous businesses and government offices to raise awareness of local culture and to counteract the refusal of the local shire council to recognise the validity of Indigenous perspectives on topics as diverse as the environment, urban development and the behaviour of Indigenous youths in public. Davina Woods takes a similar approach to non-Indigenous participation in Indigenous cultures:

> So one of the best things to do I guess is what's been happening more recently and that is more of the popular culture is taking up the Aboriginal story, the Torres Strait Islander story.

However, despite these positive standpoints on raising the validity of Indigenous perspectives through education of the broader public, considerations of language ownership can complicate this issue. It is important not to homogenise Aboriginal and Torres Strait Islander communities, because there are many different Indigenous languages, cultures, beliefs and expectations present on the continent. For some of these communities, the inclusion of non-Indigenous students in Indigenous language classrooms may be inappropriate. Marianne McKinnon-Kidd, who has experience teaching a range of languages including her own (Dharug), spoke about the importance of language to identity and the consequences this can have for language teaching:

> ... of course the people who are indigenous to that particular area, say if you were teaching at, uh, Muswellbrook or something like that, where the Wonnarua people are, well Wonnarua people would be saying, "We have to be taught it first because it's our language and it's being brought back, and they will have to wait until we've been taught." And then the last

people to get taught are going to be the non-Aboriginal people, you know—"We have to teach the Aboriginal people first, so we'll teach the Wonnarua people, then we'll teach the blow-ins, then we'll teach the white fellas, but we have to know first because it's our language and it was taken from us", you know?

Issues of language rights and ownership have been part of the platform of many Indigenous organisations for a long time. Davina Woods referred to the basic political platform of the Australian Education Union as having "always been to do with resource, rights to the resources for traditional owners; and rights to our identity; and also to our autonomy. But then our language part was one of those, you know, underpinning those three major ones." David Newry has written about the right of Indigenous communities to restrict access to their languages (Newry & Palmer, 2003). This can make it difficult for non-Indigenous teachers to teach Indigenous languages. It emphasises the need to bring local Indigenous teachers into classrooms, which benefits both them and their students by helping to "transform language hierarchies" (García & Kleyn, 2016, p. 21) and counteracting the hegemony of English. On a broader scale, the inclusion of Indigenous teachers and languages in the classroom can allow Indigenous peoples greater control over expressions of their traditional identities within the context of an English-dominant, monolingual mindset.

A more negative perspective on sharing Indigenous culture comes from Nakata (1999). Writing from a Torres Strait Islander perspective, he argues that the focus on Indigenous culture could be harming chances for equitable participation of Indigenous peoples in Australian society. Nakata believes that the focus on culture and Indigenous rights has led to a homogenisation of Indigenous perspectives by being understood as "a panacea for all our ills" (1999, p. 14), and by preventing other, potentially conflicting issues from being raised, such as the desire for effective English language education. More generally, Ruiz (1984; 2010) has argued that a rights-oriented approach to language policy tends to be excessively combative in its discourse and risks alienating those who could grant the rights sought. Both these authors conclude that only by seeing language as a *resource* can English and other languages be given equitable and productive space in education. However, language communities around the world, and indigenous language communities in particular, have tended to rely on collective rights discourses to secure rights to language, culture and education; Bauman (2001, p. 76) points out that human rights must be fought for, won and granted collectively, though enjoyed separately.

One of the biggest difficulties with this need for collective action, and one that underlies Nakata's and Ruiz's concerns, is that engaging with policy as a community is also to differentiate one's community from the ruling group. Being defined through difference gives Indigenous communities the opportunity to become political constituents and the space to engage with political processes.

But such differentiation can lead to the perception of communities as divisive groups that threaten the democracy with which they are trying to engage (Laitin, 2000). This disadvantage may be inescapable; Aboriginal and Torres Strait Islanders are perceived as a differentiated community in Australian politics, so those who advocate can only choose how to take advantage of that perception, or challenge it. Translanguaging may help by better educating minoritised groups and by contributing to social justice through the increased presence of alternative Indigenous narratives.

However, the contradiction remains: On the one hand, many Indigenous peoples use a rights discourse and a focus on culture to advocate for rights and cultural recognition, but on the other, this may undermine their need to know English well, both for educational equity and for the ability to advocate for those rights effectively in the first place (Hall, 2003; Nakata, 1999). Crucial in this discussion is that the need to know English well *and* the push for Indigenous rights may be further undermined by translanguaging discourses. This is because the translanguaging theory promoted by García and Wei (2014) and García and Kleyn (2016) "goes beyond the static definition of language as autonomous and pure, and as used 'originally' by a specific group of people whose identity depends on this" (García and Wei, 2014, p. 72). A translanguaging stance, by erasing the artificial lines between languages, may therefore weaken one of the very arguments for a claim to language and educational rights that Aboriginal and Torres Strait Islander communities have been drawing on for decades.

As a counterpoint to this, consideration of Australian contact languages (such as Aboriginal English) may benefit from a more fluid understanding of language and the disconnection of tradition from language (Sellwood & Angelo, 2013). Currently, these languages' roles as vehicles for culture and Indigeneity is almost invisible both in policy and in society more broadly (Sellwood & Angelo, 2013). This arguably further justifies Nakata's (1999) point about the restrictive nature of the policy focus on continuing culture because, while Indigenous contact languages may not have the longevity of other Aboriginal and Torres Strait Islander languages, they still provide the primary means for communication, culture and identity for thousands of people. These different aspects of the one problem underscore the need for Indigenous communities to be able to control their own languages, and to be able to access funding to revitalise, modernise, maintain or teach them as desired.

Neoliberalism and Realities of Funding

The restricted options available to communities seeking policy redress are exacerbated by the problems of a neoliberal approach to community funding, which itself may be perpetuated by the plurilingual turn in applied linguistics. New language programs, curriculum development, new teacher training and professional development for current staff, the hiring of assistant language teachers and the procurement of new language materials all require money. But unless a policy is released that systematically directs funding towards these types of pedagogical tools and training, funding tends to be piecemeal, drawn from a variety of sources and programs for which individual teachers or community members must apply. Meanwhile, the focus of the recent plurilingual turn on the capabilities of individuals risks perpetuating a neoliberal ideology by focusing on English and other languages as individual skills that aid competition in a global market (Davis, 2014; Edwards, 2011). This in turn places responsibility on individuals and institutions and can appear to absolve governmental and societal structures from the obligation to provide funding, recognition, or to otherwise direct or undergo fundamental structural change (Black, 2004).

Instead, the impetus is on communities (and teachers) to prove that they can run successful programs, which often require funding, in order to get more funding. While this is not unreasonable from a policy perspective, it disadvantages smaller communities which may not have a language centre or the funds to independently pursue language and culture programs. David Newry spoke about the Miriwoong community's pursuit of language education initiatives despite such difficulties:

> But we're just a little, a small group of people. [. . .] We're always the voice in the wilderness when we somehow – we're one of the fortunate groups that we can do what we want, you know? [. . .] But only through doing things that it is making people see that what we are doing is really positive.

In contrast with the Miriwoong community, less-fortunate groups may struggle to take advantage of community programs and pedagogical innovations that can lead to social change, and are therefore less likely to be able to demonstrate that they deserve funding. Such policy and funding considerations may have a substantial impact on Indigenous language teaching in Australia, while also suggesting an underlying problem present in political and social discourses around Indigenous community needs. The following interview excerpt underlines the problems involved in teaching Aboriginal and Torres Strait Islander language and culture in some classrooms:

> . . . when I go into the schools and teach, I don't work for the Education Department. What happens is I have my own business, it's a sole trader business, and it's like—I'm a consultant. So the teachers, they just get money from wherever they can to pay me. Whatever the program they can get the money from, they will. That's—it's a shame, because they have—they've got to find this money from somewhere. [. . .] I doubt very much that the government gives the schools funds to get someone like me in specifically to teach Indigenous culture and language.
>
> (Anonymous community leader)

The anonymous community leader had attempted to get government funding for community language programs, but found the process far too complex for little chance of reward: "we have given up [. . .] it is just ridiculous what you have to go through to put in for language funding". Communities are therefore placed in a position in which, despite continued participation in policy processes, they are underrepresented in policies which define them as 'other' and as 'problems' to be solved in order to conform to the neoliberal tests for success.

Conclusion

This chapter has drawn on interviews with four Aboriginal educators to explore the usefulness of translanguaging pedagogies in an education policy context characterised by poor policy representation, often hard-to-access funding, and a neoliberal government policy framework. The data have shown that many of the principles of translanguaging are already being drawn on by Indigenous educators, and fit naturally with a range of Aboriginal and Torres Strait Islander languages.

However, whether translanguaging pedagogies will contribute to social justice in Australia is an unresolved question. On a large scale, the diversity of Indigenous communities may be too great to generalise productively, particularly given the disagreement across and within different communities regarding the involvement or participation of non-Indigenous Australians in Indigenous traditions, cultures and languages. But, on a smaller scale, translanguaging pedagogies do have the potential to encourage participation of Indigenous teachers in and out of the classroom, and to disrupt English language hegemony by softening the boundaries between English and other languages. By acknowledging and accepting a range of language practices as legitimate, translanguaging pedagogies can give Indigenous communities greater legitimacy in educational contexts. This, in turn, may give them the confidence to participate more actively in policy processes, as well as provide them with the education to draw on a range of rights and resource-based policy discourses to position themselves more effectively in community-government relations.

Notes

1 The use of language in this chapter attempts to recognise and counteract some of Australia's colonial legacy. 'Indigenous' and 'Aboriginal' are capitalised where they refer to the Indigenous communities of Australia (a practice widely accepted as inclusive and respectful); and where possible the language or cultural group of the interviewees is provided to counteract any elision of differences between different peoples. In addition, in the context of Indigenous communities Australia is preferentially referred to as a continent rather than a nation. This is in response to the interview with Marianne McKinnon-Kidd, a Dharug woman from the Southeast region of Australia who has taught Aboriginal languages at the tertiary level. She explained that the term 'Australia' is misleading:

> ... these countries, 250 countries it's pretty hard to sort of like, talk about it as one country, when there are so many countries, but um, and even that point, to get that point across, there's a big blanket that's gone over the continent, that's got Australia written across it ...

The name 'Australia' therefore risks obscuring the existence of the hundreds of nations that existed on the continent prior to colonisation and is avoided where possible.

2 Contact languages develop from continued contact between two or more language varieties. On the Australian continent, there are several Indigenous contact languages that are English-lexified (drawing most words from English), but which nonetheless vary significantly from the languages from which they developed, and which are transferred intergenerationally.

References

AIATSIS. (n.d.). *Indigenous Australian languages*. Retrieved from http://aiatsis.gov.au/explore/articles/indigenous-australian-languages.

Australian Curriculum, Assessment and Reporting Authority. (2014). *Who are EAL/D students?* Retrieved from www.australiancurriculum.edu.au/studentdiversity/who-are-eal-d-students.

Bacchi, C. (2009). *Analysing policy: What's the problem represented to be?* Australia: Frenchs Forest, N.S.W.

Barta, T. (2008). Sorry, and not sorry, in Australia: How the apology to the stolen generations buried a history of genocide. *Journal of Genocide Research, 10*(2), 201–214. doi:10.1080/14623520802065438

Bassnett, S. (2002). *Translation studies* (3rd ed.). London, UK: Routledge.

Bauman, Z. (2001). *Community: Seeking safety in an insecure world*. Cambridge, UK: Polity Press.

Beazley, H. (1997). Inventing individual identity in the ALLP. *Literacy and Numeracy Studies, 7*(1), 46–62. Retrieved from http://search.informit.com.au.

Black, S. (2004). Whose economic wellbeing?: A challenge to dominant discourses on the relationship between literacy/numeracy skills and (un)employment. *Literacy and Numeracy Studies, 13*(1), 7–17. Retrieved from http://search.informit.com.au.

Cenoz, J. (2009). *Towards multilingual education: Basque educational research in international perspective*. Buffalo, N.Y.: Multilingual Matters.

Cope, B., & Kalantzis, M. (2009). "Multiliteracies": New literacies, new learning. *Pedagogies: An International Journal, 4*(3), 164–195. doi: 10.1080/15544800903076044

Davis, K. A. (2014). Engaged language policy and practices. *Language Policy, 13*(2), 83–100. doi:10.1007/s10993-013-9296-5

Department of Prime Minister and Cabinet. (2017). *Closing the Gap Prime Minister's Report 2017*. Australia: Commonwealth of Australia.

Dickson, G. (2012). *Ngurrju! Manymak! Pupuni! NT drops First Four Hours in English policy*. Retrieved from https://blogs.crikey.com.au/fullysic/2012/07/11/ngurrju-manymak-pupuni-nt-drops-first-four-hours-in-english-policy/.

Eco, Umberto. (2003). *Mouse or rat? Translation as negotiation*. London, UK: Weidenfeld & Nicholson.

Edwards, D. (2011). Literate or illiterate?: Seeking the literate student in government policy. *The International Journal of the Book, 8*(4), 81–90. doi:10.18848/1447-9516/CGP/v08i04/36616

Francis, N., & Reyhner, J. (2002). *Language and literacy teaching for indigenous education: A bilingual approach.* Sydney: Multilingual Matters.

García, O., & Kleyn, T. (2016). Translanguaging theory in education. In T. Kleyn & O. García (Eds.), *Tranglanguaging with multilingual students: Learning from classroom moments* (pp. 9–29). Proquest Ebook Central: Taylor and Francis. Retrieved from http://ebookcentral.proquest.com.

García, O., & Wei, L. (2014). *Translanguaging: Language, bilingualism and education.* New York: Palgrave Macmillan.

Gomberg, P. (2007). *How to make opportunity equal.* Oxford: Blackwell Publishing.

Hall, S. (2003). The work of representation. In S. Hall (Ed.), *Representation: Cultural representations and signifying practices.* London, UK: SAGE Publications.

Harris, J. (2003). Hiding the bodies: The myth of the humane colonisation of Aboriginal Australia. *Aboriginal History, 27,* 79–104. Retrieved from www.jstor.org.ezp.lib.unimelb.edu.au/stable/24054261.

Hornberger, N. H. (2008). Introduction: Can schools save indigenous languages? Policy and practice on four continents. In N. H. Hornberger (Ed.), *Can schools save indigenous languages? Policy and practice on four continents.* (pp. 1–12). New York: Palgrave Macmillan.

House of Representatives Standing Committee on Aboriginal and Torres Strait Islander Affairs. (2012). *Our land, our languages: Language learning in Indigenous communities.* Canberra: The Parliament of the Commonwealth of Australia.

Kubota, R. (2014). The multi-plural turn, postcolonial theory, and neoliberal multiculturalism: Complicities and implications for applied linguistics. *Applied Linguistics,* 1–22. doi:10.1093/applin/amu045

Laitin, D. D. (2000). What is a language community? *American Journal of Political Science, 44*(1), 142–155. doi:10.2307/2669300

Lewthwaite, B. E., Osborne, B., Lloyd, N., Boon, H., Llewellyn, L., Webber, T., Laffin, G., Harrison, M., Day, C., Kemp, C., & Wills, J. (2015). Seeking a pedagogy of difference: What Aboriginal students and their parents in North Queensland say about teaching and their learning. *Australian Journal of Teacher Education, 40*(5), 132–159. doi:10.14221/ajte.2015v40n5.8

Makoni, S., & Pennycook, A. (2007). Disinventing and reconstituting languages. In S. Makoni & A. Pennycook (Eds.), *Disinventing and reconstituting languages* (pp. 1–41). Toronto: Multilingual Matters.

Martin, C. (2015). The Northern Territory: 240,000 second-class citizens. *Meanjin Quarterly, 74*(3), 81–83.

Moore, H. (1995). Telling the history of the 1991 Australian language and literacy policy. *TESOL in Context, 5*(1), 6–20. Retrieved from http://search.informit.com.au.

Moran, M. (2016). *Serious whitefella stuff: When solutions became the problem in Indigenous affairs.* Victoria: Melbourne University Publishing.

Nakata, M. (1999). History, cultural diversity and English language teaching. In P. Wignell (Ed.), *Double power: English literacy and indigenous education* (pp. 5–21). Melbourne: Language Australia.

NT Language Support Program. (n. d.). *Iltyem-iltyem.* Northern Territory Language Support Program, Centre for Australian Languages and Linguistics, Batchelor Institute. Retrieved from http://iltyemiltyem.com/.

Newry, D., & Palmer, K. (2003). 'Whose language is it anyway?' Rights to restrict access to endangered languages: a north-east Kimberley example. In J. Blythe & R. M. Brown (Eds.), *Maintaining the links: language, identity and the land* (pp. 101–106). Bath: Foundation for Endangered Languages.

Oldfield, J. (2016). *Anangu Muru Wunka: Talking Black Fella, A critical policy analysis of the Northern Territory first four hours of English.* Paper presented at the conference Language in Focus—From Theory to Practice: New Directions in ELT and Applied Linguistics, Istanbul, Turkey.

Pearson, N. (2009). Radical hope: Education and equality in Australia. *Quarterly Essay, 35*, 1–105. Retrieved from http://search.informit.com.au.

Queensland Department of Education, Training and Employment. (2013). *Capability Framework: Teaching Aboriginal and Torres Strait Islander EAL/D learners.* Queensland: The State of Queensland.

Ruiz, R. (1984). Orientations in language planning. *NABE Journal, 8*(2), 15–34. Retrieved from www.tandfonline.com

Ruiz, R. (2010). Reorienting language-as-resource. In J. E. Petrovic (Ed.), *International perspectives on bilingual education: Policy, practice, and controversy* (pp. 155–172). Charlotte, NC: Information Age Publishing.

Sellwood, J., & Angelo, D. (2013). Everywhere and nowhere: Invisibility of Aboriginal and Torres Strait Islander contact languages in education and Indigenous language contexts. *Australian Review of Applied Linguistics, 36*(3), 250–266. doi:10.1075/aral.36.3.02sel

Simpson, J., Caffery, J., & McConvell, P. (2009). *Gaps in Australia's Indigenous language policy: Dismantling bilingual education in the Northern Territory.* AIATSIS Research Discussion Paper No. 24.

Zuckermann, G., Shakuto-Neoh, S., & Quer, G. M. (2014). Native tongue title: Compensation for the loss of Aboriginal languages. *Australian Aboriginal Studies, 1*, 55–71. Retrieved from http://search.informit.com.au.

PART II
Plurilingual Student Repertoires

5

THE TRANSLINGUAL ADVANTAGE

Metrolingual Student Repertoires

Emi Otsuji and Alastair Pennycook

This chapter looks at the metrolingual practices of students in two tertiary institutions in Tokyo and Sydney. Focusing as much on out-of-class as in-class language use, we look at the diverse repertoires of students as they go about their daily university-related lives. The argument here is that a focus only on the medium of instruction, or translingual educational practices, may overlook the diverse semiotic resources students bring to their educational experiences. Contemporary students in particular, with their interlinked online and offline worlds, their ease of communication in and across the boundaries of educational institutions, inhabit worlds where a diversity of linguistic and other semiotic resources are easily available. They engage in diverse forms of popular culture—from music to TV dramas—and chat to friends elsewhere using a range of creative textual means. When it comes to study itself, students' multilingual worlds confer not so much a 'bilingual advantage' as this has been narrowly defined from a more cognitive perspective, but rather a 'translingual advantage' that makes it possible to draw on a range of resources to construct meaning and develop learning.

The Learning Affordances of Semiotic Assemblages

In line with the 'multilingual turn' (May, 2014) in applied linguistics, and the upsurge in sociolinguistic studies of diverse multilingualisms (under a variety of super-poly-hyper-trans-metro labels; Pennycook, 2016), there has been an increased interest in multilingualism in tertiary contexts. The constant emphasis on internationalisation in higher education (both as an economic necessity for underfunded education sectors as well as a goal to diversify student experience) and increased student mobility (both as a result of changing migration patterns and the possibilities for study elsewhere provided by state and private means) have led to major shifts in the potential language makeup of universities and other education providers. Into this mix come continuing concerns over the global role of English in facilitating such exchanges while limiting the media through which education is delivered. In the context of Europe, a key idea behind the promotion of student mobility was student plurilingualism, incorporating the language of the country of study rather than the widespread use of English as the tertiary medium of instruction. The role that English plays, therefore, particularly in contexts where the language of instruction is already caught up in complex language politics (such as Catalonia or the Basque region), is often fraught (Doiz, Lasagabaster & Sierra, 2014; Doiz and Lasagabaster, 2017; Moore et al., 2013).

Although Busch (2011) notes in her review of multilingual education practices in Europe a shift "from minority to multilingual education which valorises the heteroglossic repertoires of the learners as a linguistic and communicative resource" (p. 548), studies of multilingualism at the tertiary level still suggest a prevailing monolingual ideology. Pauwels (2014b) notes that university language teachers in her U.K. study seemed uninterested in the diverse linguistic profiles—the *hyperlingualism* (2014a)—of some of their multilingual students, seeing them instead as a problem. This invisibility of student multilingualism has been challenged from several directions, Preece (2010, p. 36) arguing, for example, for ways of "imagining higher education as a multilingual space" that views the languages of minority students as an asset rather than a problem. While monolingual ideologies appear to prevail at many institutional (university policy) and sub-institutional (classroom practice) levels, it has also become clear that beliefs in the possibility, benefits and practicality of monolingual classroom practices overlook both the affordances of multilingual pedagogies and the realities of learning practices. The idea of translanguaging in higher education—by which is generally meant the mixing of languages in pedagogical contexts—has received increased attention of late, with the predominant argument being that university classrooms could benefit from getting beyond monolingual ideologies that emphasise one language of instruction so that more flexible forms of bilingualism (or translanguaging) can prevail.

As van der Walt (2013) argues, there are many reasons to challenge the assumptions around English as a default language of higher education, and to explore instead the possibilities of multilingualism at many levels. In their study of three professors at a bilingual university in Puerto Rico, Mazak, Mendoza and Mangonéz (2017) show how their translanguaging practices open up a space for the acknowledgement of Spanish as both an everyday language and a legitimate academic language alongside English as the officially sanctioned language of science and technology. Gu's (2014) study of mainland and Hong Kong university students shows how they established "a translanguaging space through hybrid language use," drawing on "their cultural and linguistic repertoires to transcend cultural, linguistic and regional boundaries and construct a multilingual identity" (p. 326). Makalela's *ubuntu* translanguaging pedagogy, drawing on local South

African language practices as well as a broader African epistemology of being (*ubuntu*) aims to "disrupt perceived language boundaries among preservice student teachers and to recreate complex multilingual spaces that reflect the *ubuntu* principles of ecological interdependence" (2017, p. 17).

This chapter draws on this work, stressing the importance of translingual spaces in higher education, and suggests, along with van der Walt (2013), that the "possibilities for multilingual education are limited only by our own fixed ideas about language, learning and the nature of education" (p. 180). Our focus, however, has several distinctive elements: We are particularly interested in focusing not so much on the medium of instruction but on the translingual practices (Canagarajah, 2013) of students in their daily lives. By translingual practices we refer to the ways in which people draw on a wide variety of semiotic resources in everyday tasks. Like Canagarajah (2013), we are interested in a broader semiotics that includes space, objects and other affordances for learning. He, Lai and Lin (2017) draw attention to the relations between translanguaging and multimodality, showing how the use of varied linguistic resources may be integrated with other resources through PowerPoint, gesture, film, graphics and so on to create a transmodal whole.

Although the students discussed in this study might easily be categorised as an elite class of the mobilely educated, we are interested in their own 'multilingualism from below' or the metrolingual practices they engage in (the ways in which semiotic resources, everyday tasks and social space are intertwined; Pennycook and Otsuji, 2015) around their tertiary studies. These terms could benefit from much more extensive disentangling than we have space to do here (see for example Pennycook, 2016) and there are clearly extensive overlaps between translanguaging and metrolanguaging. We prefer the latter term more generally because of its link to the idea of the city, and therefore space and urban complexity. It is also better able to avoid the slide back towards normative accounts of language use (translanguaging sometimes becomes little more than an alternative term for bilingualism). We have, nonetheless, used translanguaging, translingual practices and the translingual advantage in this chapter to align with the more common current usage. We see translingual practices as a particular type of broader metrolingual practices, referring here to the diverse resources that transnationally mobile students bring to the table. We are particularly interested in the roles that semiotic assemblages (Pennycook, 2017; Pennycook and Otsuji, 2017)—the coming together of diverse semiotic and material resources—may play in the learning process.

Our focus is on the translingual practices of students in and around universities. To understand university multilingualism, we need to focus not only on the medium of instruction, or the languages used in classrooms, but also on the spatial repertoires of students, that is the available resources related to activities in particular online and offline places (Pennycook and Otsuji, 2015). In order to grasp the spatial repertoires of different learning contexts, we need to know what it is our students engage in more broadly, from popular culture to social networks. The online and offline worlds of students are deeply intertwined, and neither should be seen as more real or virtual than the other. Students are online in our classes, and their offline lives are part of their online activities. In a transnational context of elasticity and at a personal age of flexibility, students are often keen to try stuff out, exploring identities, messing around with language, and engaged with popular culture. They are sitting in our university and other classes, watching us (now and then), checking their mobile devices (more often) and living in multiple linguistic, cultural and spatial worlds. Varied modes of popular culture form not just a backdrop to their daily lives, not just a pastime when they are not doing something else, but a fabric around which parts of their lives are built (Dovchin, Pennycook & Sultana, 2018; Dovchin & Pennycook, 2017).

The different resources these students bring to their learning contexts are better understood not so much in terms of the reductive discussions of a 'bilingual advantage'—where languages are considered to confer a cumulative cognitive benefit on their users—but rather in terms of what we call the *translingual advantage*, whereby translingual resources become part of a set of distributed linguistic and learning practices. If, as MacSwan (2017) argues, "multilingualism, not monolingualism, is universal, and . . . each of us, even so-called monolinguals, has multiple overlapping rule systems acquired through our participation in divergent speech communities" (p. 179), then the notion of a bi- or multilingual advantage dissolves in a general multilingualism. The problem in much of this discussion is that in response to negative views about multilingualism, a line of argument has grown up proposing a 'bilingual advantage' based largely on studies of word and sentence manipulation in cognitive isolation, or positing an advantage through executive control functions in order to manage two or more languages (Bialystock, 2007; and see Paap et al., 2015 for a critique). While such studies are well intentioned in their attempts to persuade parents, educators and institutions that bilingualism is an inherently good thing (King and Mackey, 2007), they tend to overlook several of the most important dimensions of bilingualism: While elite bilingualism (de Meija, 2002) (the bilingualism of those who speak a majority language and learn one or more other prestige languages in formal contexts) may confer various advantages (though generally on the already-advantaged), bilingualism often occurs in contexts of disadvantage, prejudice, and inadequate conditions of learning, literacy and schooling.

It is, therefore, much more important to view bilingualism in terms of "a set of resources which circulate in unequal ways in social networks and discursive spaces, and whose meaning and value are socially constructed within the constraints of social organisational processes, under specific historical conditions" (Heller, 2007, p. 2). If we view bilingualism only in additive and cognitive terms (speaking more than one language brings benefits), we miss the point that bilingualism is about social practices, language in real life, discrimination and inequality (Piller, 2016). We cannot deal with 'bilingualism' as an abstract quality of linguistic manipulation outside the contexts of language practices. We also need to investigate how people use their linguistic resources: If people can call on a range of semiotic resources in their learning, how do they deploy these to their advantage? Drawing on Paulsrud et al.'s (2017, p. 15) point that "inviting students' whole linguistic repertoires into the classroom" provides students with wider learning possibilities, we argue that the real advantage lies not, therefore, in some additive, numerical bilingualism by which 'knowing languages' increases cognitive capacity but rather in terms of the aptitude people develop to manipulate a diversity of linguistic resources in their learning processes.

The Everyday Language Practices of Students: Chotto Nihongo, Chotto Korean

The data introduced in the study was part of our broader research on metrolingualism that looked at everyday multilingualism in shops, markets, streets, cafes, construction sites and other workplaces in Sydney and Tokyo (Pennycook and Otsuji, 2015). As part of a wider study of metrolingual university practices, we asked students in Sydney and Tokyo to keep language diaries, recounting their various uses of languages. We were interested in trying to find out what kinds of daily semiotic practices students engaged in. Students were asked to use a diary app to log their daily activities for a week, with particular reference to language. These language journals were then followed up with interviews and closer studies of language learning practices when possible. Subsequent to the interviews, some students shared with us Facebook pages, text-chat exchanged with friends using various phone apps, notes taken during classes as well as audio conversations recorded with classmates, friends and families.

In order to explain more clearly what we are looking at here, let us start with Abiola, a student of Nigerian background studying in Sydney. Abiola lives in university accommodation and associates regularly with students of other language backgrounds. He notes frequent moments where he "learned some Japanese phrases" from a Japanese flatmate; a Jordanian friend was "teaching myself and my friends some phrases in Arabic"; Indian friends taught "some common Hindi phrases that are used in everyday communication"; another flatmate "taught some conversational terms in French". He also teaches friends phrases in Yoruba. These are the casual multilingual learning practices among international students, taking an interest in simple phrases and terms, though for many such as Abiola this seems not so much an exoticisation of difference as part of a broader history of multilingual practice. He notes with some pride that when he greeted a Chinese friend in Mandarin, she responded in Mandarin.

Aside from this casual multilingualism, three other domains are influential: He likes to listen to music, and during the period of his language diary, this involves music in English, Yoruba, Spanish (Cuban) and Hindi. In his studies, he also encounters different languages, noting that he enrolled in a mathematics course via edX tutored by a Chinese professor: "She explains in Mandarin and with the aid of a translator and close caption, it was translated to English". And third, he regularly calls home to speak to his father as well as an aunt, for which he uses Yoruba and English (following the standard Arabic greeting among Muslims). This, then, is our starting point—the metrolingual life of a student as he calls home, chats to others, studies, listens to music and generally engages in the social, cultural and educational life among international students. There is a capacity to use Yoruba and English for a range of tasks, a comfort to study in the context of other languages such as Chinese, and playfulness with friends and flatmates with the various linguistic resources that surround him.

Likewise, Ria, an exchange student from a university in central Java, studying at a Japanese university[1] in Tokyo describes her linguistic repertoire in the following terms "I can speak Indonesian and English and *nihongo chotto* [Japanese a little]" and "I can understand *chotto* [a little] Korean and can speak *chotto* Indonesian dialect [Javanese]". Ria's "*chotto* Korean" repertoire stems from her passion for Korean dramas and music from her childhood (dramas from age 14, music from age 16). This role of Korean dramas fostering a knowledge of things Korean, including language, particularly in Asia but also elsewhere, has been noted in a number of studies (Choi, 2016; Dovchin, Pennycook & Sultana, 2018). Ria watches Korean dramas or variety shows almost everyday at breakfast. Similar to Abiola (discussed above), Ria is also an avid listener to many different kinds of music: "I listen to music all the time—Korean, English, Indonesian and Japanese music, any type of music" (interview), "Went home while listening to songs in my iPad (Japanese/Indonesian/English/Korean)" (diary entry). With her iPhone and iPad full of downloaded music and videos (including Bollywood films alongside Korean dramas), she learns Korean and other languages multimodally. Apart from these forms of casual learning, she also uses online resources, particularly in Indonesian, when completing English assignments for economics and technology. Various devices such as an iPad, computer and mobile phone make possible Ria's multilingual and multicultural lifestyle and learning.

Her linguistic resources can be characterised by a diversity of languages and registers as well as what we might call *chotto-ness*. The Japanese term (ちょっと) *chotto*, meaning 'a little' and heard commonly in phrases such as ちょっと待って (*chotto matte*: Wait a minute) or ちょっとちがいます (*chotto chigaimasu*: Slightly wrong) or in other phrases as a hedge, softener, diminutive or filler, is used by Ria to refer to her partial capacity in various languages (Japanese, Korean and Javanese). Akin in some ways to what Blommaert (2010) calls *truncated repertoires*— referring to the fact that multilingual repertoires always contain 'bits' of languages rather than some impossible notion of whole languages—we prefer this notion of *chotto-ness* for its less negative associations (*truncated* was never intended negatively but struggles to throw off such implications) and its more emic implications.

This *chotto* repertoire is used in different domains: Classroom discussions with her classmates, text chats with her friends, and her Facebook postings. The day after she took part in the university festival, running an Indonesian food stall, she wrote: "A大学B祭[2] [sic]D２！みんな、ありがとう！ Soto Ayam sold out dua hari 800porsi! Yay Alhamdulilua (😊😊😊)" together with pictures from the day (a bowl of Soto Ayam (Indonesian chicken soup) and her Japanese and Indonesian friends). Her post is characterised by various *chotto* resources: Japanese (A大学B祭 [sic]D-２！みんな、ありがとう！ [University A, B festival, D-2! Thank you everyone]), English (sold out, yay) and Indonesian (dua hari 800 porsi [two days 800 portions]), Arabic, (Alhamdulilua [praise God]), emoji (smiley icons) and pictures. This casual multilingual, multimodal and multisensory (the food and the color of hijabs in the pictures) post, together with her profile photo with Mt. Fuji in the background and the cover photo with the Union Jack and Big Ben (she is an avid Manchester United fan), is for her an everyday semiotic assemblage (the momentary coming together of material and semiotic resources; Pennycook and Otsuji, 2017) drawing on the wider spatial repertoire of on- and offline resources.

Like Abiola, she also calls home, with obvious linguistic implications: During Ramadan, she called her family: "As Ramadhan started, I started doing fasting since today. Because it's the first day of Fasting, I did skype with my family so I won't feel lonely". She also cooked Indonesian food (checking the recipe on YouTube) and went out with her Malaysian friends where she spoke both Indonesian and Malaysian (mutually intelligible). As these students go about their daily lives, they move in and out of online and offline worlds (Dovchin, Pennycook & Sultana, 2018), with aspects of their lives part of what they do online (a Skype call home, a Facebook posting about a festival) and part of what they do online integrated with the daily fabric of their lives (music, Korean language, cooking). They celebrate and play with this linguistic *chotto-ness*. For them, spatio-temporal boundaries are often indistinct and integrated in their casual multilingual everyday life in and around their tertiary studies. All of this, we argue, that occurs in such liminal spaces around education has implications for the translingual advantage that they bring to the educational contexts themselves.

Multilingual and Mulltimodal Repertoires and Affordances

The ways in which these students deploy multilingual and multimodal resources can be looked at not only from the point of view of everyday metrolingual practices but also from a perspective of learning affordances, of sets of possibilities they bring to their educational practices. This use of multiple resources in aiding learning is what we are here calling the *translingual advantage*. In the examples below we can see how students' learning is closely integrated with translingual, trans-modal and trans-semiotic resources that include space, objects and other affordances for learning. Caroline is an exchange student enrolled in the same program as Ria, taking subjects such as Japanese, Attic (Ancient) Greek, and science. She is of Chinese Singaporean background and, according to her, speaks *Singlish*, which she describes as "mostly English with questionable grammar and interjections/phrases in Chinese/Malay/Hokkien" (Questionnaire).

Because quite a few classmates are also Chinese speakers, she notes that her language becomes "peppered with Chinese and a touch of Hokkien" and that she and her classmates swiftly switch between English, Japanese and Chinese. Excerpt 1 is a conversation with her classmate Helen when she was waiting for her next class in a computer lab with other classmates. Helen is from China and speaks Mandarin Chinese, English and Japanese. In the excerpt, Caroline is eating a snack while she and Helen are browsing Games on Steam (Electronic Game Distribution Service).

Excerpt 1 (C: Caroline, H: Helen)

English: Plain, Mandarin Chinese: *Italics*, Japanese: <u>Underline</u> (translation in brackets)

1. C: *好吗?* (is it OK?)
2. H: Mm, yeah.
   [a rustling sound of the snack packet C is eating]
3. C: Daedalic's good.
4. H: Seriously?
5. C: Mm.
   [a rustling sound of the snack packet]
6. H: What's this? Like, *这个是什么?* (What is this thing?)
7. C: Europa?
8. H: No, no, no. This one.
9. C: DLC. Download content. Downloadable content.
   [a vibration sound from the mobile phone/a rustling sound of the snack packet]
   [a pause while opening the file]
10. H: *这是什么?* (what is this?)
11. C: Terraria <u>みたい</u>. (similar to Terraria) I think. I'm not sure.
    [a rustling sound of the snack packet]

The above excerpt confirms Caroline's statement that she and her Chinese-speaking friends swiftly move between Chinese, English and Japanese language resources. From the exchange, it is obvious Caroline is more knowledgeable than Helen about video games: Asking Helen if she is OK "*好吗?*" (line 1), telling Helen that "Daedalic [a software development company] is good" (line 3), urging Helen to download DLC to complete downloading the video game features, "DLC. Download content. Downloadable content" (line 9), and commenting that the game is similar to Terraria, "Terraria みたい." (line 11). She achieves all this by drawing on various linguistic resources (Chinese, English and Japanese). At the same time, Helen also employs a number of linguistic resources when asking Caroline questions or simply in back channeling, i.e., "Mm, yeah", "Seriously" or "What's this? Like, 这个是什么? (What is this thing?)" (lines 2, 4 and 6).

The mixed linguistic resources are deployed pragmatically, strategically, out of convenience or perhaps as Caroline notes "not a conscious decision". Our aim here, however, is not to identify which language was used, or why, when and how they are switched or mixed, but rather to appreciate how these students at a Japanese university who also share various Chinese and English resources seem comfortable drawing on their multiple resources as they negotiate various social relations. As we have argued elsewhere, the idea of a *metrolingua franca* (Pennycook & Otsuji, 2014; 2015) as a set of linguistic and non-linguistic resources that can be drawn on in different moments better describes this kind of context than any attempt to determine one particular language (English, Japanese or Chinese as a lingua franca).

Apart from the linguistic resources employed by Caroline and Helen in the above excerpt, there is a strong presence of other material resources and activities such as a rustling sound of a bag of snacks and the sound of a mobile phone vibrating to mark the completion of the download. In the interaction, therefore, not only linguistic resources but also materials (mobile phone, computer lab, food) as well as activities (waiting, eating, browsing, and talking) are closely amalgamated. Their linguistic and non-linguistic activities are afforded by (and sometimes limited by) spatio-temporal and material conditions. This multilingual and multimodal multitasking is part of the way these students navigate through their multiple linguistic, cultural and spatial worlds.

In Caroline's view English, Japanese and Chinese complement each other since each has meanings that cannot be expressed in the other. Thus, when it comes to learning, she views being a linguistically resourceful student (Pennycook, 2012, 2014; Otsuji, 2011) as an advantage: "rich linguistic resources help me understand studies more easily". She takes notes in three languages (Chinese, English and Japanese) in most of her classes. The following is an excerpt from Caroline's language diary on the day she had an Attic (Ancient) Greek class. Caroline's diary clearly shows how she takes advantage of her "rich linguistic resources". She views learning Greek through Japanese not as a hindrance but as an advantage.

Excerpt 2: Language Diary

Several things stand out in this extract. Caroline has a strong sense of linguistic awareness: She is very cognizant of the kinds of linguistic operations she is engaged in, and is able to see why she does things (sometimes just pragmatic, sometimes more strategic) and the kinds of linguistic manipulations her studies involve. With

> Specifically, my weekly dose of Attic Greek. Class is conducted in Japanese; the text written on the black board is mostly Greek and/or kanji. Sometimes I process the kanji as Chinese because it's easier to understand that way, and the meaning is no different. My notes are written in English for ease of reference, though sometimes I copy the teacher's explanation in Japanese because it's easier to understand as is, or because he's going too fast for me to translate it on the spot without losing some content. I also carry with me both a Japanese textbook (the prescribed one) and an English one I borrowed from the school library. I could write an essay on how helpful it's been to learn Greek using both English and Japanese. Having two ways to look at new vocabulary helps me to grasp its meaning more accurately. When we do our translation exercises (written, then read out), I translate the sentence word for word into either English or Japanese, whichever is most suitable, then synthesise sentences in both languages. 10/06/2015 (Wednesday)

her knowledge of Chinese (Hokkien and Mandarin) lurking in the background, she here uses her English and Japanese resources to bear on her learning of Greek. As she explains, this is not only so that she can use the language she is more comfortable in (English) as well as Japanese when it's quicker and more convenient, but also so that she can use her knowledge of the two languages to grasp the meanings of Greek terms more accurately. This is again what we would call the translingual advantage: Not so much an increased cognitive capacity brought about by the addition of languages but the capacity to manipulate linguistic resources on the fly.

Her deployment of various semiotic resources does not stop here, however, since she also uses a wider semiotic range including space (classroom), objects (textbooks, blackboard), images and other affordances for learning. In her notes from the Greek lesson, her linguistic resources are integrated into a wider multimodal semiotic learning landscape (Figure 5.1).

Here, the chapter numbers of the textbook are written in Japanese/Chinese (第三課, 第四課 [Chapter 3, Chapter 4]), an English summary of the story is provided next to the chapter number (第三課), "man on his horse on a path from Egypt, accompanied by his slave." Caroline's main strategy here is to draw aspects of the story and to add labels in Greek (or to write words in Greek and to add labels). Thus, the river flowing under the bridge on the left middle of the page is marked π οταμός below the two wavelets that designate water. The slave following the horseman is labelled δοῦλος and the figure of justice on the left of the group of three on the right of the picture has the caption δικαιοσύνη. Meanwhile more functional vocabulary is explained over to one side: γάρ; because, indeed, that is; τε: and.

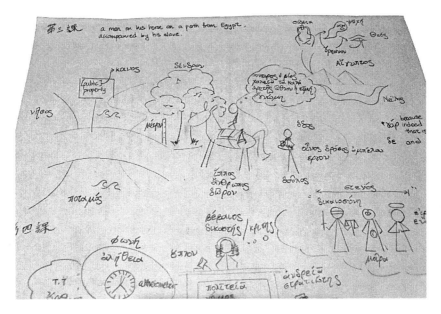

FIGURE 5.1 Greek class notes

Although she is also a student capable of using various technologies and multimedia options, Caroline here prefers to use a blank (unlined, plain) sheet of paper to draw, annotate and recreate a multimodal and multilingual text that captures the summary of the story, the movements of the protagonists, and the environment where the story took place, while also creating for herself a multilingual and multisemiotic learning space. This supplements the claim she made in her diary, "Having two ways (English and Japanese) to look at new vocabulary helps me to grasp its meaning more accurately." For Caroline, there are much more than just two multi-semiotic resources at play here. Her everyday translingual practices in and outside the classroom (waiting for a class and doing preparations and assignments at home) create particular affordances for learning.

Notes taken by Kate, a student doing a double degree program (Design and International studies with Japanese) at an Australian university, also shed light on these processes. Having moved to Australia from Hong Kong at the age of 16, she also uses both English and Chinese (spoken Cantonese and standard written Chinese) in her studies. When she studies Japanese, her Chinese knowledge becomes useful for learning vocabulary due to the proximity of the words and characters between the two languages but when she learns sentence structures, she translates the sentences into English. This, according to her, is because there are more conjunction words in English than in Chinese. In preparing for the Japanese language proficiency test, Kate created grammar notes, summarising grammatical points (Figure 5.2).

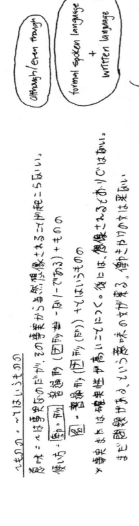
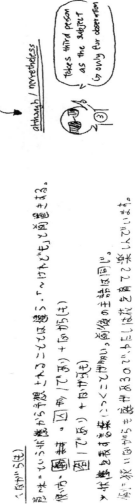

FIGURE 5.2 Grammar notes

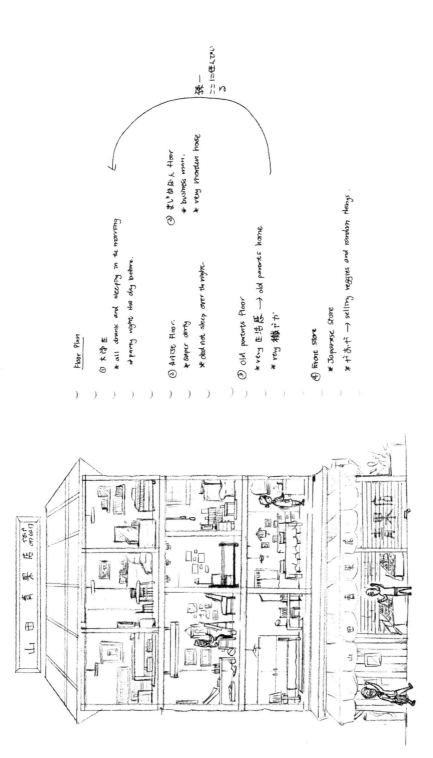

FIGURE 5.3 Sketch and notes involving the use of drawing comics in preparation for assignment

When studying a conjunction "〜ものの・〜とはいうものの", not only does she supply an English translation (although/even though), but she also uses her design skills to add small drawings of people to remind herself of the important points. These varied semiotic resources (drawings, underlining, font colour, speech bubbles, Japanese and English resources) as well as the spatial organisation of the page (dividing the page into two sections), while ostensibly insignificant, are conscious pragmatic and strategic choices for her. These multimodal and interactive/dialogic study notes show how different linguistic resources can be integrated with other multimodal elements in the process of studying.

Enrolled in both Design and International Studies majoring in Japanese, Kate integrates her knowledge, ideas and skills in the process of her study. She is often inspired by Japanese designs, popular culture, as well as by her own experiences as they relate to Japan in conducting her design degree project (Figure 5.3). Figure 5.3 shows the sketch and notes she made in preparing her assignment which involved drawing comics. The idea and the story are inspired by her visit to Japan, and Japanese artists, especially the artist Mateusz Urbanowicz, who is also the background artist for the recent epic animation movie *Kimino na wa*.

The story she creates is set in a Japanese share house, which has a greengrocer on the ground floor. The store front of 山田青果店, Yamada greengrocer's, or やおや which sells vegetables and other related food commodities, is inspired by one of the shops she visited when she was in Japan. The shared house is occupied by a wide range of people from different generations (old and young), occupations (大学生 [a university student], an artist, a business man), rhythms (sleeping in the morning, staying up all night), life styles (modern, 生活感 [lived-in feel], very dirty), relations (an old couple and their 孫 [grandchild]) and characters (まじめな人 [square person] and very 穏やか [calm]) and the story will evolve around these occupants and space. With the deployment of these varied images and text, including Japanese, this floor plan is an artifact of Kate's ability to assemble various semiotic resources: The online-offline world (her own experience, pen and blank sheet, as well as online research about Japanese animation), and resources acquired from studying Japanese and Design subjects. These are all part of her wider semiotic capital, and it is the ways these are deployed in the process of learning that we call the 'translingual advantage'.

Translingual Advantages

The four students we have discussed here—Abiola, with his various language exchanges, study practices, music and calls home to family in Nigeria; Ria, with her various language abilities drawn from popular culture and her calls home to family in Indonesia; Caroline, with her mixed language practices with fellow students and particular learning strategies; and Kate, with her deployment of multilingual and multimodal texts—all share a number of common practices. Their diverse linguistic repertoires can be characterised by a certain *chotto-ness*, a range of bits of languages that they pick up and use in different circumstances. As we suggested, this is very much in line with the observations made by Blommaert that "shifting our focus from 'languages' (primarily an ideological and institutional construct) to resources (the actual and observable ways of using language)" (2010, p. 102) allows us to be less concerned about how many languages someone speaks and more interested in how they use their various linguistic resources. We prefer the idea of *chotto-ness*, however, to the notion of truncated repertoires since it suggests less of an etic description of the shortcomings of a repertoire and more of an emic category that shows how speakers talk casually about the bits of language they use.

These students also all demonstrate a keen awareness of language and the ways they can use their varied linguistic resources in their studies. Caroline, for example, is very clear that using English and Japanese together to study Greek brings her a number of advantages, particularly in terms of understanding the meaning. It is worth noting that, while some parts of her multilingual and multimodal strategies are on display on the page (images, Greek, English and Chinese text), the role that Japanese is playing here, as the language in which the class is being conducted, is invisible. Kate, meanwhile, is equally clear that her knowledge of English and Chinese contributes greatly to her learning of Japanese. Into this mix, these students also bring a variety of other semiotic resources. If we focus predominantly on the medium of instruction—whether this involves a variety of linguistic resources or not—or the language of assignments and evaluation, we may miss this liminal space between studying and daily student life, where multilingual resources from a range of social and cultural interactions become part of student learning practices. All four students call on a range of semiotic resources (multimodal and multilingual) in their everyday learning practices. This suggests the need for a shift from cognitive-oriented assumptions premised on numerical bilingualism (knowing another language aids cognition) to a practice-based focus on the development of a translingual aptitude to deploy a range of linguistic and non-linguistic resources.

Expanding on García and Klein's (2016) case for the importance of translingual pedagogies and Paulsrud et al.'s (2017, p. 15) emphasis on "inviting students' whole linguistic repertoires into the classroom", we can suggest some pedagogical implications from this discussion of metrolingual learners. As educators, we would do well to avoid the demolinguistic labels that characterise our students as bilingual, second language learners, or speakers of named languages (García, in press); rather, we need to appreciate the diversity of linguistic resources and forms of popular culture with which they may be engaged. These resources are not only linguistic but multimodal: Students may employ a complex array of resources in their learning, and as educators we need to be wary of that trap that links learning only to forms of language and literacy with which we may be familiar. The translingual advantage we have been proposing here is a multimodal affair, so as educators we need ways to appreciate and facilitate what learners may be bringing to the table.

We also need to think beyond the idea that students simply bring these resources to the classroom: Their linguistic and learning practices are also emergent in the pedagogical context. The idea of semiotic assemblages suggests not only that multiple resources come together at any moment, but also that the dynamic effects of such assemblages are also productive: Learning affordances are emergent from the interactions of semiotic assemblages. So again, as educators, if we cannot predict such moments, we need at least to make their emergence possible. If we think in terms of spatial repertoires and distributed language and learning, then these resources are affordances of the learning spaces we create, not just things we or our students bring to class. The challenge from a pedagogical point of view, therefore, is not merely to open up learning spaces where students can engage in translingual practices or deploy their translingual repertoires, but rather to consider how to make use of such practices in the transformation of the language and learning ideologies of the classroom and the institution. This is a move from translanguaging to *translingual activism* (Pennycook, in press), an emphasis not only on the learning affordances brought by the translingual advantage but the transformational affordances of alternative pedagogical practices.

Notes

1 The university offers an undergraduate degree program taught in English. The degree is open for Japanese local and international students.
2 Ria here confused the homonyms (both are pronounced *Sai*) 歳 (age) with 祭 festival.

References

Bialystok, E. (2007). Cognitive effects of bilingualism: How linguistic experience leads to cognitive change. *International Journal of Bilingual Education and Bilingualism, 10*(3), 210–223.
Blommaert, J. (2010). *The sociolinguistics of globalization.* Cambridge: University Press.
Busch, B. (2011). Trends and innovative practices in multilingual education in Europe: An overview. *International Review of Education, 57,* 541–549.
Canagarajah, S. (2013). *Translingual practice: Global Englishes and cosmopolitan relations.* New York: Routledge.
Choi, J. (2016). *Creating a multivocal self: Autoethnography as method.* New York: Routledge.
De Meija, A. (2002). *Power, prestige, and bilingualism: International perspectives on elite bilingualism.* Clevedon, UK: Multilingual Matters.
Doiz, A., Lasagabaster, D., & Sierra, J. (2014). Language friction and multilingual policies in higher education: The stakeholders' view. *Journal of Multilingual and Multicultural Development, 35*(4), 345–360.
Doiz, A., & Lasagabaster, D. (2017). Teachers' beliefs about translanguaging practices. In C. Mazak, & K. Carroll (Eds.), *Translanguaging in higher education: Beyond monolingual ideologies* (pp. 157–176). Bristol, UK: Multilingual Matters.

Dovchin, S., & Pennycook, A. (2017). Digital metroliteracies: Space, diversity, and identity. In K. Mills, A. Stornaiuolo, A. Smith, & J. Z. Pandya (Eds.), *The Routledge handbook of digital writing and literacies in education* (pp. 211–222). New York: Routledge.

Dovchin, S., Pennycook, A., & Sultana, S. (2018). *Popular culture, voice and linguistic diversity: Young adults on- and offline*. London, UK: Palgrave-Macmillan.

García, O. (in press). Decolonizing foreign, second, heritage, and first languages: Implications for education. In D. Macedo (Ed.), *Decolonizing foreign language education*. New York: Routledge.

García, O., & Klein, T. (2016). Translanguaging theory in education. In O. García & T. Kleyn (Eds.), *Translanguaging with multilingual students: Learning from classroom moments* (pp. 9–33). New York: Routledge.

Gu, M. (2014). From opposition to transcendence: the language practices and ideologies of students in a multilingual university, *International Journal of Bilingual Education and Bilingualism*, *17*(3), 310–329.

He, P., Lai, H., & Lin, A. (2017). Translanguaging in a multimodal mathematics presentation. In C. Mazak & K. Carroll (Eds.), *Translanguaging in higher education: Beyond monolingual ideologies* (pp. 91–118). Bristol, UK: Multilingual Matters.

Heller, M. (2007). Bilingualism as ideology and practice. In M. Heller (Ed.), *Bilingualism: A social approach* (pp. 1–22). New York: Palgrave.

King, K., & Mackey, A. (2007). *The bilingual edge: why, when, and how to teach your child a second language*. New York: Harper Collins.

MacSwan, J. (2017). A multilingual perspective on translanguaging. *American Educational Research Journal*, *54*(1), 167–201.

Makalela, L. (2017). Translanguaging practices in a South African institution of higher learning: A case of *Ubuntu* multilingual return. In C. Mazak & K. Carroll (Eds.), *Translanguaging in higher education: Beyond monolingual ideologies* (pp. 11–28). Bristol, UK: Multilingual Matters.

May, S. (2014). Introducing the 'multilingual turn'. In S. May (Ed.), *The multilingual turn: Implications for SLA, TESOL and bilingual education* (pp. 1–6). New York: Routledge.

Mazak, C., Mendoza, F., & Mangonéz, L. P. (2017). Professors translanguaging in practice: Three cases from a bilingual university. In C. Mazak & K. Carroll (Eds.), *Translanguaging in higher education: Beyond monolingual ideologies* (pp. 70–90). Bristol, UK: Multilingual Matters.

Moore, E., Nussbaum, L., & Borràs, E. (2013). Plurilingual teaching and learning practices in 'internationalised' university lectures. *International Journal of Bilingual Education and Bilingualism*, *16*(4), 471–493.

Otsuji, E. (2011). Metrolingualism and Japanese language education: Linguistic competence across borders. *Literacies*, *9*, 21–30.

Paap, K., Johnson, H., & Sawi, O. (2015). Bilingual advantages in executive functioning either do not exist or are restricted to very specific and undetermined circumstances. *Cortex*, *69*, 265–278.

Paulsrud, B. A., Rosén, J., Straszer, B., & Wedin, Å. (2017). Perspectives on translanguaging in education. In B. A. Paulsrud, J. Rosén, B. Straszer & Å. Wedin (Eds.), *New perspectives on translanguaging and education* (pp. 10–19). Bristol, UK: Multilingual Matters.

Pauwels, A. (2014a). Rethinking the learning of languages in the context of globalization and hyperlingualism. In D. Abendroth-Timmer & E. Henning (Eds.), *Plurilingualism and multi-literacies: International research on identity construction in language education* (pp. 41–56). Frankfurt am Main: Peter Lang.

Pauwels, A. (2014b). The teaching of languages at university in the context of super-diversity, *International Journal of Multilingualism*, *11*(3), 307–319.

Pennycook, A. (2012). *Language and mobility: Unexpected places*. Bristol, UK: Multilingual Matters.

Pennycook, A. (2014). Principled polycentrism and resourceful speakers. *The Journal of Asia TEFL*, *11*(4), 1–19.

Pennycook, A. (2016). Mobile times, mobile terms: The trans-super-poly-metro movement. In N. Coupland (Ed.), *Sociolinguistics theoretical debates* (pp. 201–206). Cambridge, UK: University Press.

Pennycook, A. (2017). Translanguaging and semiotic assemblages. *International Journal of Multilingualism*, *14*(3), 269–282.

Pennycook, A. (in press). From translanguaging to translingual activism. In D. Macedo (Ed.), *Decolonizing Foreign Language Education*. New York: Routledge.

Pennycook, A., & Otsuji, E. (2014). Market lingos and metrolingua francas. *International Multilingual Research Journal*, *8*(4), 255–270.

Pennycook, A., & Otsuji, E. (2015). *Metrolingualism: Language in the city*. London, UK: Routledge.

Pennycook, A., & Otsuji, E. (2017). Fish, phone cards and semiotic assemblages in two Bangladeshi shops in Sydney and Tokyo. *Social Semiotics*, *27*(4), 434–450.

Piller, I. (2016). *Linguistic diversity and social justice: An introduction to applied sociolinguistics*. Oxford: University Press.

Preece, S. (2010). Multilingual identities in higher education: Negotiating the 'Mother Tongue', 'Posh', and 'Slang'. *Language and Education*, *24*(1), 21–40.

van der Walt, C. (2013). *Multilingual higher education: Beyond English medium orientations*. Bristol, UK: Multilingual Matters.

6

AN EXPANDED VIEW OF TRANSLANGUAGING

Leveraging the Dynamic Interactions Between a Young Multilingual Writer and Machine Translation Software

Sara Vogel, Laura Ascenzi-Moreno, and Ofelia García

In the 21st century, two of the central forces shaping K-12 literacy pedagogy in the United States are the increasingly diverse and rich multilingual practices of students, as well as our growing use of digital technologies to communicate and make meaning (Deumert, 2014; García, Bartlett & Kleifgen, 2007; Jewitt, 2008; New London Group, 1996). Even if much scholarship has focused on the trends of multilingualism and multimodalities as separate entities, there are many intersections. Digital tools like machine translation software are being used in schools by multilingual students, and their often-monolingual teachers. Frameworks for multilingual teaching and learning involving intentional use of machine translation tools, however, are not yet fully incorporated into curriculum, school policies and practice.

In this chapter, we analyse a case study of how an emergent bilingual who had arrived recently in the United States from China used machine translation software (Google Translate) in a sixth-grade general education classroom during writing activities. Two of the authors of this article who are university-based researchers, were working with his teacher on the implementation of translanguaging pedagogy. Translanguaging pedagogy is an approach that calls on teachers to draw upon students' diverse language practices and to mobilise them intentionally as a critical resource in students' overall development (Creese & Blackledge, 2014; García, Johnson, & Seltzer, 2017; García & Kleyn, 2016; Gort, 2015; Gort, forthcoming; Paulsrud, Rosén, Strasser, & Wedin, 2017).

We focus on the use of machine translation software because in texts about translanguaging pedagogy written for teachers, Google Translate is recognised as a valid and valuable resource (Celic & Seltzer, 2012; García, Johnson & Seltzer, 2017). Even though we have much anecdotal evidence of machine translation's ubiquity in multilingual K-12 classrooms in the U.S., there is a lack of scholarship written from a translanguaging pedagogy perspective that focuses on its use.

We analyse field notes, observations, student work, and interviews with the teacher and our focal student to take stock of how the student used machine translation to write. We read his practices through the lens of Dant's (2004) theory of "human-machine assemblages" and the embodied social actions they enable. Additionally, we rely on Thibault's (2011) distributed language view, positing that meaning-making involves the integration of different time and spatial scales which includes both human-bodies in interaction with each other and with artifacts. In this article, we extend the linguistic concept of translanguaging (Otheguy, García & Reid, 2015) to encompass a semiotic reading, viewing translanguaging through the expressivity of a student body as he interacts with Google Translate. Additionally, our data analysis also traces the role his teacher played in the student's engagement with the tool, as the teacher shifted his view of translanguaging to encompass machine translation as part of the students' available semiotic repertoire.

Our work attempts to demonstrate how conversations about pedagogy in multilingual classrooms cannot be conducted apart from student engagement with digital tools. We hope this study also provokes reflection on how both machine translation and multilingualism prompts teachers to rethink what counts as translanguaging. Teachers should view bilingual students who use machine translation as active learners who are drawing on their available semiotic repertoire to make meaning and learn. If used intentionally, students' interactions with machine translation might become embodied as resources in students' semiotic repertoires. Thus, teachers should consider how they might, as we call it, "teach into" machine translation practices, to better support their bilingual students.

Theoretical Framework

To understand how the student at the center of our case study used machine translation software to engage in classroom-based work, and how the teacher came to view it as part of translanguaging, we found it necessary to bring several theories into conversation with each other. Firstly, we had to consider theories of translanguaging pedagogy, which were guiding our own approach to the professional development we provided the teachers at the school. The student's use of machine translation prompts us to additionally think about theories of multimodal communication and multiliteracies, and theories regarding human-technology interaction.

In the following section, we introduce the lenses guiding this work.

Translanguaging as Pedagogy

Until recently, bilingual language development was theorised as additive or subtractive (Lambert, 1974) conceptions that both imply linear acquisition of static language features. As part of a "multilingual turn" (May, 2013) in the field of sociolinguistics, static, structuralist conceptions of language and the hierarchical ideologies accompanying them have been challenged (Makoni & Pennycook, 2007). Language learning is seen as dynamic, meaning individuals learn to use different language features in social interaction and in order to negotiate meaning-making contexts (García, 2009; García & Li Wei, 2014; García & Kleyn, 2016). Translanguaging has emerged as a term to focus on the diverse language practices of people. Such practices defy categorisation into socially constructed, named language categories (Otheguy, García & Reid, 2015).

Translanguaging has had a number of important applications in the teaching of emergent bilingual students. In multilingual classrooms, despite official language allocation policies that dictate specific languages to be used at particular moments or locations, translanguaging is often the norm (Palmer, Martínez, Mateus, & Henderson, 2014; Pontier & Gort, 2016). Bilingual learners arrive in classrooms with rich language practices and backgrounds, and engage in social "acts of knowing and doing" in order to integrate and appropriate new language features into their bilingual repertoires (García & Li Wei, 2014).

Translanguaging has also framed a transformative pedagogical stance (García, Johnson & Seltzer, 2017; García & Kleyn, 2016; García & Li Wei, 2014; Gort & Sembiante, 2015; Mazak & Carroll, 2017). In order for students to bring the entirety of their academic and social selves to the learning process, teachers working within this paradigm center dynamic bilingualism at the heart of teaching and learning, and intentionally draw upon students' diverse language practices. For example, in a classroom in which translanguaging pedagogy has taken root, teachers make space for students to dive into content (take notes, read, write, perform, etc.) using their full repertoire, which includes features that are said to be from their home languages and from new languages.

Highlighting the Semiotic Repertoire in Translanguaging Pedagogy

In some conceptualisations, translanguaging is defined as what a bilingual person does when she deploys her full "linguistic repertoire" to make meaning. Such a definition focuses on bilinguals' lexical, morphological, syntactical, and other features that are "linguistic" in nature (Otheguy, García & Reid, 2015). Most research conducted on translanguaging pedagogy has underscored how students draw on their full linguistic repertoire for meaning-making in multilingual classrooms, and how teachers support and build on those practices through translanguaging pedagogy (Blackledge & Creese, 2014; Creese & Blackledge, 2010;

García, Johnson & Seltzer, 2017; García & Kleyn, 2016; Gort & Sembiante, 2015; Sayer, 2013).

In other conceptualisations of translanguaging, the bilingual's repertoire is construed more broadly, going beyond the linguistic, to encompass how she "call[s] upon different social features in a seamless and complex network of multiple *semiotic* signs, as they adapt their languaging to suit the immediate task" (García & Li Wei, 2014, our emphasis). Such a conception recognises that people draw not just on resources "within them (e.g., the linguistic features of their repertoire), but also those that they embody (e.g., their gestures, their posture), as well as those outside of themselves which through use become part of their bodily memory (e.g., computer technology)" (García, 2016).

This more ample perspective of translanguaging, resting on semiotic theories of meaning-making, takes up Thibault's distributed language view. Thibault's view of language emphasises the material dynamics of language, that is, the bodily interactions between persons, artifacts, and technologies responsible for meaning-making. Thibault conceptualises first-order languaging behavior, which includes human-bodies in interaction with each other, as well as with artifacts and technologies. The first-order languaging that Thibault contemplates "is not limited to vocalizing but includes a whole range of bodily resources that are assembled and coordinated in languaging events together with external (extra-bodily) aspects of situations, environmental affordances, artifacts, technologies" (p. 7). He privileges such languaging over what he calls "second-order languaging dynamics"—what society traditionally thinks of as languaging. Second-order languaging is comprised of intrinsically normative patterns which constrain first order languaging dynamics, and which emerge from the cultural dynamics of entire populations. Because Thibault's distributed language view makes space for co-acting agents (artifacts, technologies), we find this theory appropriate to apply in our case study given the way machine translation figures into our focal students' meaning-making.

Other scholars have similarly highlighted the need to include semiotic resources in theories about how individuals make meaning (Androutsopoulos, 2010; Bezemer & Kress, 2016; Blommaert, 2014), especially given the ways that rapid technological change brought on by globalisation has transformed the media through which we communicate and learn. In what they call the "continua of biliteracy", Hornberger (2003, p. xii) and Hornberger and Link (2012) highlight multimodal meaning-making as they conceive of the many dimensions which must be taken into account in order to understand biliteracy. They define biliteracy as "any and all **instances** in which communication occurs in two (or more) languages in or around writing", (Hornberger, 2003, our emphasis). The continua of biliteracy framework acknowledges that the media through which one develops biliteracy includes a range of practices beyond reading and writing traditional text. Hornberger and Link call on their readers to pay attention to "different communicative modes including technological ones, as they are acquired and used not in a dichotomised sequence but more often in criss-crossed, hybrid mixes, and languaging practices" (2012, p. 267).

Drawing on the continua of biliteracy, the "pluriliteracies" approach evolved to unite research in multiliteracies and multimodalities with growing understandings of bilingual language and literacy development (García, Bartlett & Kleifgen, 2007). The architects of pluriliteracies predicted that new pedagogies for literacy practices would emerge out of "the linguistically integrated space of the classroom, coupled with the possibilities afforded to all new languages by new technologies" in order to "increase the potential for communication, knowledge and understandings among all participants" (p. 218). Years after the emergence of pluriliteracies theories, there are just a few studies addressing how translanguaging pedagogies that privilege the entire "linguistic" repertoire address the realities of multilingual classrooms (Martín-Beltrán, 2014; Martínez-Roldán, 2015; García & Kleyn, 2016). Very little research, however, has explicitly focused on those biliteracy instances during which bilingual learners translanguage by drawing on their whole semiotic repertoire—including their interactions with digital technologies—and how teachers might leverage such broader semiotic practices for learning. In this case study, we focus on just one of those human-technology interactions, use of machine translation software.

The Bilingual Learner's Language—Machine Translation Assemblage

Machine translation has become a ubiquitous tool. The online Google Translate software alone boasts 500 million users and translates over 100 billion words per day (Turovsky, 2016). At present, most studies of machine translation in the context of teaching and learning are written from the perspective of researchers and practitioners of higher education foreign language programs and courses. These studies reveal the anxieties that professors and instructors have regarding machine translation, such as the fear that students will plagiarise, that machine translation will replace human acts of interpreting, that texts will be produced with errors, or that students will become dependent on the technology (Clifford, Merschel, & Munné, 2013). Many of the studies call for an acceptance of these technologies, and encourage educators to view them as an opportunity for learning, rather than as a threat (Case, 2015; García, 2010; Mundt & Groves, 2015).

Our research is guided by theories that go beyond the premise that machine translation is a disruptive tool. We reframe machine translation software as one of many meaning-making *modes*, or "socially shaped, culturally available material resources" (Bezemer & Kress, 2016, p. 7) that bilingual students draw upon. Bezemer and Kress argue that all modes offer different potentials, called *affordances*, for meaning-making, which depend on the object's material qualities and the conventions by which the object has been historically used. To explain the concept of affordance, they offer the example that a book can be read, but also used as a doorstop due to its heavy, solid properties.

But the term "affordances" has some limitations, as it considers only what the properties of an object "offer" the human user, rather than what sociologist Tim Dant refers to as the "forms of social actions" that get embodied in the human when he or she comes together with a machine in a temporary "assemblage"—the coming together of human and technology elements "within which the human remains complete in his or her self" (2004, p. 62). Dant writes about the driver-car, the assemblage created when a driver uses a car, which "is neither a thing nor a person; it is an assembled social being that takes on properties of both and cannot exist without both." This assemblage—rather than the human or the machine alone—produces social actions such as driving, speeding, polluting, transporting, etc. (Dant, 2004). At the same time, the technology does not have independent agency, but the assemblage itself enables "a range of humanly embodied actions" only possible when the human and technology interact (Dant, 2004, p. 22).

In the past, Dant's theory has been applied by Deumert (2014) in the context of communication with mobile devices. We use the concept of assemblage to analyse the emergent bilingual student in our study's use of machine translation. The theory of human-machine assemblages recognises that machine translation doesn't just *afford* students with a resource to support traditional interactions with text, but that in the interaction between student and tool, specific kinds of embodied social actions emerge. As Dant writes:

> The assemblage of the driver-car produces the possibility of action that once it becomes routine, habitual and ubiquitous, becomes an ordinary form of embodied social action. People who have become familiar with the driver-car through participating in the assemblage become oriented to their social world, partly at least, through the forms of action of which it is capable.
>
> (2004, p. 23)

In the case study that follows, we consider the specific embodied social and bodily actions that emerged from the student's use of machine translation, and consider how participating in the bilingual learner-machine translation assemblage, and privileging Thibault's first-order languaging (and not just the second-order languaging that we usually mean by language), might orient both learners and their teachers to their social world in ways that open up new biliteracy instances and possibilities for teaching and learning.

Context and Methods

Our case study focuses on a middle school student and recent emergent bilingual arrival from China, we examine how he used machine translation during one of his classes, and the possibilities for teaching and learning that opened up once his teacher's practice shifted to more intentionally incorporate the student's machine translation engagements. We draw on multiple sources of data to examine the student's interactions, including field notes of meetings with teachers, observations of instruction, analyses of student work (including the revision history feature of the online documents software he was using), and interviews with the teacher and the focal student.

Downtown East (all proper nouns describing the school site and participants are pseudonyms) is a vibrant school located in the heart of Chinatown in New York City. Whereas the majority of students are Asian (around 56 per cent), the school houses sizable populations of Latino, White and Black students. Most of the students are multilingual; many count what are considered Chinese dialects or Spanish as among the languages they speak at home. Although the school does not have a bilingual program in either Chinese or Spanish, the English as a New Language (ENL) teachers have begun to recognise their emergent bilingual students' translanguaging, and readily use their language practices to support the development of English, which is the goal of the classroom. Furthermore, the arts-infused literacy curriculum engages students to actively use language across content areas.

The school in which the study took place was involved in the City University of New York, New York State Initiative on Emergent Bilinguals (CUNY-NYSIEB) (for more on CUNY-NYSIEB, see also García & Menken, 2015; García & Sánchez, 2015; García & Kleyn, 2016). Schools that participated in the CUNY-NYSIEB project had a very large population of emergent bilingual students. The CUNY-NYSIEB team offered support to educators in order to transform their pedagogical practices by focusing on the translanguaging of their bilingual students and its pedagogical potential.

Two of the authors made up the CUNY-NYSIEB team assigned to work in this particular school, whereas García served as the project's co-principal investigator. This study took place over the course of a school year, prompted by a school-based need; the school leader wanted middle school teachers to address the needs of emergent bilingual students in their classes through translanguaging pedagogy. Ascenzi-Moreno and Vogel gathered middle school teachers and asked them to describe the needs of emergent bilingual students in their shared sixth grade class. Through this conversation, one student stood out in particular. Fu-han had recently arrived from China at the end of the previous academic year. The teachers had serious concerns about how to integrate him into the increasingly challenging work of middle school literacy and social studies content in English, and asked for our assistance in modifying lessons to incorporate translanguaging pedagogy. There were two focal teachers who worked with us closely on this project, Ross and Chandler, and in this case study, we focus on Fu-han's work in Ross' English Language Arts (ELA) class.

As a result of our conversation with teachers about Fu-han, we conducted a preliminary observation of the student. We then came back together as a working group (CUNY-NYSIEB faculty along with the two focal teachers and an additional ENL teacher at the school) to assist Ross in adapting one of his upcoming English Language Arts persuasive writing units for Fu-han. As we suggested ways Ross could insert opportunities for translanguaging within this unit, it became clear that since Ross did not speak Chinese, he would have to promote Fu-han's use of machine translation and specifically of Google Translate to facilitate his own teaching and communication with Fu-han. After Ross implemented initial translanguaging strategies, we observed the student at work again in the ELA classroom.

In debriefing our field notes, we noted that the English product resulting from Fu-han's engagement with Google Translate seemed to be treated by both student and teacher as an end point. We wondered how instead it could be a starting point for developing the language Fu-han needed to deeply engage with content-based assignments. We suggested to Ross that he could ask Fu-han to more explicitly and critically grapple with the Google Translation itself. Subsequent to the shift in pedagogical strategy by Ross, we interviewed the focal student through an interpreter, since none of us are Mandarin speakers. The goal of this interview was to more deeply understand Fu-han's engagement with Google Translate and its role in his learning. We also interviewed Ross about the role that machine translation played in his teaching. Both interviews were conducted individually and lasted approximately 45 minutes.

In what follows, we present a narrative of our findings—first those findings related to shifts in Ross' pedagogy, and then those findings which demonstrate the embodied social actions that Fu-han's use of Google Translate enabled—read through the lenses of the theories we presented above.

Ross' Shift Towards Treating Machine Translation Engagements as "Biliteracy Instances" to "Teach Into"

Fu-han was a sixth-grade boy from Fuzhou, China, who completed the first half of sixth grade in his home country before coming to the U.S. six months prior to our study. According to his ENL teacher, Fu-han speaks mostly Mandarin, but also some Fujanese. Our work began with an observation of Ross' English Language Arts course, as they were working on a persuasive writing unit. On the day we arrived, we noted that while other students in the class were engaged in content-based skills, Fu-han was reading an unrelated book in Chinese, or speaking in Mandarin to partners at his table. Armed with our notes from the observation, we began to assist Ross in finding spaces within the curriculum for translanguaging. We helped him brainstorm alternative products for the persuasive writing unit that Fu-han might create in lieu of a full formal persuasive essay in English, and suggested Fu-han might produce a book which would include an extended response about a topic in Chinese accompanied by images captioned in English.

Ross incorporated several translanguaging strategies (Celic & Seltzer, 2013) into his teaching, such as strategically partnering the student with others in the class who could speak Chinese and English. He also used Google Translate to produce bilingual graphic organisers and provided English sentence stems to assist Fu-han in his writing. Crucially, in order to facilitate Fu-han's research and writing in Chinese, Ross gave Fu-han a laptop to use.

His teacher asked him to summarise the information he researched about endangered elephants, a topic he chose from his teacher's short list. Ross also asked him to describe his emotional responses to the information he researched. As Fu-han navigated his work on the persuasive unit study, he used Google Translate to conduct research and engage in writing about endangered elephants. During one visit, we observed Fu-han's process. Fu-han drew on many linguistic resources to support his work in the class, including his oral language skills, as he conversed mostly in Mandarin with bilingual partners at his table to help him get a sense of the teacher's prompts which were specifically directed at the focal student. On the laptop, he toggled back and forth between Google Translate and the tabs on the browser that displayed websites about elephants. From what we could tell as observers of this session, Fu-han used his Chinese reading and writing skills to help him search for information on the website Baidu (a Chinese search engine), and to write and take notes responding to the teacher's prompts. He would type in Chinese directly into Google Translate (sometimes sentence by sentence, other times word by word) and would then write the English machine translation into his notebook, as in Figure 6.1.

Following this process with Google Translate, Fu-han produced an essay in English. However, we also noticed he was deleting his Chinese writing (in an

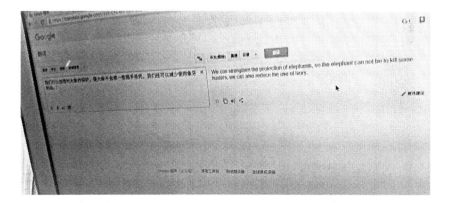

FIGURE 6.1 Student work sample #1. The student writes his ideas in Chinese in the left box on the screen, then copies the resulting English from the right side. After this process, he erases the Chinese.

interview months later, reflecting on that moment, Fu-han told us he deleted the Chinese because it was not part of the assignment). Ross, the teacher, also told us that he (not the student) did a great deal of the editing of the Google Translated writing piece, and that he hoped to see Fu-han leverage Google Translate to practice using own words in English more often.

> He was obviously using Google Translate for a lot of it. I think ideally he could hand in both pieces [Google Translated English and Chinese] . . . or he could hand in a piece that he wrote in Chinese but also a piece that he tried . . . not to rely too heavily on the Google Translate. I mean it's easy to do that because it's easy, but I'd love to be able to see maybe him trying to put some of it into his own words in English . . . so he has opportunities to practice that English and to try to get better at it as well.
>
> (8 April 2016)

We identified the need to bring Fu-han's interactions with Google Translate closer to the core of Ross' practices so that as the teacher he might recognise the student's engagement with Google Translate as a legitimate biliteracy instance (Hornberger, 2003) that needed support.

We told Ross about our initial observations of Fu-han's use of Google Translate, and discussed with him how he might further engage with Fu-han's processes. We hoped that Ross might help to place value on Fu-han's Chinese responses as well as help him further refine his language abilities in English with assistance from Google Translate. Based on our conversations, and with our help, Ross created a shared, collaborative online document that explicitly asked Fu-han for a few versions of a response to a story—a Chinese version, a version which would tap into the English that he knew off the top of his head, and then a Google Translated version of his work.

What follows is an artifact of Fu-han's responses to comprehension questions about *The Empty Pot*, a story about a Chinese boy by the American author Demi. Fu-han now not only included a Google Translated version of the story in English (the last column), but also his own response in Chinese, as well as his own response using the English he knows. This serves as an example of the type of language work in which Fu-han engaged as the teacher's role shifted towards leveraging Fu-han's engagements with Google Translate as legitimate "biliteracy instances", and as Ross recognised machine translation as a semiotic resource that was part of Fu-han's repertoire of meaning-making.

We looked at the revision history of the Google Document where Fu-han wrote his responses. Revision history indicates a chronological sequence of edits made to a document. We can infer from this data that his first step was to write his responses in Chinese. He then proceeded to the column where he was asked to "respond in English in your own words". The revision history demonstrates

Responses to "THE EMPTY POT"

Reading strategy (阅读策略)	中文	在回应自己的话 (Respond in English in your own words.)	English (Google Translate)
Did someone realize something? How might this change things?	男孩注意到了他的种子长不出来。这样他可能会失去变成皇帝的继承人的机会。	The boy found the seed is not growing, he think he may not be the emperor's heir.	The boy found his species does not grow, he felt could not be the emperor's heir.
What have you learned about a character? How do you know this?	男孩是一个很诚实的孩子，因为他的种子是长不出来的，所以他就拿着一个空的花盆去见皇上。	the boy is a honest kid, because the seed is can't growing, so he just take a empty pots go to see the emperor.	The boy is a very honest boy, because his seed is not out long, so he took an empty pot to see the emperor.
What themes do you notice? Why?	这个故事围绕着小孩和种子。因为这个故事大部分在讲小孩想了什么办法让种子长大。	The story is about the boy and his seed, because the story talking about what the boy wanted to let the seeds grow method.	The story revolves around children and seeds, because the kids want to tell the story mostly in what way to let the seeds grow.

FIGURE 6.2 Student work sample #2

he was working on his responses in that column phrase by phrase, and also doing some revision and editing which would lead us to conclude that he was writing, rather than copy-pasting pieces of text into that column. Lastly, Fu-han worked on the final column—the Google Translated version—where the revision history of the document demonstrates that blocks of text were placed in all at once, suggesting that the responses under this column were probably Google-translated versions of his Chinese responses.

What we are able to surmise is that when Fu-han is asked to respond in his own words, he often opts for words that are available to him through language that he hears in oral interactions with his teachers and peers. For example, in the first response, he chooses the word, "seed", whereas Google Translate gave him the word "species", The same is true for his choice of, "kid," over the word, "boy", the word that we surmise was offered by Google Translate.

Ross found the Google Doc graphic organiser a helpful strategy because, as he said, it gave Fu-han "more opportunities to work in English in his own words to try on his own . . . Maybe I would do that sort of moving forward. Not have Google Translate be the end product necessarily" (8 April 2016). Ross' recognition of machine translation engagements as legitimate biliteracy instances, and as translanguaging, opens up space for what we are calling "teaching into" language. By "teaching into" we refer to the opportunity for teachers to engage the students' full semiotic repertoire and, together with the student, to examine and discuss both student-generated and machine translation-enabled language outputs. While machine translation is often viewed as a means to an end, if we focus on the translanguaging that is enabled by the technology, we recognise it as a process laden with learning potential. When an educator "teaches into" machine translation interactions, he or she places attention on the student's developing biliteracy practices simultaneously with content objectives.

We were excited about Ross' pedagogical shifts because they helped him recognise the student's machine translation as a legitimate biliteracy instance. In the following quote, he refers to the students' interactions with Google Translate as posing an entry point for his providing continued support to the student in reading and writing.

> Until the end of the year, I would definitely like to see him produce work like this. We're going to be working on a short story, we're going to be working on a memoir. I would like to have him try, after the Google Translate, to try to put the work in his own words in English so he has more practice to do that. So I can get a little more of his voice, so I can maybe even assess him a little more. What are some things he does really well? What are some things I might be able to support him with?
> (8 April 2016)

We knew Ross' pedagogy could go even further towards supporting the student's fluid use of Google Translate. We hoped to learn more about the student's engagements with machine translation during an interview with him to gain more insights about how the strategies Ross used to "teach into" language could truly leverage the student's full semiotic repertoire.

Embodied Social Actions Emerging from the Bilingual Learner—Machine Translation Assemblage

About a month after Ross introduced the new format for supporting Fu-han's work with Google Translate, we conducted an interview with Fu-han through a Mandarin-speaking interpreter, Chiahao Lin, to learn more about the student's use of Google Translate[1]. Our interview revealed how the student was enacting particular social actions which we are calling "tinkering" and "evaluating"—actions that get embodied as part of Fu-han's semiotic repertoire, that is, of his translanguaging. We describe both of these actions in the sections that follow.

Tinkering

During our interview, we learned that Fu-han had studied English in China throughout elementary school, and had learned to use technology and computers through his own exploration, and also with the support of his father. Fu-han's interview reveals that he draws on his knowledge of what school and society name English, Chinese, and technology to "tinker" with machine translation to obtain more accurate results. Based on how "correct" Fu-han deems the Google

Translation to be, he uses another machine translation program to assist him. As the interview goes on, we see that Fu-han chooses when to translate words, phrases, or whole sentences.

In the following quotation, taken from the interview, we see that Fu-han is an active user of machine translation and combines it with his knowledge of what he views as Chinese, English, and machine translation:

I: For the essay about the elephant, did you have the version you wrote in Chinese? Is that the same in Chinese and in English?
F: A little bit different, because sometimes it's not correct from Google Translate. I could tell it's not correct when I used Google Translate at home.
I: So some parts are not correct, and the Chinese writing should be closer to what you want to say, right. When you notice the incorrect [parts] from the Google Translate, what did you do?
F: I will try to use other translation software.
I: OK
F: If it's still not good, I will write it by myself.
I: How did you write it by yourself?
F: Translate the words I need because it's easier to translate one word.
I: How about the whole sentence?
F: It will have more nonsense when connecting more sentences, but it's better to translate the word only.

(04/07/16)

Fu-han is already independently exploring Google Translate as part of his semiotic repertoire. In doing so he is constructing his own understandings of its capabilities to translate Chinese into English and vice versa. This action, tinkering, is now a social action that is "embodied" for Fu-han, possible when he comes together into an assemblage with the Google Translate software. Through Fu-han's tinkering with Google Translate, he comes to new understandings of how he can use the software to extend his languaging.

Evaluating

Fu-han's work with Google Translate went beyond his using it as a tool for the simple translation of words from Chinese to English. His interaction with Google Translate was also an opportunity for him to evaluate the capabilities of the software to produce intelligible translations, to analyse the accuracy of Google-translated pieces in English, to embed the translations with his own language, and to use these interactions to refine his own language practices. We refer to these particular translanguaging processes that emerged as "evaluation". Evaluation represents another biliteracy instance and embodied social action resulting from the formation of an assemblage between the emergent bilingual student and the software.

Through our interview with Fu-han, his "evaluation" interactions with Google Translate were evident. He used his knowledge of features from the school language—English—to read the English translated text and to rewrite aspects he did not deem adequate. He also acknowledged that he needed to copy some of the Google Translated text without alteration. In the following quote from the interview Fu-han describes his process of writing using Google Translate.

F: I write by myself first, then using Google Translate.
I: Which way do you do it more?
F: Half and half.
I: Because you understand, you don't need the Google Translate all the time?
F: And it will be more concise for the writing I do by myself.

This quote reveals that at the center of the writing process for Fu-han is his evaluation of the machine translation-produced text. He fluidly and flexibly incorporates from both his own linguistic repertoire and the output from Google Translate to produce the best outcome. In the interview he also notes that, for him, efficiency is important: the more that he can write without the assistance of Google Translate, the faster he will be able to get his thoughts down. Fu-han actively evaluated Google-translated texts drawing on his bilingual repertoire, thus embedding his languaging within the translations produced by the machine translation software.

Implications

In our study, we consider the specific social actions that emerge when the focal student, Fu-han, comes together with machine translation software in an assemblage. Those social actions become embodied semiotic resources for Fu-han in a way similar to the way in which the experience of the driver-car is incorporated into a person's body and then carried "into all their other perceptions and engagements with the material world in a way that they take for granted and treat as unremarkable" (Dant, 2004, p. 22). In tinkering and evaluating with machine translation, Fu-han developed a method for employing Google Translate to write text that furthered his own languaging, as well as met his expectations for accuracy of language in the context of his English class.

Teachers' translanguaging pedagogy must explicitly support emergent bilingual students' social actions with machine translation and the biliteracy instances that grow from them. But in order for this student-machine assemblage to develop so that it is part of the student's semiotic repertoire, time and space are needed to enable students to tinker and seriously evaluate all their languaging. Teachers should provide resources for emergent bilingual students to develop ways of working with technologies, assuming that students' linguistic and semiotic repertoire will shape the way they use the tool, and that the tools in turn, will shape their linguistic and semiotic repertoire.

Fu-han's abilities with machine translation evolved with his use of it, and were shaped by factors such as his literacy in Chinese, his familiarity with English, and his comfort with technology. With a greater understanding of the specific embodied social actions that emerged from the student's machine translation use, Ross can now further modify his templates and activities to build on and leverage those actions.

The following are some of the ways we imagine Ross could "teach into" Fu-han's biliteracy by recognising his first-order languaging behavior, which includes human-bodies in interaction with each other, as well as with artifacts and technologies:

a) Building on Fu-han's "tinkering" with machine translation, Ross could direct the student to write as much as he can in English and to use Chinese or Google Translate fluidly for specific words (rather than whole passages) whenever he did not know the word or concept in English, producing a linguistically translanguaged text.

b) Leveraging Fu-han's budding "evaluating" action with machine translation, Ross could prompt him to write a version of a piece in English (with or without machine translation) and then to compare its content against his Chinese or translanguaged response to make sure that all the ideas he intended to capture are captured in the English version. If not, Fu-han could then translate these concepts from Chinese to English.

c) Also building on his "evaluating", Ross could ask Fu-han to combine a response written in his own words through his own translanguaging with a Google translated text. In this exercise, the student would be asked to explicitly merge his own words (without regard to the categories of named languages) with a text translated through machine translation.

These activities leverage the student's entire *semiotic* repertoire, including his interactions with machine translation. They recognise that the product and processes of the bilingual learner-machine translation assemblage are valid and valuable classroom biliteracy instances, and that used appropriately, they can be seen as part of translanguaging.

As we detail, Fu-han's assemblage with machine translation opened up space for "teaching into" multiple biliteracy instances. For this "teaching into" to occur, we believe that teachers must be observant of students' work with technology and deepen their roles in supporting that work. One shift that we envision is that teachers focus on the processes students use to craft language, not only when self-directed, but also when used in combination with machine translation. This means the actions that the bilingual student engages in with machine translation become just as important, and perhaps more important than the product itself. It is in these actions that students' translanguaging and its potential become apparent.

Conclusion

The original aim of our work with the focal teacher in this case study was to infuse translanguaging strategies into his teaching of English Language Arts to support a newcomer focal student. As we observed the student at work, we noticed his translanguaging practices went beyond his simply drawing on his linguistic repertoire.

We viewed his use of Google Translate through the lens of theories on human-machine assemblages and the distributed language view, which allowed us to focus on the unique embodied social actions enabled by technology use. These actions become part of the student's semiotic repertoire, and therefore, of their translanguaging potential. As a result of the assemblage, complex biliteracy instances (Hornberger, 2003) also emerged and became sites for teacher intervention, support, and "teaching into".

Given this evidence, we advocate for definitions of translanguaging that integrate all parts of the semiotic repertoire of bilingual learners, including artifacts and technology. The role of teachers within this broadened vision for translanguaging is to support, to be inquisitive about, and communicate with students about the various embodied social actions and forms of languaging that occur when bilingual learners and machine translation come together.

Note

1 Chiahao Lin, was recruited to conduct the interview in Mandarin with the focal student based on an interview protocol designed by the research team in English. After conducting the interview, he translated the interview into English for analysis. We use, "I" for interviewer within excerpts of the translated transcript.

References

Androutsopoulos, J. (2010). Localizing the Global on the Participatory Web. In N. Coupland (Ed.), *The handbook of language and globalization* (pp. 201–231). Malden, MA: Wiley-Blackwell.

Bezemer, J., & Kress. G. (2016). *Multimodality, learning and communication. A social semiotic frame.* London, UK: Routledge.

Blackledge, A., & Creese, A. (2014). *Heteroglossia as practice and pedagogy.* Heidelberg: Springer.

Blommaert, J. (2014). From mobility to complexity in sociolinguistic theory and method. *ResearchGate.* Retrieved from www.researchgate.net/publication/265850000_From_mobility_to_complexity_in_sociolinguistic_theory_and_methodhttps://www.researchgate.net/publication/265850000_From_mobility_to_complexity_in_sociolinguistic_theory_and_method.

Case, M. (2015). Machine translation and the disruption of foreign language learning activities. *eLearning Papers, 45,* 4–16.

Celic, C., & Seltzer, K. (2013). *Translanguaging: A CUNY-NYSIEB Guide for Educators,* www.cuny-nysieb.orghttp://www.cuny-nysieb.org/.

Clifford, J., Merschel, L., & Munné, J. (2013). Surveying the landscape: What is the role of machine translation in language learning? *@tic. Revista D'innovació Educativa, 10*, 108–121.

Creese, A., & Blackledge, A. (2010). Translanguaging in the Bilingual Classroom: A Pedagogy for Learning and Teaching? *The Modern Language Journal, 94*(1), 103–115.

Dant, T. (2004). The Driver-car. *Theory, Culture and Society, 21*(4), 61–79.

Deumert, A. (2014). *Sociolinguistics and mobile communication*. Edinburgh: University Press.

García, O. (2009). *Bilingual education in the 21st century: A global perspective*. Malden, MA and Oxford, UK: Wiley/Blackwell.

García, I. (2010). Can Machine Translation Help the Language Learner? Presented at the ICT for Language Learning, Florence, Italy. Retrieved from http://conference.pixel-online.net/ICT4LL2010/common/download/Proceedings_pdf/TRAD02-García.pdf.

García, O. (2016). A sociolinguistic biography and understandings of bilingualism. Unpublished Manuscript.

García, O., Bartlett, L., & Kleifgen, J. (2007). From biliteracy to pluriliteracies. In P. Auer & Li Wei (Eds.), *Handbook of applied linguistics* (pp. 207–228). Berlin: Mouton de Gruyter.

García, O., & Kleyn, T. (Eds.). (2016). *Translanguaging with multilingual students: Learning from classroom moments*. New York: Routledge.

García, O., & Menken, K. (2015). Cultivating an ecology of multilingualism in schools. In B. Spolsky, O. Inbar & M. Tannenbaum (Eds.), *Challenges for language education and policy: Making space for people* (pp. 95–108). New York: Routledge.

García, O., & Li Wei. (2014). *Translanguaging: Language, bilingualism and education*. London, UK: Palgrave Macmillan Pivot.

García, O., & Sánchez, M. (2015). Transforming schools with emergent bilinguals: The CUNY-NYSIEB Project. In I. Dirim, I. Gogolin, D. Knorr, M. Krüger-Potratz, D. Lengyel, H. Reich & W. Weiße (Eds.), *Intercultural education: Festchrift for Ulla Neumann* (pp. 80–94). Berlin: Waxmann-Verlag.

García, O., Johnson, S., & Seltzer, K. (2017). *The Translanguaging classroom. Leveraging student bilingualism for learning*. Philadelphia, PA: Caslon.

Gort, M. (Ed.). (2015). Transforming literacy learning and teaching through translanguaging and other typical practices associated with "doing being bilingual" [Special issue]. *International Multilingual Research Journal, 9*(1).

Gort, M. (Ed.). (forthcoming). *The complex and dynamic languaging practices of emergent bilinguals: Translanguaging across diverse education and community contexts*.

Gort, M., & Sembiante, S. F. (2015). Navigating hybridized language learning spaces through translanguaging pedagogy: Dual language preschool teachers' languaging practices in support of emergent bilingual children's performance of academic discourse. *International Multilingual Research Journal, 9*(1), 7–25.

Hornberger, N. H. (Ed.). (2003). *Continua of biliteracy: An ecological framework for educational policy, research, and practice in multilingual settings*. Bristol, UK: Multilingual Matters.

Hornberger, N. H., & Link, H. (2012). Translanguaging and transnational literacies in multilingual classrooms: A biliteracy lens. *International Journal of Bilingual Education and Bilingualism, 15*(3), 261–278.

Jewitt, C. (2008). Multimodality and literacy in school classrooms. *Review of Research in Education, 32*, 241–267.

Lambert, W. E. (1974). Culture and language as factors in learning and education. In F. E. Aboud & R. D. Meade (Eds.), *Cultural factors in learning and education* (pp. 91–122). Bellingham, Washington: 5th Western Washington Symposium on Learning.

Makoni, S., & Pennycook, A. (Eds.). (2007). *Disinventing and reconstituting languages*. Clevedon, UK: Multilingual Matters.

Martín-Beltrán, M. (2014). "What do you want to say?" How adolescents use translanguaging to expand learning opportunities. *International Multilingual Research Journal*, 8, 208–230.

Martínez-Roldán, C. (2015). Translanguaging practices as mobilization of linguistic resources in a Spanish/English bilingual after-school program: An analysis of contradictions. *International Multilingual Research Journal*, 9(1), 43–58. doi:10.1080/19313152.2014.982442

May, S. (Ed.). (2013). *The Multilingual Turn: Implications for SLA, TESOL, and Bilingual Education* New York: Routledge.

Mazak, C., & Carroll, K.S. (Eds.). (2017). *Translanguaging in Higher Education: Beyond Monolingual Ideologies*. Bristol, UK: Multilingual Matters.

Mundt, K., & Groves, M. (2016). A double-edged sword: The merits and the policy implications of Google Translate in higher education. *European Journal of Higher Education*, 6(4), 1–15.

New London Group. (1996). A pedagogy of multiliteracies: Designing social futures. *Harvard Educational Review*, 66(1), 60–93.

Otheguy, R., García, O., & Reid, W. (2015). Clarifying translanguaging and deconstructing named languages: A perspective from linguistics. *Applied Linguistics Review*, 6(3), 281–307.

Palmer, D. K., Martínez, R. A., Mateus, S. G., & Henderson, K. (2014). Reframing the Debate on Language Separation: Toward a Vision for Translanguaging Pedagogies in the Dual Language Classroom. *The Modern Language Journal*, 98(3), 757–772.

Paulsrud, B.A., Rosén, J., Straszer, B., & Wedin, A. (Eds.). (2017). *Translanguaging and Education: New perspectives from the field*. Bristol, UK: Multilingual Matters.

Pontier, R., & Gort, M. (2016). Coordinated translanguaging pedagogy as distributed cognition: A case study of two dual language bilingual education preschool co-teachers' languaging practices during shared book readings. *International Multilingual Research Journal*, 10(2), 89–106.

Sayer, P. (2013). Translanguaging, TexMex, and bilingual pedagogy: Emergent bilinguals learning through the vernacular. *TESOL Quarterly*, 47(1), 63–88.

Thibault, P. (2011). First-order languaging dynamics and second order language: The distributed language view. *Ecological Psychology*, 23, 1–36.

Turovsky, B. (2016, April 28). Ten years of Google Translate. Retrieved January 10, 2017, from http://blog.google:443/products/translate/ten-years-of-google-translate/.

7

KEEPING THE PLURILINGUAL INSIGHT

Visualising the Literacies of Out-of-School Children in Northern Ghana

Brendan Rigby

Photography, like the act of literacy, records both the abstract and concrete. Both actions use devices to create knowledge, make meaning and "add to the truth and reality of representation" (Henry Fox Talbot, 1844: Plate X). Both acts also rely on objects to achieve their purpose. Photography relies on a device to produce photographs, while literacy relies on objects with which to scratch, incise and click. Photography and literacy require individuals to have competencies with which to manipulate relevant objects, whether pen or camera. The camera, at the forefront of a global visual culture, is quickly replacing the keyboard as the primary material for creating meaning.

This chapter explores the possibilities and complexities of participatory visual research with out of school children from two communities in northern Ghana. It discusses the place of literacy in plurilingualism, and how children switch between different literacies and languages across contexts. To improve and develop children's literacy, we need to understand their worlds. In order to understand their worlds, we need to elevate children's perspectives, in which they actively participate in documenting and understanding their literacy and language practices. Digital technology offers an opportunity to collaborate with children in revealing literacy and challenging durable notions of what literacy is and how children use it both inside and outside the classroom.

In particular, this chapter will focus on the photographic portfolio of one particular child, Amina. Her portfolio of over 300 digital photographs reveals the depth and nuance that just one perspective of literacy can offer. Digital visual research has the potential to reveal where, when and how children move between languages and literacies in out of school contexts. However, it also represents challenges in regards to ethics, representation, ownership and interpretation. Digital visual research offers unprecedented opportunities to collaborate with children in the research process, and open up different ways into research questions, dialogue and discussions. There are also unprecedented pedagogical possibilities of engaging children as researchers in their own right (Dyer, 2008).

The project involved ten children who were enrolled in a semi-formal literacy intervention implemented by a Ghanaian non-government organisation. This intervention, known as Complementary Basic Education (CBE), provided nine months of literacy and numeracy teaching to out of school children. The research methodology involved inviting the ten children to use second-hand digital cameras for a period of three weeks. They were asked to document how and where they use literacy, which was translated in their local language, Dagbanli, as "reading and writing". The children were interviewed using their photographs for elicitation. Their parents/guardians were also interviewed regarding schooling, education and literacy in their community.

The Location of Literacies Within Plurilingualism

This account draws theoretically on New Literacy Studies (Barton, 2001; Heath, 1983; Street, 1984), multimodality (Kress & van Leeuwen, 1996) and sociocultural approaches to literacy research in development contexts (Maddox, 2007; Robinson-Pant, 2008). These studies have revealed situated, socially-mediated literacy events, practices and discourses that are often excluded in formal schooling curricula, pedagogy and policy. The New Literacy Studies have contributed to a deeper and more nuanced conceptualisation of literacy *without* schooling, identifying power relations and discursive practices that configure, exclude and marginalise. Street's (1984) framework for identifying autonomous and ideological models of literacy is enduring, and has provided an important counter-balance to a durable notion of literacy as decontextualised and functional. In the context of globalisation and the evolution of digital communication technologies, further research has extended the framework for the study of literacy to include multimodal practices (Kress & van Leeuwen, 1996) and multiliteracies (New London Group, 1996).

The application of plurilingualism to digital and multimodal forms of literacy production and practice expands this notion of language competence (Kress, 2003; Prinsloo, 2004; Prinsloo & Stein, 2004). An individual's repertoire then not only includes language competence, but also capabilities to use a range of material devices and objects to make meaning through expanded literacy actions. The notion of pluriliteracy has found purchase in emerging research and is conceptualised in the same way as plurilingualism (García, Bartlett & Kleifgen, 2007; Meyer, Coyle, Halbach, Schuck & Ting, 2015; Scribner & Cole, 1978). García, Bartlett & Kleifgen (2007) framed a pluriliteracies approach to learning that emphasised the hybridity of literacy practices in sociocultural contexts afforded by digital devices. Meyer et al. (2015) argued that an increasingly digital and image-based society calls for pluriliterate citizens. Pluriliteracy calls attention to the multisemiotic and multimodal forms of representation and communication.

Recent literacy research has also reconsidered the materiality of literacy, and the way matter and materials interact, shape and influences our social worlds. There is a rise in post-humanist approaches to understanding the role matter and materials play in shaping lived experiences, especially those involving communication, language and literacy (Brandt & Clinton, 2002; Coole & Frost, 2010; van Enk, Dagenais & Toohey, 2005). Literacy researchers have applied sociocultural approaches as part of a hybrid theoretical and methodological toolbox to further explore the relations between school and out of school contexts to support pedagogic changes that value vernacular and everyday literacies. However, the changing pace at which digital technology is enabling uncountable literacy practices means that research will struggle to keep up. A focus on the pluriliterate practices of individual out of school children can offer valuable insights into understanding how the materials of literacy move, are produced and reproduced in different contexts. Digital photographs are material traces of both past and present events. A photograph is fundamentally *matter*, whether physical or digital. However, it is an incomplete snapshot, a trace of a particular time and place. Photographs move whether physically by hand or digitally over email, social media and other electronic modes. Digital photographs of literacy practice can reveal how matter and materials infuse and shape literacy, and this is critical to understand as digital technology continues to exert influence on how children are engaging and using literacy in both school and their everyday lives.

The Emergence of Universal Primary Schooling and Literacy

The documentation and analysis of local, everyday literacy practices is situated within the broader, global context of norms, systems and policies. A pluriliterate approach to understanding an individual's local practices cannot lose sight of the global stage. These two spheres interact to create educational settlements brokered by global actors. The participating out of school children were attending a complementary form of schooling as a direct result of the Universal Primary Education (UPE) agenda. Although Ghana has made progress to achieving UPE, it is estimated that 10–20 per cent of primary-aged children are out of school (UNESCO, 2016).

Although plurilingual frameworks prefigure individual children as active agents, these are not operating within contained or sealed borders (Coste & Simon, 2009). A global network of education actors has evolved rapidly since 1946, the composition and functioning of which is complex and ever-changing. This, in turn, makes identity building and agency of an individual a much more complex and perhaps less understood process (Coste & Simon, 2009). This is especially heightened in development contexts on which the multi/pluri turn has not focused (Kubota, 2014). Development contexts are defined as those in which multilateral, bilateral and non-government organisations actively work towards human rights, global development objectives and more generally to end poverty. Common parlance for these contexts includes "developed countries", "Global South" and "third world countries".

The majority of out of school children are growing up in multilingual contexts even if they are not afforded opportunities of formal schooling. In countries such as Ghana, semi-formal schooling is shaping the literacies of tens of thousands of children. In the Northern Region of Ghana, children in rural communities are moving between at least three languages, including English, Dagbanli and Qu'ranic Arabic. English is the official language of Ghana and there are 11 government-sponsored languages. Government-sponsored languages are supported by the Bureau of Ghana Languages, and can be used as the language of instruction in the first three years of primary school. The boundaries between these languages are not defined by geography, and are shaped by past and present policies, migration and social change. Global actors such as UNICEF and UNESCO (1957, 2016) continue to play a significant role in determining the movement of literacy in development contexts such as Ghana, through policy advocacy, programmatic interventions and research dissemination.

Participatory Visual Methodology as the Means

By designing and using a sociocultural approach to literacy research within the broader paradigm of plurilingualism, this chapter will demonstrate how to keep individual practice in-sight, and encourage scholars to collaborate with individuals and communities to explore emerging communication practices. It will explore digital traces of connections as represented by photographs, between global and local sites of pedagogy, discourse and practice. Although these children are out of school, they are enrolled in a local literacy and numeracy intervention. It is a local site of language and literacy practice that is informed by a global initiative funded by national governments and multilateral agencies to achieve universal primary education.

A participatory visual research methodology was designed for which participatory digital photography was the primary method (Wang & Burns, 1997). This research approach invites community members to be active participants in research design and/or data production, analysis and interpretation. Visual research indicates that the methods and/or data are image-based, usually drawings, art, videos, cartoons, photographs and other modes. Participatory digital photography enables participating children to mediate the production of data through the lens of digital cameras. It shifts the emphasis away from text, which generally mediates all aspects of research from data generation to dissemination, to the visual (Burnett & Myers, 2002; de los Ríos, 2017; Kaplan & Howes, 2004; Pauwels, 2015; Prosser, 1996; Strawn & Monama, 2012; Zenkov & Harmon, 2009). The text associated with the production of this research has the same value as the images. Neither is given preference in data production and analysis. Participatory digital photography represents a flexible, fluid and iterative methodological process that expands the notions of audience, practice and competence.

Visual research that is participatory and utilises digital photography offers new ways into research questions, particularly in exploring everyday communication events and practices (Gauntlett & Holzwarth, 2006). Hymes' (1964) call for "fresh kinds of data" to explore communication practices has languished, as the ethnography of literacy has remained relatively stable and static in its theoretical and methodological orientations. Ethnographic approaches place a premium on observation and interviews within bounded contexts. These methods are underwhelming for revealing and exploring contemporary literacy and language landscapes. In addition, ethnographic approaches in education side-line children as participants (Lodge, 2009). Participatory visual research has the potential to create a new ethnography of communication that is empowering, fluid and pedagogical. It also has important implications in building pluriliteracies, as a method such as digital photography simultaneously enables participants and creates new pedagogical activities and literacy practices.

Ten children were invited to participate as photographers of literacy. They were given one hour of basic training in how to use a small digital camera. This occurred in a school building with their parents/guardians, teacher and a translator present. They practiced in the school building, experimenting with depth of field, different camera angles and composition. The participants were asked to take photographs of their practice and understanding of reading and writing. They were told that photographs can be taken both in school and out of school contexts. The instructions were given in English and translated into their mother tongue, Dagbanli. The translator checked for understanding with the children, their parents/guardians and the teacher.

After a three-week period, the photographs were analysed and coded for the literacy themes in each photograph. Actions, objects and places were identified in each photograph and assumptions were checked in the interviews with participants. Two rural communities were purposively selected out of 25 in the Savelugu-Nanton District of the Northern Region of Ghana. The main criterion was that both communities have an active Complementary Basic Education (CBE) program running during the fieldwork period between February and April 2015. Complementary Basic Education is a specific term referring to an arrangement in which non-state education service providers implement an alternative primary education program that targets out of school children (Rose, 2009; DeStefano & Moore, 2010). A CBE program sits outside of the formal primary education system, but is often officially considered equivalent to a predetermined number of years of primary schooling. A Ghanaian non-government organisation, School for Life, offers a CBE program that is considered to be equivalent to two to four years of formal primary schooling. Children who attend CBE are still considered out of school and not counted in the official enrolment figures. School for Life offers a modified literacy and numeracy program over nine months, which includes a local language as the medium of instruction, three hour-timetables with classes held during the afternoon to account for household labour children perform and a culturally relevant curriculum including appropriate teaching and learning materials (TLM).

The two communities selected, Botingli and Bunglung, had concurrent CBE programs provided by School for Life with funding from UNICEF Ghana. The two communities were located four kilometres east of Savelugu, the capital of the local district. The Dagomba are the dominant ethnic group in this district, primarily practice Islam and whose mother tongue is Dagbanli. Botingli is accessed along a dirt road that ends when the community is reached. It is a small community that sits near a river and comprises roughly 20 Dagomba households. There is no running water or electricity with the exception of a small number of solar-powered streetlights. Botingli does not have a primary or secondary school; however, a community member funded the construction of a building for informal Qu'ranic Arabic classes. There is also a mosque in the centre of the community funded by an external donor in Saudi Arabia. Less than two kilometres south of Botingli is Bunglung. The community is divided by a larger unpaved road that connects Savelugu to Nanton. It is roughly twice the size of Botingli, is connected to the electrical grid and has a primary school. There are roughly 30 Dagomba households in Bunglung including a mosque.

Analysing Visual Data of Literacy: A Case Study

Ten children, five from Botingli and five from Bunglung, were randomly invited to participate in the research. They were between eight and twelve years of age, although their age is uncertain, as many of the children were not registered at birth. They had either never attended formal schooling or had dropped out before completing, but were attending School for Life's CBE program. Semi-structured interviews were conducted with 10 parents/guardians of the children who participated in the research. An independent translator was recruited from Tamale for the interviews.

Photo-elicitation interviews were conducted with each participating child, which lasted no more than 1.5 hours. The participating children were asked open-ended questions about particular photographs. For example, "tell me about this photo", "why did you take it?" and "what were you doing?" CBE classroom observations were conducted over two months and totaled around 40 hours. Ethical issues and procedures including informed consent were considered on-going and not one-off. A robust ethical framework was developed, which was guided and informed by university ethical regulations, professional guidelines and approaches taken by the research community. Last, photography exhibitions of selected photographs were also organised in Bunglung, Botingli, Melbourne and Sydney.

The ten participating children produced over 4,000 digital photographs, which were coded both manually (physically sorting each printed version of the photographs) and digitally (using Atlas.ti). Over-arching patterns, themes and results were analysed. However, for the purposes of this chapter, the focus is on the portfolio of one participant, Amina. In this section, a selection of photographs are shown that are representative of Amina's portfolio. Over the course of three weeks, she produced 333 digital photographs. Of those, an even number were produced in two languages, English and Dagbanli (see Figure 7.1). However, only 31 per cent of her photographs contained any representation of language. The remaining 69 per cent contained no representations of written languages.

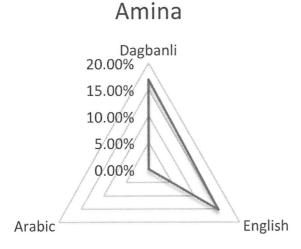

FIGURE 7.1 Representation of languages

The contexts in which these photographs were produced is revealing. Only 43 per cent of the portfolio was produced in school-based contexts (see Figure 7.2). That is, either in the context of CBE, primary school or junior high school. Although Amina does not attend formal primary schooling, Bunglung has primary school and junior high school buildings. A classroom in the primary school was used for their CBE classes during after-school hours. It is evident from Amina's photographs that she moved within these buildings both during CBE classes and during other times of the day. She also produced 46 per cent of her photographs in out of school contexts, including in her home and community. Dagbanli was correlated to the context of CBE, and English was correlated to the context of primary school. However, these where usually one and the same in terms of context, as Amina was moving in and out of school buildings for CBE classes.

Amina lives with her mother in Bunglung, and is the daughter of her mother's first husband. Amina has a twin brother. She indicated that she had never attended formal schooling, but her mother contradicted this, indicating that Amina attended at least until grade two. Amina has also been attending Qu'ranic

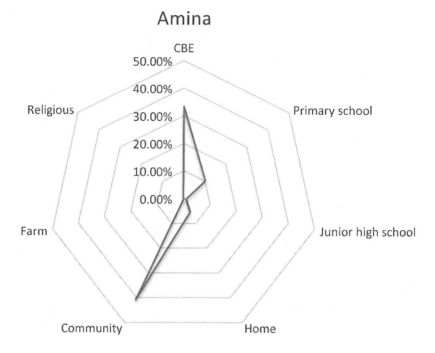

FIGURE 7.2 Contexts of production

Arabic schooling for the past five years, but cannot say why she does not attend formal schooling. Amina's mother stated that Amina refused to go to formal schooling because her twin brother had refused. Amina's mother described the purpose of Arabic schooling as a means to make a living. Although the content of Arabic schooling was different to primary schooling and CBE, it represented a form of schooling for which Amina's mother perceives a future economic value. Being able to read and write in multiple languages would have an economic benefit for her family in the future.

Qu'ranic Arabic schooling is very common in Dagomba communities, and is seen by other parents/guardians as a form of moral education. Although Amina did not produce any photographs of Arabic schooling, materials or texts, she described the type of tasks they engaged in while in class and what they do with Arabic outside of the classroom. The reading and writing children engaged in are defined by rote learning and memorisation.

The following photographs are a sample of the first Amina produced (see Figures 7.3–7.5) and are all out of school, featuring both English and Dagbanli language. The first photographs Amina produced are of a bright red and white sign located on the main road through Bunglung (see Figure 7.3). It is a World Vision sign, announcing the five interventions that the organisation implements in the community. It is written in English and welcomes visitors to Bunglung.

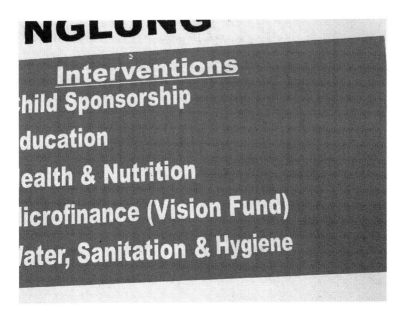

FIGURE 7.3 A photograph of one of Bunglung's English language signs. This shows a section of World Vision Ghana's sign, listing the range of development interventions being implemented in Bunglung. Image credit, Amina.

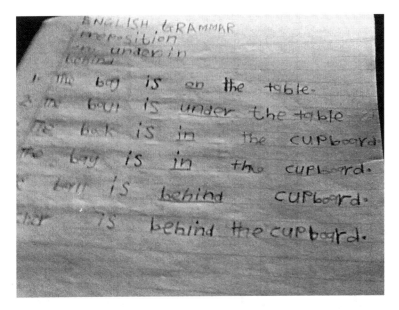

FIGURE 7.4 A photograph of Amina's writing book, in which she copied English text from one of Bunglung primary school's blackboards. The photograph was taken at home. Image credit, Amina.

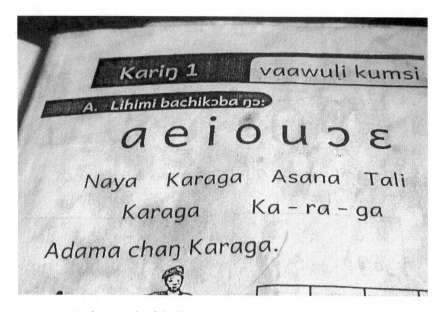

FIGURE 7.5 A photograph of the first page of Amina's School for Life textbook. The instructions read "Look at the letters of the alphabet". The vowels of Dagbanli are listed followed by key characters and place names used in the textbook. "Naya", "Asana" and "Tali" are names of people in the textbook's stories. "Karaga" is a small town in the northern region of Ghana. The last sentence translates to "Adama goes to Karaga". Image credit, Amina.

It is a non-school context, and the children recognised the word "Bunglung" and could recognise some of the phonemes and letters, which share similarities to Dagbanli. Amina often produced photographs of written language inscribed on other objects. It was not writing of her own, but produced by other people (see Figure 7.7). Her interaction with these materials through the lens of the camera became a literacy event itself, and she reconciled her competency using a device. In the photo-elicitation interview with Amina, as with the other participants, she referenced how conscious she was of the instructions given to her to photograph *karimbu sabbu*. Amina wanted to meet expectations while also reconciling her own representations of reading and writing. The camera supported this reconcilitation, enabling her to explore different spaces, sites and materials of reading and writing.

At the same time, Amina produced photographs of her own literacy actions. She produced a photograph of a page of an exercise book on the ground of her home (see Figure 7.4). The page features her writing in English. Under the heading of "ENGLISH GRAMMAR", the first sentence says, "The bag is *on* the table". According to Amina, she saw these sentences written on a blackboard in a primary school classroom. She decided to copy them. When asked about why she took the photograph Amina responded, "I learn it. I learn English from the writing".

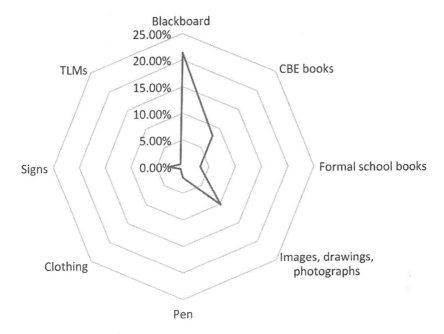

FIGURE 7.6 The materials of literacy

Amina's CBE class is held in one of the classrooms of the local primary school. The formal school day ends around 13:00 each weekday. Between 14:00 and 14:30, CBE starts in the same classroom that the grade six class also occupied. Therefore, in many of the photographs from Bunglung in school-based contexts, there is an overlapping of languages being represented, Dagbanli and English, as the purpose of the classroom changes from formal primary schooling to the CBE program.

Navigating the Pluriliterate Self

Amina navigates her way through and between languages, literacy materials and schooling spaces (see Figures 7.4–7.7). She used a methodological tool given to her by the researcher to represent this movement. Her literacy repertoire was not confined to a school context nor to a CBE context, but went beyond these boundaries. Amina was able to reveal her pluriliterate self through photography.

Despite being out of school, Amina represented a connection with English language and formal schooling through her photographs (see Figure 7.7). She displayed an individual competence in utilising the camera to represent her

FIGURE 7.7 A photograph of a blackboard in Bunglung's primary school. The English text reads "Homework: Basic five pupils in a class were asked to name their favourite subjects. The result is shown below". Image credit, Amina.

competencies and aspirations. Formal schooling represented the opportunity to "be someone in the future". Amina said that she wants to go to school and wants to be educated. School for Life represents an opportunity to attend formal schooling.

> When you attend, when you have not begun formal schooling, and you start with School for Life, at the end of your training there you can go to formal school and that can be the way for you to be someone in the future.
> (Amina)

When asked about her understanding of literacy, which is translated in Dagbanli as *karimbu sabbu* (translated as "reading and writing"), Amina stated that they are complementary. She reads at home after she is finished with her household work and homework. Amina also stated that she is sometimes asked in the community to demonstrate her literacy. "Sometimes people call us to ask us questions on what we read and write, and then I explain it to them". Amina's mother characterised literacy as actions of copying; of copying what is taught at school. "She practices by repeating what she learned in school, either by writing or reading at home". Literacy was defined as the ability of a student to copy what a teacher has written and then being able to read it (see Figure 7.10). These notions of literacy reflect school-based understandings that are underpinned by the particular curriculum being taught, the content of the teaching and learning materials and the pedagogical methods used by the teacher. In unpacking plurilingualism and pluriliteracy this reveals the school-based influences that can shape a child's competencies in contexts of high out of school populations. Pluriliteracy is not a concept that is confined to digitally-rich image and text environments. Amina's portfolio demonstrates the length to which we can trace this notion across contexts using innovative research methods.

English is used in the school contexts to access the curriculum and textbooks. Yet, examining the English documented in classrooms by Amina, it could be predicted that it will be very difficult for her to make sense of the written text into the future. It appears to be directly copied by the formal school teachers from school textbooks and the subject content is very different from the curriculum and content of CBE textbooks (see Figure 7.8). However, Amina navigates the two languages through the process of copying. Copying from the

FIGURE 7.8 A photograph of School for Life students writing on a blackboard in Bunglung's primary school. On the right side of the blackboard, the students had written "Kom", meaning "water", "KOKO" means "gruel", "buku" means "book" and "Silimiga" means "white man". Image credit, Amina.

blackboard and copying from textbooks in both English and Dagbanli. The navigation is also revealed when comparing Figures 7.7 and 7.8. The blackboard is from the classroom, but at two different times during the day or week. In Figure 7.7, the primary school teacher had copied this text from a book onto the blackboard. In figure 7.8, children from the CBE class were writing Dagbanli words from their textbook onto the blackboard without the teacher present. They are individual words and are not connected into simple sentences.

Amina also expressed non schooled-based representations of literacy and the materials that inhabit literacy. Over 10 per cent of the photographs she produced featured images, pictures and/or drawings. Although not significant in terms of frequency, Amina's capturing of a television set (TV) highlights moments of out of school multimodal literacies. She rarely produced photographs of multimodal literacies in school compared to the three boys in Bunglung. However, a television as an object only appeared in Amina's and one other participant's portfolio. Amina produced four photographs that contained a TV (see Figure 7.9). Amina shows a television sitting almost in the entirety of the frame. The television is switched on, and the event being broadcast can be identified. The photograph

FIGURE 7.9 A photograph of Amina's family's TV, which was broadcasting live events from Accra to celebrate Ghana's Independence Day. Image credit, Amina.

was produced on 6 March 2015, the same day as Ghana's 58th Independence Day. Celebrations were being broadcast live from Black Star Square in Accra. The three other photographs of the tv show different scenes from the celebrations. The last photograph in this series is focused on the text at the bottom of the screen. "LIVE FROM BLACK STAR SQUARE". Amina was unaware of what event was being broadcast, and described it as "a drama, play on TV".

The interviews with both Amina and Amina's mother were conducted after the participatory photography finished. I asked Amina's mother about Amina's practice of literacy in the community. Her response, which was given in Dagbanli and translated into English, highlights the pedagogical aspects of participatory digital photography, revealing unanticipated outcomes in terms of the participating children's learning.

Brendan: How does Amina use literacy in the community?
Amina's mother: In the meantime, the only outward display of literacy is in this photographing thing you have introduced to them and the community has benefited a lot from it.
Brendan: How would you say the community has benefited?
Amina's mother: This photographing thing you brought will surely do one thing. The next time they are recruiting children for School for Life, they are going to get so many. Secondly, it's united the children because those who have the cameras, anytime they went out to take their pictures, you see the others just follow them to observe and see how they are taking them. The children really enjoyed doing these things.

Although Amina's mother did not identify any other literacy events, Amina produced photographs of literacy actions and also possessed an orthodox understanding of literacy. When asked what she enjoyed about participating, Amina responded that she liked photographing "the act of writing". This is reflected in her photographs, in which she captures people in the act of writing and also the finished action (see Figures 7.10–7.12). This is representative again of her competency to recognise literacy actions that others take or have taken, and from which she draws meaning. Figure 7.11 and 7.12 are photographs of her writing both in action and as a completed action. Figure 7.12 is a paragraph copied from her CBE textbook. Figure 7.10 is of her teacher writing multiplication problems from the CBE numeracy textbook. Numeracy is also represented as a way to develop and access literacy in Dagbanli, while also developing Amina's numeracy skills. She did not differentiate between literacy and numeracy, but rather saw them as one and the same.

Amina, much like the other nine participating children, drew on a range of multimodal, literacy and language practices in her documentation. Her portfolio offers a brief glimpse into the microcosm of competencies in languages and literacies that are beginning to emerge in her learning. There are multiple sites in this small

FIGURE 7.10 A photograph of Amina's School for Life teacher writing multiplication problems on the blackboard. Image credit, Amina.

FIGURE 7.11 A photograph taken by one of Amina's peers. It is of Amina writing in a book during a School for Life class. Image credit, unknown.

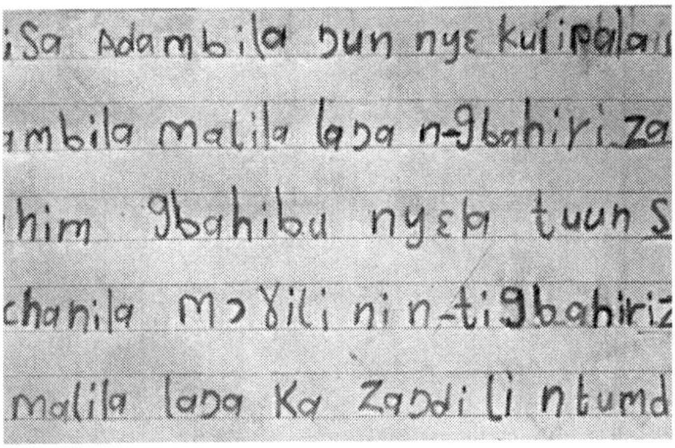

> iSa Adambila ɔun nyɛ kuiŋɔla
> mbila malila laɔa n-gbahiri za
> him gbahibu nyɛla tuun s
> chanila mɔ yili ni n-ti gbahiriz
> malila laɔa ka zaɔdi li ntumd

FIGURE 7.12 A photograph of a paragraph of Dagbanli text copied by Amina from the School for Life textbook. Image credit, Amina.

community in which different communicative modes are apparent, verbal, written and multimodal. The digital camera offered the opportunity for Amina to explore and represent those modes and sites, and how she understands literacy. She understands that literacy is something that both other people do and that she does, often through copying text. Amina represented literacy in a variety of materials, from sign posts and blackboards to televisions and textbooks. At the same time, her emergent practices and understandings are regulated by global policy frameworks and discourse situated around historical movements towards universal primary schooling and notions of literacy embedded in assumptions about language of instruction. These are not temporally bound, and have shifted and moved across different times and spaces influenced by global and local actors. Although she is an active agent of her pluriliterate practices, these are neither local nor global but are influenced by a range of social, cultural and political factors. Her photographs also demonstrate the width and breadth that the notion of pluri-literacy can be applied. It is not a concept that can necessarily be confined to digitally-rich media and text environments.

Participatory digital photography is a complementary methodology to literacy and language research and teaching, which enables not only data production but also pedagogical offerings in participatory research. Cameras can act as pedagogical tools, offering students the opportunity to reflect on their own communicative practices, engage a broad audience in the discussion and sharing of photographs and identify the traces linking local and global practices. Digital cameras regulate and encourage a global, common practice regardless of context. The act of photography can become part of a student's communicative repertoire and allow the expression and representation of complex ideas, thoughts and competencies.

This exploration of Amina's plurilingualism, as she traverses English, Dagbanli and Qu'ranic Arabic, is mediated by multivariate actions involving literacies, images and objects. Out of school children in these two communities in northern Ghana are developing competencies between different forms of schooling, both informal and semi-formal. Each form of schooling is linked to a particular language, and ascribed a particular form of literacy through teaching and text. Amina used her limited but visible plurilingual and pluriliterate resources to participate in this research and represent her literacy. Digital photography made visible her resources and competencies, which could allow her teacher to differentiate her learning and support her development. Amina and her peers demonstrate a deeper and more nuanced understanding of everyday literacies, embodied in materials and objects across different contexts. Global traces are evident in and among local variations and understandings that influence how these children develop their perspectives of literacy. Amina's language use and choice is routinised through schooling, yet not contained or static. In conceptualising and advancing plurilingualism, it is crucial that we pay attention to the multivariate ways children make meaning through different modes and media. That we pay attention to the multitude of minute details that children use in language and literacy practices to represent their realities.

References

Barton, D. (2001). Directions for Literacy Research: Analysing Language and Social Practices in a Textually Mediated World. *Language and Education*, *15*(2&3), 92–104.

Brandt, D., & Clinton, K. (2002). Limits of the local: expanding perspectives on literacy as a social practice. *Journal of Literacy Research*, *34*(3), 337–356.

Burnett, C., & Myers, J. (2002). "Beyond the frame": exploring children's literacy practices. *Literacy*, *36*(2), 56–62.

Canagarajah, S., & Liyanage, I. (2012). Lessons from pre-colonial multilingualism. In M. Martin-Jones, A. Blackledge & A. Creese (Eds.), *Routledge handbook of multilingualism* (pp.49–65). Abingdon: Routledge.

Coole, D., & Frost, S. (2010). Introducing the new materialisms. In D. Coole & S. Frost (Eds.), *New materialisms: Ontology, agency, and politics* (pp.1–46). Durham: Duke University Press.

Coste, D., & Simon, D-L. (2009). The plurilingual social actor. Language, citizenship and education. *International Journal of Multilingualism*, *6*(2), 168–185.

DeStefano, J., & Moore, A. S. (2010). The role of non-state providers in ten complementary education programmes. *Development in Practice*, *20*(4–5), 511–526.

Dyer, C. (2008). Literacies and discourses of development among the Rabaris of Kutch, India. *Journal of Development Studies*, *44*(6), 863–879.

van Enk, A., Dagenais, S., & Toohey, K. (2005). A socio-cultural perspective on school-based literacy research: Some emerging considerations. *Language and Education*, *19*(6), 496–512.

García, O., Bartlett, L., & Kleifgen, J. A. (2007). From biliteracy to pluriliteracies. In P. Auer & L. Wei (Eds.), *Handbook of applied linguistics, vol. 5: multilingualism* (pp. 207–228). Berlin: Mouton-DeGruyter.

Gauntlett, D., & Holzwarth, P. (2006). Creative and visual methods for exploring identities. *Visual Studies*, *21*(1), 82–91.

Heath, S. B. (1983). *Ways with words: Language, life, and work in communities and classrooms*. Cambridge: University Press.

Hymes, D. (1964). Introduction: Toward ethnographies of communication. *American Anthropologist, 66*(6), 1–34.

Kaplan, I., & Howes, A. (2004). 'Seeing through different eyes': exploring the value of participants research using images in schools. *Cambridge Journal of Education, 34*(2), 143–155.

Kress, G. (2003). *Literacy in the new media age*. London, UK: Routledge.

Kress, G., & van Leeuwen, T. (1996). *Reading images: The grammar of visual design*. London, UK: Routledge.

Kubota, R. (2014). The multi/pural turn, postcolonial theory, and neoliberal multiculturalism: Complicities and implications for applied linguistics. *Applied Linguistics, 37*(4), 474–494.

Lodge, C. (2009). About face: visual research involving children. *Education 3–13: International Journal of Primary, Elementary and Early Years Education, 37*(4), 361–370.

Maddox, B. (2007). What can ethnographic studies tell us about the consequences of literacy? *Comparative Education, 43*(2), 253–271.

Meyer, O., Coyle, D. Halbach, A., Schuck, K., & Ting, T. (2015). A pluriliteracies approach to content and language integrated learning—mapping learner progressions in knowledge construction and meaning-making. *Language, Culture and Curriculum, 28*(1), 41–57.

New London Group. (1996). A pedagogy of multiliteracies: Designing social futures. *Harvard Educational Review, 66*(1), 60–92.

Pauwels, L. (2015). 'Participatory' visual research revisited: A critical-constructive assessment of epistemological, methodological and social activist tenets. *Ethnography, 16*(1), 95–117.

Prinsloo, M. (2004). Literacy is child's play: Making sense in Khwezi Park. *Language and Education, 18*(4), 291–304.

Prinsloo, M., & Stein, P. (2004). What's inside the box? Children's early encounters with literacy in South African classrooms. *Perspectives in Education, 22*(2), 67–84.

Prosser, J. (1996). What constitutes an image-based qualitative methodology? *Visual Sociology, 11*(2), 25–34.

de los Ríos, C. V. (2017). Picturing ethnic studies: Photovoice and youth literacies of social action. *Journal of Adolescent & Adult Literacy, 61*(1), 1–10.

Robinson-Pant, A. (2008). 'Why literacy matters': Exploring a policy perspective on literacies, identities and social change. *Journal of Development Studies, 44*(6), 779–796.

Rose, P. (2009). NGO provision of basic education: alternative or complementary service delivery to support access to the excluded? *Compare, 39*(2), 219–233.

Scribner, S., & Cole, M. (1978). Literacy without schooling: Testing for intellectual effects. *Harvard Educational Review, 48*(4), 448–461.

Strawn, C. & Monama, G. (2012). Making Soweto stories: photovoice meets the new literacy studies. *International Journal of Lifelong Education, 31*(5), 535–553.

Street, B. (1984). *Literacy in theory and practice*. Cambridge: University Press.

Talbot, H. F. (1844). *The pencil of nature*. London, UK: Longman.

UNESCO. (1957). *World illiteracy at mid-century: A statistical study*. Paris: UNESCO Publishing.

UNESCO. (2016). *Education for people and planet: Creating sustainable futures for all*. Paris: UNESCO Publishing.

Wang, C., & Burris, M. A. (1997). Photovoice: Concept, methodology, and use for participatory needs assessment. *Health Education & Behavior, 24*(3), 369–87.

Zenkov, K., & Harmon, J. (2009). Picturing a writing process: Photovoice and teaching writing to urban youth. *Journal of Adolescent & Adult Literacy, 52*(7), 575–84.

PART III
Plurilingual Classroom Practices and Teacher Perspectives

8
TRANSLINGUAL INNOVATION WITHIN CONTACT ZONES

Lessons from Australian and South African Schools

Sue Ollerhead, Mastin Prinsloo, and Lara-Stephanie Krause

Introduction

In keeping with a global trend toward increasing plurilingualism in school contexts, students from multilingual migrant backgrounds who speak English as an additional language (EAL) are a rapidly expanding feature of the wider school population in Australia, where the school system continues to be dominated by a monolingual English ethos (Coleman, 2014). Consequently, concerns have grown around giving Australian school teachers the knowledge and skills they need to assist such students to access school curriculum content in English. In contrast, in multilingual South Africa where 11 official languages co-exist, the majority of school children grow up speaking languages other than English in their home settings, yet find themselves in a similarly monolingual school system where they are taught and tested through the medium of Standard English, often by teachers from similar backgrounds who are themselves not fluent users of Standard English.

We undertake a contrastive study in this chapter, across our respective sites in Sydney, Australia and Cape Town, South Africa, focusing on implications for pedagogy and school language policy development. Faced with expectations from policy-makers in both contexts that schools should migrate EAL children quickly and successfully to Standard English-language proficiency, we contrast the challenges experienced by teachers of addressing such concerns across the two sites of our research. In the Sydney setting, we focus on the ways in which teachers sometimes overlook the linguistic resources their students bring with them to the classroom. In the Cape Town setting, we describe research conducted with teachers who themselves speak English as an additional language, and who grapple daily with the linguistic demands of a curriculum that mandates Standard English as the medium of instruction and assessment. In both cases, we discuss how teachers understand and respond to the process of "translanguaging" (García & Wei, 2013), a term and practice that refers to the flexible and dynamic classroom use of students' available language resources and repertoires, for purposes of supporting their learning in English across the curriculum as well as enhancing their multilingual resources. We identify as a critical issue, the call for all teachers, irrespective of their linguistic environment, to be equipped with the pedagogical language knowledge necessary to draw upon students' full range of linguistic resources to support learning. Similarly, we identify as a crucial issue the conceptualisation of teacher interactions with students as "contact zones" (Pratt, 1991) where languages and cultures come together, often in contexts of conflict and misunderstanding, in social spaces characterised by unequal power relationships.

Parallel Monolingualism, Monolingual Habitus and Standard Language

In the past, educators and researchers have shown a strong preference for the construction of parallel monolingual spaces (Heller, 1999) for learning, with strict monitoring of those spaces for their monolingualism. Martin-Jones (2007) refers to such a view as a "container metaphor of competence": Manifest in terms such as "full bilingual competence", "balanced bilingualism", "additive bilingualism" and "subtractive bilingualism" (p. 167), in effect all conceiving of languages and linguistic competencies as separate containers, side by side, that are more or less full or empty. Such conceptualisations of language use often co-exist within educational contexts that operate according to a monolingual habitus. The term "habitus" (Bourdieu, 1991), refers to the dispositions, actions and perceptions that individuals acquire through social experience. A monolingual habitus thus refers to the unquestioned assumption that a single language—in this chapter, English—is the basis for the operating norm (Gogolin, 1997). The idea of a "standard" language, that form of a country's language that is taught and tested in schools, is integral to the maintenance of such habitus. Joseph (2016) contends that the notion of a standard language positions students hierarchically according to their ability to master the "largely arbitrary rules" (p. 26) of that language, which ultimately acts to oppose or slow down innovation. Says Joseph:

> This resistance to innovation means that it is the past of the language being incorporated into its present (standard) state, and indexing users of the standard form as educated and (although fallacious) as more intelligent than non-standard speakers.
>
> (p. 27)

Over the last two decades, however, a surge in language learner identity research has sought to disrupt and counter such rigid conceptions of language use.

Globalisation, Mobility and Contact Zones

The impact of globalisation has seen previous ideas of stable and bounded language groups replaced by notions of language shift and variation. Rapid increases in mobility and migration have resulted in people building new social networks that link their countries of origin with the new countries in which they settle. These globalised societies are characterised by increased contact between individuals, which turns urban spaces into what Pratt (1991) terms "contact zones", characterised by cultural and linguistic diversity. If one endorses de Fina's (2016) definition of language learner identities as being "conveyed, negotiated and regimented through linguistic and discursive means" (p. 163), then a new, more fluid iteration of how identities are indexed and expressed through the manipulation of linguistic resources in response to global developments is needed. The term "translanguaging" has arisen from such a need. Bilingual talk around monolingual texts in school and community settings is, indeed, characteristic of most multilingual social contexts, as was already seen in Gregory and Williams' *City Literacies* (2000), a study of language and literacy based on long term ethnographic engagement with the Bangladeshi settlement in East London, UK, notable for its emphasis on the interaction of home and school languages and literacies in the learning lives of children. More recently, this multilingual fluidity has come to be attended to by researchers within the discursive terms around "translanguaging" as a phenomenon.

Translanguaging and Translanguaging Pedagogy

Translanguaging is a process whereby multilingual learners access a range of available linguistic features or semiotic modes for communication and learning (García, 2009). In the act of translanguaging, learners "shuttle between languages" that behave as an integrated system (Canagarajah, 2011, p. 401). Translanguaging is thus a dynamic process in which a user's repertoire of linguistic practices can only emerge and grow through practice and socialisation with other language users. This shuttling between languages allows users to adapt their complex linguistic and cultural practices to diverse contexts and varied local practices, allowing them to inhabit manifold and fluid identities. This affirmation of multiple linguistic identities serves not only to balance the power-relations between languages in the classroom (Canagarajah, 2011), but also increases students' participation and motivation (Blackledge and Creese, 2010; Lin, 2012), thus ultimately enhancing learning. Most important for school contexts are the ways in which translanguaging allows teachers and students to engage with pedagogies that harness the full range of learners' linguistic practices.

García, Johnson and Seltzer (2016) describe "translanguaging pedagogy" as an instructional and assessment framework that allows teachers to support multilingual students in reading and comprehending complex texts, developing linguistic practices for academic language contexts, allowing "space" for their multilingual practices and facilitating and supporting their identity development. To meet these goals, García et al. (2016) recommend supportive materials such as multilingual readers and interactive word walls, as well as specific strategies, such as having students do pre-writing activities using all of the languages in their repertoire, then choosing a language in which to publish, making connections between cognates, and brainstorming using different languages. Of particular interest to this chapter is the writing of "identity texts", a process outlined by Cummins (2001) in which multilingual students create texts in both English and their home languages as ways of sharing their cultural and linguistic identities and experiences. Says Cummins (2001):

> Students invest their identities in the creation of these texts which can be written, spoken, visual, musical, dramatic or combinations in multimodal form. The identity text then holds a mirror up to students in which their identities are reflected back in a positive light.
>
> (p. 12)

Having established translanguaging pedagogy as a viable approach to catering for linguistic diversity in classroom settings, we now turn our attention to its application in case studies from two diverse settings, namely Australia and South Africa.

The Australian Context

Australia is a culturally and linguistically diverse country, where approximately 20 per cent of its population speaks a language other than English (LOTE) at home. In New South Wales, Australia's most populous state, LOTE students comprise 33 per cent of the school-going population, and 20 per cent of all students are learning English as an additional language (EAL) (NSW Department of Education, 2016). EAL students are described as needing "targeted support" to develop proficiency in Standard Australian English, the variety of spoken and written English taught and examined in Australian schools. Various educational stakeholders have made much of the fact that EAL students perform poorly on national standardised testing measures such as the National Australian Program for Literacy and Numeracy Assessment (NAPLAN). As a consequence, they are often positioned in deficit terms as "challenging" or "problematic" learners to have in the classroom (Creagh, 2014; Dobinson & Buchori, 2016). Far less credence is given to the fact that even though EAL students are only part way through their English language learning journey, they are subject to the same national tests as first language English speakers.

Notably absent from language education discourse in Australia is an acknowledgement of EAL learners' plurilingual resources, a recognition of the linguistic capital that they bring to classrooms, or any discussion of pedagogical implications for how these linguistic resources could be used to enhance the learning of both EAL *and* mainstream learners. This absence is incongruent with numerous studies that point to the cognitive advantages of speaking more than one language, including the fact that bilingual brains are more flexible, more creative, and better at problem solving (Baker, 2006; Hakuta & Diaz, 1985). Says Misty Adoniou in *The Conversation* (2014): "It would appear that we are so busy defining them (EAL learners) as problems that need to be fixed, that we have lost sight of the fact that they are the most linguistically savvy learners in our schools". There is very little recognition of what Genesee (1987) describes as the cognitive complexity that EAL learners face when having to master three things concurrently at school, namely: Becoming highly proficient in academic English; acquiring complex academic skills and content taught in English, and developing new social skills that will allow them to integrate with their English-speaking classmates and teachers.

Such challenges particularly apply to students from refugee backgrounds entering secondary school when they arrive in Australia. Many require intensive language support to access the school curriculum, and may also have emotional, welfare and other educational support needs as a result of their refugee experiences and disrupted or limited prior schooling. In Australia, this additional language support is provided through initial intensive English tuition at specialised schools known as Intensive English Centres (IECs). The case study presented below concerns one such school located in a large metropolitan area of Sydney.

The Setting and Participants

Metro Intensive English College (pseudonym) is located in a culturally diverse, working class suburb of Sydney. It caters for newly arrived students to Australia, many of whom have refugee backgrounds and have experienced little, or severely disrupted, schooling, as well as a smaller cohort of International Students from China who are seeking to complete their secondary education in Australia. At the time of the study, the school was experiencing an increased intake of refugee-background students from Syria. The school provides lessons in all high school subjects within a specialised language-enriched program, called a "language outcomes framework". The framework provides explicit language support through focusing on the structure of texts, key vocabulary and grammar in all subjects. All teachers at the school are required to have a specialised qualification in teaching English to speakers of other languages (TESOL).

The Australian Study

This research comes from a broader study in which academics, teachers and trainee teachers collaborated on an 18-month participatory action research project at Metro Intensive that trialled, observed and documented the most effective pedagogies for new arrival EAL students. Despite the linguistic diversity at Metro, from an etic perspective, the school's 'operating norm' appeared largely monolingual in its goal of transferring standard English language skills to newly arrived students to "get them ready" for mainstream Australian schools within a maximum period of 12 months. Notably, this goal was perpetuated by a teaching cohort that was largely multilingual, with only three out of 17 staff not speaking one or more languages in addition to English. The aim of this research was to investigate the extent to which teachers utilised both their own linguistic funds of knowledge as well as those of their students, to inform their classroom teaching practices.

The study's participants were 17 classroom teachers at Metro Intensive, including the principal and head teacher, both of whom had teaching roles in addition to their administrative duties.

Research Design and Data Collection

This study was designed as an "issue driven case study" (Rodriguez and Hye-Sun, 2011, p. 497) that draws upon an interpretive methodology to gain insight into teachers' linguistic resources, or 'funds of knowledge' (Moll, Amanti, Neff & Gonzalez, 1992). Case study methodology provided a basis for collecting factual information as well as teacher narratives which shed light on their approach to working with plurilingual resources and translingual pedagogies.

Seventeen teacher participants were given a survey to complete, which sought data on the nature and degree of their linguistic funds of knowledge (e.g. languages spoken, self-assessment of literacy/oracy) as well as their attitudes and practices related to translingual pedagogy. Two examples of key survey items were: a) In what different ways do your students use languages other than English during classroom learning? and b) What do you feel to be the benefits/drawbacks to students using languages other than English language in the classroom?

Following the survey, focus group interviews were held with two groups of three classroom teachers. These semi-structured interviews probed questionnaire responses and elicited more fulsome narratives from teachers regarding their use of plurilingual resources in the classroom. This narrative-based research offered valuable ways to explore the multiplicity and complexity of social identities of the teachers (Rodriguez & Hye-Sun, 2011, p. 496).

The survey and interview data was complemented by an analysis of four classroom teaching "video vignettes". These vignettes were five-minute long video-recorded segments in which Metro teachers provided "mini-lessons" in particular language support strategies. Each video showed a teacher using a particular linguistic strategy in a classroom or one-on-one tutoring session, overlaid with the narration of a metalinguistic rationale for the strategy chosen. Metro Intensive posted these video vignettes on their intranet as a source of professional learning for all teachers. Selected vignettes were also posted on YouTube to showcase the range of teaching practices implemented at the school. The video vignettes analysed in this study were all available via YouTube and thus available in the public domain.

Data Analysis

The instances of discourse analysed as data were both narrative and non-narrative in nature (i.e. teachers explaining their attitudes towards their students' linguistic resources, or funds of knowledge in interviews, as well as short phrases regarding their practices in response to survey questions). Hence, transcripts were analysed using an eclectic approach borrowing from narrative analysis (NA) and also from Critical Discourse Analysis (CDA) (Fairclough, 1995), in order to derive themes. From this hybrid analysis, broad preliminary themes emerged, meriting further examination of: a) Teachers' perceptions about the utility of their own linguistic funds of knowledge; b) teachers' harnessing of their students' linguistic resources; and c) teachers' enactment of translanguaging pedagogies and practices in the classroom.

Findings and Discussion

Teachers' Perceptions About the Utility of their Own Linguistic Funds of Knowledge

Collectively, the 17 teachers surveyed possessed a rich array of linguistic resources, and all but three participants spoke languages additional to English. These languages included Spanish, Malay, Chinese, Japanese, Mandarin, Cantonese, French, Russian and Thai. Although participants articulated some appreciation of the linguistic resources they brought to their teaching, they generally perceived no role for these additional languages in the Intensive English Centre. They articulated their roles as ostensibly "immersing" students in English, so that they would be ready to think and learn in English when they reached mainstream schooling:

> We need them to get used to thinking in English so that they will speak, write and reason in English too. We would just confuse them if we used our other languages with them in the classroom.
>
> (Harold)

This response is significant in that it reflects a siloed approach to language use, described as "parallel monolingualism" (Heller, 1999), where the linguistic resources students already hold are seen at best as separate from, at worst as distractions to, learning the target language. Such a view is at odds with more dynamic conceptualisations of bi- or multilingualism, in which repertoires of bilingual practice emerge and expand through socialisation and practice (García, 2009).

Teachers' Harnessing of their Students' Linguistic Resources

While teachers were patently aware of their students' linguistic diversity, in some cases they characterised this diversity in slightly dismissive terms, as seen in responses such as "My students speak too many different languages to mention" or "My students speak mostly Chinese".

While two participants commented on the utility of students' first languages for cultural exchange and to foster a sense of belonging, the remainder reflected a "language as problem" (Ruíz, 1984) perspective when asked about their students' use of their first languages (L1s), as illustrated in the following:

T1: Overuse or reliance on using the first language can slow English language learning.
T2: They become too comfortable speaking their first language and lose interest in the language they are trying to learn.
T3: It (the L1) interferes with their learning of English, and you don't understand them, so it is a distraction.
T4: It can exclude other students from different language groups, and lead students not to think in English.
T5: It leads to exclusion of the teacher, of others, to disengagement.

Collectively, these responses pointed to teachers' general disinvestment in students using their L1s in the classroom, where any engagement with languages other than English were perceived as obstacles towards the ultimate goal of attaining the "standard" academic English proficiency. The assertion by some teachers that students' L1 use led to the teacher "not understanding" students or "being excluded" from them, suggests that some participants were reluctant to hand over the English-medium classroom to linguistic forces beyond their control. This chimes with Hornberger's (2008) assertion that the monolingual classroom positions teachers in an inequitable position of power in relation to their students, as opposed to classes that adopt translanguaging pedagogies, where teachers are seen as linguistic learners alongside their students (García & Wei, 2013).

Teachers' Enactment of Translanguaging Pedagogies

When asked about the different ways in which students' L1s were used in the classrooms, teachers referred almost uniformly to their translation by L1 teacher aides, who were present for part of the days in almost all classrooms, and would translate complex instructions or concepts in English into students' L1s. Said teacher Lucy: "On the rare occasion I will ask a student to translate for another student; but generally aides help lower level students".

This consignment of the L1 to the role of a scaffolding or translation tool for students who "can't yet understand instructions in English", contrasts with García's vision of translanguaging as a pedagogical strategy that is used for students of all levels of L2 language development, even those highly proficient in the L1. Rather than acting merely as an aid or a scaffold, García (2009) points to the utility of the L1 as a tool for enriching and enhancing learning, through for example encouraging students to engage critically with challenging texts and to develop 'bilingual voices'.

On the surface, teachers' responses suggested that very few translanguaging practices were implemented at Metro Intensive. This assumption was challenged, however, on examination of a series of video vignettes produced by Metro Intensive teachers which revealed that, despite the monolingual ethos of the organisation and the guarded approach to the use of languages other than English, elements of effective translanguaging were emerging in the midst of quality, culturally responsive teaching practices. The vignettes comprised five-minute-long video-recorded segments in which teachers provided "mini-lessons" on a particular language support strategy. The video vignettes analysed in this study were all available via YouTube and thus available in the public domain. Below is an example of one such lesson.

Richard's Neurological Impress Vignette

This vignette showed senior teacher Richard demonstrating a reading strategy to a newly arrived student with little first language literacy using a strategy called "neurological impress". This is a form of paired reading in which a student and teacher read the same text almost simultaneously. Sitting side-by-side, the teacher reads a text slightly faster and louder than the student while both follow the text with their fingers. Reading along with a more fluent reader is thought of as "an impress, an etching in of word memories on the natural process" (Heckelman, 1969). In addition, positive reinforcement from the teacher helps to build students' self-confidence and enjoyment of reading.

During Richard's demonstration, he sits at a desk with a new student, Suraya, who has recently arrived in Australia from Syria. At 14 years old, she has received just three years of formal schooling in Arabic. Alongside Suraya sits Arabic aide Joumana, who translates Richard's English instructions for the lesson into Arabic. The transcript from the micro-lesson below contains both Richard's instructions to Suraya (marked "I") and his metalinguistic explanation for each step in the lesson (marked "ME").

Richard [I]: Right, we're going to write down in English a story that you tell me about yourself. And then we're going to read it many times in English, together. Then you make a recording on your mobile phone. [He takes out mobile phone and points to the record button]. Take it home for homework. Listen and practice. [L1 aide Joumana translates all of these steps into Arabic for Suraya].

Richard [ME]: The translator listens to each of her sentences in Arabic. Together, they jointly construct the text. The interpreter (translator) sits with her, gets basic things about the kid's story, like "My name is . . . I come from. . . . I lived in. . . ." Also things they like, if they had any pets or something, just things that are important to them as their own life story.

[Suraya tells Joumana a sentence in Arabic and Joumana relays it back to Richard in English]

Joumana: I lived in Aleppo.

Richard: Okay, tell me about Aleppo. [Joumana translates and Suraya responds]

Richard: Okay, so it was a big place and it had a big park.

[Richard types Suraya's sentences translated into English by Joumana. He cuts and pastes some pictures of Aleppo into the text. Then he prints out the five-lined text and hands it to Suraya. Joumana translates the text into Arabic for Suraya so that she can tell if it is accurate. Richard reads the first sentence aloud:]

Richard: My name is Suraya. I lived in Aleppo . . .

Suraya: My name is Suraya. I lived in Aleppo . . .

[Suraya repeats each line in English, using her finger to track each word. Each line is repeated several times until the reading is fluent.]

Richard [ME]: Finally, we neurologically impress the text as a result of the repetition. We then transfer the text to an audio recording. So we draw on multimodal resources rather than just linguistic, to aid reading and writing in English.

A close analysis of Richard's neurological impress vignette reveals that it contains all the elements of an identity text activity, a classic translanguaging pedagogical strategy, as Cummins (2001) described it, of developing parallel texts across L1 and the language of learning. In this activity, Suraya was able to draft her initial spoken text in her language of choice, Arabic. Using her L1 allowed her more freedom to express her ideas and identity. Suraya then worked with Richard and Joumana to translate the text into English, which was then transposed into another semiotic mode, in this case a digital audio recording. By including aspects of Suraya's life history in the text, including details about her home city Aleppo accompanied by pictures, Richard was able to draw upon not only Suraya's linguistic resources, but also her cultural funds of knowledge (Moll et al., 1992) to affirm and support her identity development as a language learner. Says Richard:

Somehow just by drilling it again and again, and by it (the text) coming from within them, their own cognition and experience, it makes it all come together. It can be a very powerful tool . . . and a very affirming one.

Although Richard did not express any explicit awareness of translanguaging pedagogy in his demonstration, his culturally responsive teaching approach authentically introduced Suraya's use of her L1 as a means of affirming her cultural and linguistic identity. In so doing, Suraya was able to harness four key resources, namely: Her L1 knowledge of Arabic, her emerging knowledge of English, her cultural and historical knowledge of Aleppo, and her digital proficiency with a mobile phone to competently create an oral, written and digital audio text that expressed her identity. It was clear that harnessing all of these resources combined to enhance Suraya's comprehension and communication to the extent that she was able to create a written and digital artefact, resulting in a sense of accomplishment and satisfaction. Richard's video vignette lesson serves to explicate the powerful impact that cultural and linguistically responsive teaching practices have on language learning. This would suggest that in order for teachers to ascribe to the benefits of translanguaging pedagogy in the classroom, those involved in language education need to bridge the theory-practice divide by disseminating more widely local instances of translanguaging strategies in situated contexts, so that teachers can see concrete benefits to adopting strategies that may at first seem counter-intuitive in traditionally rigid, monolingual school systems.

The South African Context

Prinsloo's work with colleagues and students has explored the complexities of language and literacy in multilingual contexts in South Africa, where English is the prescribed language of instruction. He has drawn links with similar work in Africa, Asia, South America and elsewhere, where the languages of the indigenous majority get transposed in schooling by an ex-colonial language, in policies and practices supported and perpetuated by contemporary governmental strategies.

In a school-based comparative study of English-language instruction at three sites, distinguished from each other along socioeconomic and linguistic lines, Prinsloo (2012) focused on English-language instruction as a bounded monolingual practice, endorsed and sustained in schools, but diverse and specific in effects and outcomes in diverse contexts. In a maths class in a school in Khayelitsha, a teacher struggled to find the words in mono-lingual English to explain a maths problem, where both he and his children were not fluent or regular English speakers. In a slightly more up-market school nearby in the Cape Flats, where many of the children were Xhosa-speakers, transported daily to the school from Khayelitsha, they were taught by a teacher who spoke no Xhosa, and the language of learning and teaching was monolingual English. Most of the teaching happened at this school on the assumption that the children brought almost nothing with them to the school by way of linguistic resources and background knowledge. The teacher focused on surface features of language and literacy coding and decoding and on surface features of language meanings. In contrast to these two examples, a middle-class school not far away taught children who were, along with the teachers, predominantly monolingual English speakers. The teachers here moved fluidly in and out of more formal genres and registers and "everyday English" in their teaching. The teachers' language was fluid and dialogical, acknowledging and drawing on children's out-of-school interests and knowhow, while for the few students at the school from social backgrounds that were not white or monolingual middle-class, the language and practices of the school were assimilationist, inviting the children to identify as English-speakers and to assimilate the cultural capital brought to school by the other children. The researcher concludes that children (and teachers) who already have knowledge of prestige varieties of English from out of school are positioned advantageously in comparison to poorer students who do not have that access, when monolingual standard English is the hegemonic norm.

In contrast, in recent work, Krause and Prinsloo (2016) have started to examine the practices of translanguaging that are prevalent in some schools in Khayelitsha. Linguistically, the township is predominantly associated with Xhosa, though the local language diverts from the standard, which was codified in a 19th-century rural setting. Inequality has a strongly linguistic dimension in this setting, where access to an imagined Standard English, as taught to the well-off in suburban schools, acts as a profoundly reified and instrumental motivation for families living on the periphery to send their children to suburban or inner-city schools. However, "township schools" in Khayelitsha and other settlements that house the urban poor are the only option available for the many children whose parents cannot afford to send them elsewhere and most of them stay isolated from the city centre, along with their parents, due to the geographical distance and a lack of financial means. The school that was studied follows the early-transition language policy model with Xhosa as the Language of Learning and Teaching (LoLT) for the first three years of schooling, followed by a switch to English as the LoLT thereafter. This model assumes the possibility and desirability of two languages being learned and practiced side by side in one societal setting without significant mingling or interfering of their respective spheres.

We draw here on data collected by Lara-Stephanie Krause working as a graduate student researcher, first reported in Krause (2014) and in Krause and Prinsloo (2016). The research shows that, despite the school explicitly subscribing to a separatist language policy and ideology that endorses monolingual English as the language of instruction, classroom talk was characterised by patterns of translanguaging, where teachers and students spoke a varying mix of resources conventionally associated with Xhosa and English. However, as Krause and Prinsloo (2016) noted, such translanguaging in this school was happening 'under cover' as it were, not supported in the explicit language ideas of the teachers and not permitted in examinations and other formal writing tasks but sustained and nurtured in classroom pedagogical practices.

As one brief example of translanguaging, a Grade 5 Mathematics classroom explained a calculation on the board:

> Alright let's carry on! He showed us ba we are adding two hundred and thirty four, five, thirty eight. Zisteps zakhe ebethetha apha besimva sonke. Waze wabhala usixteen phaya right? Ecaleni ukusikhumbuza. That is what you do, siyavana?

English Translation:

> Alright let's carry on! He showed us that we are adding two hundred and thirty four, five, thirty eight. These are his steps that he was talking about here, we all heard him. Then he wrote sixteen there right? On the side, to remind us. That is what you do, do we understand each other?

Most of the numbers the teacher referred to were either in English or using terms where a Xhosa prefix met the English number (e.g. usixteen). Drawing on Bailey's (2007) account of Bhakhtin's concept of "heteroglossia", Krause and Prinsloo (2016) describe such terms as "heteroglossic", because they are individual lexical items which are built from linguistic features conventionally associated with different languages. Indeed, Xhosa-speakers in the Western Cape commonly count using either English names for numbers or heteroglossic terms where English terms are incorporated into Xhosa syntactical patterns (as in *usixteen*). In everyday language, the boundaries between language are far more permeable than is allowed in standard language contexts.

The official language policy at the school, as described by the principal, restricts the language use of this teacher in the classroom. He is supposed to focus on speaking English. The excerpt shows, however, that the classroom register is translingual. The teachers' languaging is fluid, sometimes leaning more towards English, then again more towards Xhosa. For explanatory purposes, teachers frequently either repeat a monolingual statement translingually or vice versa. Other times they vary the level of translanguaging in the repetition. The principal explicitly disapproves of what his teachers do:

> All the learning area, the language of the learning area is English. Only Xhosa as a learning area that must be taught in Xhosa. And it's not happening, that's why we have problems. And we know that not to

happen, we know that it's a failure of the teachers, because the teachers think they have, they got a sympathy for the children, they undermine the knowledge of the children. They also think that children will not be able to understand them. Now they want to get onto the level of the children, the time is going. That's why we have a problem.

So translanguaging as currently advocated in the literature (García & Lin, 2017; García & Wei, 2013; Lewis, Jones & Baker, 2012) as the way out of restricting, monolingual teaching strategies is in fact often common practice in these township classrooms, with teachers applying the language resources at their disposal to make learners understand subject content. Through their fluid language practices they counteract the rigidity of the school's separatist language policy that treats languages as bounded objects and assigns them to specific learning spaces at the school. However, the institutional language ideologies that materialise in the school's language policy and in testing regimes, turn such skilful language practices from an asset into a disadvantage. When it comes to writing and testing, the teachers insist that everything has to be in standard English (Krause and Prinsloo, 2016, p. 353):

R: Mhm so when they answer in Xhosa you gonna mark it wrong?
T: Yes.
R: So even if the content is correct?
T: It's correct but it's wrong.

Teachers know from experience that translanguaging in class clashes with the language requirements learners have to fulfil in written exams. However, they continue to employ the multiplicity of linguistic resources at their disposal. Translanguaging moves teachers away from monolingual teaching strategies towards a more integrated, less boundaried use of language resources in teaching and learning, but this productive pedagogy runs up against separatist language ideologies that inform school management (embodied here by the principal and his views), language policy and resulting assessment practices. Teachers know that they are transgressing the principal's language policy as well as they know that their students are struggling with monoglossic examination requirements. Thus, translanguaging and the monoglossic ideological constraints they encounter land up in an unproductive balance with the students suffering at the point of testing (Krause & Prinsloo, 2016, p. 355).

The view from Khayelitsha suggests that the practices that lead to the reproduction and enactment of monolingual language ideologies can be challenged when it comes to developing appropriate educational strategies in multilingual contexts. As Silverstein (1996) pointed out, for monolingual standard language ideologies to maintain their hegemony, they have to be perceived as widely available and attainable to hide the power relations behind such attitudes. In the examples from Khayelitsha shown here, the inappropriateness of such language attitudes are not hard to see. Through the experiences of teachers' translanguaging practices, "under the covers", as it were, strategies for effective pedagogy in multilingual contexts can be shown to be emergent.

Conclusion

We have presented a study of a school in Sydney in this chapter, where refugees, immigrants and other EAL students are learning and being tested and we contrasted that study with one of children and youths at a school in Khayelitsha, Cape Town. We review here some of the key points that emerge across the two sites and draw conclusions of a general nature from a contrasting of these two studies. In both settings, it is apparent that the students struggle with standard language requirements while their existing language resources are underused. At the Intensive English Centre in Sydney, the teachers and students bring a diversity and multiplicity of language resources other than Standard English to the classroom, yet those resources get marginalised by the hegemonic weight of Standard Australian English in the classroom and the wider society. In contrast, at the school in Cape Town, the teacher and students all speak the local Xhosa language of their homes and neighbourhood. In both cases, school policy or teacher expectation is that all teaching and testing should be in English only. In the Cape Town school, the inequitable impacts of language ideology on schooling practice are somewhat easier to see. We can clearly see here the incongruities between what language resources the teachers and students bring to the classroom and the insistence by the school principal on English-language-only instruction. His insistence along with the wider policy framework in education in South Africa reflects the wider language hierarchies in South African society, unmistakeably shaped by colonial and apartheid regimes of the past and enduring in the post-apartheid present in South Africa, where language differences emerge as markers of social inequality and where the ex-colonial language, English, is the official language of learning and teaching, serving as a gatekeeper to success and employment. The Cape Town study helps us to see that the conceptions of language that inform policy at school level and in inter-school testing protocols are imbued with the effects of social power and do not always make sense in terms of effective pedagogy, curricula and testing. For learners' full linguistic repertoires to be legitimately used as resources for learning, a shift at both policy and teacher-training level is required. The prevalence of the English language in post-apartheid South African society, in commerce, employment and tertiary education makes "home-language" instruction in schooling in indigenous African languages such as Xhosa less appealing as a strategy to resolve language-of-learning challenges in schools, but the Khayelitshan teachers' unofficial, illegal and subversive use of translanguaging pedagogic strategies in the classroom shows us just how necessary and important such language strategies can be for effective teaching when students are not at ease with the language of instruction in its standardised form. Without any specific training to do so, the Khayelitshan teachers use translanguaging to overcome obstacles in helping students to both understand content as well as to learn specific features of the form of the standard English language that they are required to use for testing purposes.

From the perspective of the study of the school in Sydney, we can see similar workings out of the effects of power on ethnolinguistic groups of people, where educational structures legitimise and delegitimise particular uses of language. Arguments for translanguaging teaching strategies under the conditions described here make considerable sense, where the students and teachers among them hold diverse resources across multiple named languages. Such a curriculum would give space to teaching practices that incorporate students' language resources, experiences and knowhow, where diversity is viewed as an important cultural resource in children's development. Teachers need to be trained to recognise and work with these resources in a sustained and productive way. In Australia, the notions of "intensive English immersion" or "English only instruction", espoused at both policy and practice levels, fail to capture the reality of situations in which multilingual students and teachers come together in contact zones where numerous cultural and linguistic resources are at play. Not allowing space for these resources, by framing them as "deficit" in comparison to standard English, results in teaching practices that fail to harness multilingual students' full potential.

This chapter argues for more explicit teacher training in translanguaging pedagogy for teachers working in linguistically diverse contexts. Such training should start with the sharing of instances of powerful and innovative translanguaging practices in local contexts that enhance learning and communication. Viewing multilingual resources as an asset, rather than a problem, and harnessing them within innovative and flexible translanguaging approaches, will do much to realise the "linguistic savviness" of EAL students entering monolingual English-based school systems.

Being multilingual does not necessarily make one more receptive to translingual pedagogy. We need to disrupt the notion that the use of learners' language resources other than Standard English is a problem in effective learning. Our view is that language and ethnicity have porous borders that allow for the negotiation of more fluid and hybrid identities and resources. Shifts in institutional culture and resources are required to enable students from multilingual communities to achieve the identity transformation on offer in higher education. To this end, translanguaging pedagogy and practices offer us alternative ways in which to operationalise this vision. In order to do this, we need to first interrogate teachers' linguistic ideologies, to provide a solid basis in translanguaging theory and operationalise it in terms of accessible classroom strategies so that teachers are equally invested in a pedagogy that harnesses the linguistic savviness that, to date, remains largely untapped for many EAL students in classrooms around the world.

References

Adoniou, M. (2014, July 15). *Improving kids' literacy: A little knowledge can go a long way.* Retrieved from http://theconversation.com.

Bailey B. (2007). Heteroglossia and Boundaries. In M. Heller (Ed.), *Bilingualism: A social approach* (pp. 257–274). Basingstoke, UK: Palgrave Macmillan.

Baker, C. (2006). *Foundations of bilingual education and bilingualism.* Clevedon, UK: Multilingual Matters.

Blackledge, A., & Creese, A. (2010). Translanguaging in the bilingual classroom: A pedagogy for learning and teaching? *The Modern Language Journal, 94,* 103–115.

Bourdieu, P. (1991). *Language and symbolic power.* Cambridge, MA: Harvard University Press.

Canagarajah, A. S. (2011). Codemeshing in academic writing: Identifying teachable strategies of translanguaging. *The Modern Language Journal, 95,* 401–417.

Coleman, J. (2014). Realising the pedagogical potential of multilingual pre-service primary teachers. *Exchanges: the Warwick Research Journal, 2,* 35–52.

Creagh, S. (2014). A critical analysis of problems with the LBOTE category on the NAPLaN test. *The Australian Educational Researcher. 41*(1), 1–23.

Cummins, J. (2001). *Negotiating identities: Education for empowerment in a diverse society* (2nd ed.). Los Angeles: Californian Association for Bilingual Education.

De Fina, A. (2016). Linguistic practices and transnational identities. In S. Preece (Ed.), *The Routledge handbook of language and identity* (pp. 163–178). Oxford, UK: Routledge.

Dobinson, T., & Buchori, S. (2016). Catering for EAL/D Students' language needs in mainstream classes: Early childhood teachers' perspective and practices in one Australian setting. *Australian Journal of Teacher Education, 41*(2), 32–52.

Fairclough, N. (1995). *Critical discourse analysis: The critical study of language.* London, UK: Longman.

García, O. (2009). Education, multilingualism and translanguaging in the 21st century. In T. Skutnabb-Kangas & R. Phillipson (Eds.). *Social justice through multilingual education* (pp. 140–158). Clevedon, UK: Multilingual Matters.

García, O., Johnson, S., & Seltzer, K. (2016). *The translanguaging classroom: Leveraging student bilingualism for learning.* Philadelphia, PA: Caslon.

García O., & Lin, A. (2017). Translanguaging in bilingual education. In García, O., Lin, A., & May, S. (Eds.), *Bilingual and multilingual education, encyclopedia of language and education.* New York: Springer.

García, O., & Wei, L. (2013). *Translanguaging: Language, bilingualism and education.* London, UK: Palgrave Macmillan.

Genesee, F. (1987). *Learning through two languages: Studies of immersion and bilingual education.* Cambridge, MA: Newbury House Publishers.

Gogolin, I. (1997). The monolingual habitus as the common feature in teaching in the language of the majority in different countries. *Per linguam: A journal of language learning, 13*(2), 38–49.

Gregory, E., & Williams, A. (2000). *City literacies: Learning to read across generations and cultures.* London, UK: Routledge.

Hakuta, K., & Diaz, R. M. (1985). The relationship between bilingualism and cognitive ability: A critical discussion and some new longitudinal data. In K. E. Nelson (Ed.), *Children's language,* (Vol. 5) (pp. 319–344). Hillsdale, NJ: Erlbaum.

Heckelman, R. G. (1969). A neurological-impress method of remedial-reading instruction. *Academic Therapy, 4*(4), 277–282.

Heller, M. (1999). *Linguistic minorities and modernity: A sociolinguistic ethnography*. London, UK: Longman.

Hornberger, N. H. (2008). Ecology of language. In A. Creese, P. Martin & N. H. Hornberger (Eds.), *Continua of biliteracy: Encyclopedia of language and education*, (Vol. 9) (pp. 275–290). New York: Springer.

Joseph, J. E. (2016). Historical perspectives on language and identity. In S. Preece (Ed.), *The Routledge handbook of language and identity* (pp. 19–33). Oxford, UK: Routledge.

Krause, L. (2014). *Xhosa is my identity, English is my future: Complexities around language values and practices at a South African township school* (unpublished Masters thesis). Germany: University of Leipzig.

Krause, L., & Prinsloo, M. (2016). Translanguaging in a township primary school: Policy and Practice. *Southern African Linguistics and Applied Language Studies, 34*(4): 347–357.

Lewis, G., Jones, B., & Baker, C. (2012). Translanguaging: Developing its conceptualisation and contextualisation. *Educational Research and Evaluation: An International Journal on Theory and Practice, 18*(7): 655–670.

Lin, A. (2012). Multilingual and multimodal resources in L2 English content classrooms. In C. Leung & B. Street (Eds.), *"English" in Education* (pp. 79–103). Bristol, UK: Multilingual Matters.

Martin-Jones. (2007). Bilingualism, education and the regulation of access to language resources. In M. Heller (Ed.), *Bilingualism: a social approach* (pp. 161–82). New York: Palgrave Macmillan.

Moll, L., Amanti, C., Neff, D., & Gonzalez, N. (1992). Funds of Knowledge for teaching: Using a qualitative approach to connect homes and classrooms. *Theory into Practice, 31*(2), 132–141.

New South Wales Department of Education. (2016, August 20). *Enrolment of LBOTE students in NSW government schools (2013–2015)*. Retrieved from https://data.cese.nsw.gov.au.

Pratt, M. L. (1991). Arts of the contact zone. *Profession, 91*, 33–40.

Prinsloo, M. (2012). What counts as English? In B. Street & C. Leung (Eds.), *English— a changing medium for education* (pp. 22–40). Clevedon, UK: Multilingual Matters.

Rodriguez, T. L., & Hye-Sun, C. (2011). Eliciting critical literacy narratives of bi/multilingual teacher candidates across the U.S. *Teaching and Teacher Education, 27*, 496–594.

Ruíz, R. (1984). Orientations in language planning. *NABE: The Journal for the National Association for Bilingual Education, 8*(2), 15–34.

9

PLURILINGUALISM AND AGENCY IN LANGUAGE EDUCATION

The Role of Dramatic Action-Oriented Tasks

Enrica Piccardo and Angelica Galante

Introduction

The acceleration of mobility in the global village is bringing to the fore aspects of linguistic and cultural coexistence that have certainly prevailed for a very long time in most societies but that, until recently, had been pushed to the background, or bluntly ignored. Currently, diversity as a construct that informs and shapes the lives of both individuals and communities is emerging as a key notion in our societies, one that is essential to our wellbeing and peaceful coexistence. However, at the same time, the tendency towards linguistic and cultural homogenisation that accompanies the globalisation phenomenon is putting that same diversity at risk; this threatens social harmony in a way similar to that in which the reduction of biodiversity is threatening the balance of the entire planet (Skutnabb-Kangas, 2000, 2002).

This tension between the opposite poles of homogenisation and increasing diversity contributes to a new scenario, which presents both great potential and serious challenges. On the one hand, we witness, helplessly, the damage done over time by oppressive linguistic and cultural policies, while becoming increasingly aware of how an apparently small change in policies can have a great negative and even irreversible impact in a relatively short time span. This is the case, for instance, with language loss due to family and/or community linguistic choices and pressure (Cummins, 2000; 2001). On the other hand, we have come to realise the need for all language stakeholders to take active measures if we are to counteract and prevent this loss of diversity and its consequences. Yet, a prerequisite for planning such measures is an appropriate conceptual framework to support us in the theorisation of the complexity of the social reality we are faced with.

In this chapter, we first discuss the value of plurilingualism as a conceptual framework. We then move to the related concept of agency and present its implications for language learning and teaching. Finally, we focus on the synergies between drama and agency as one possible pedagogical venue to operate a shift towards plurilingual language education.

Plurilingualism as a Conceptual Framework

Heterogeneous communities are the norm rather than the exception in many parts of the world. Characterised by mobility, immigration, technology and globalisation, societies have become increasingly diverse. As a way to address diversity and reject the *monolingual disposition* (Gogolin, 1994), which prevents one from seeing, let alone valuing, different languages in society or education, plurilingualism has been recognised as an important framework for language teaching (Canagarajah & Liyanage, 2012; Moore & Gajo, 2009, Piccardo, 2013). The multi/plurilingual turn (Conteh & Meier, 2014; Kubota, 2016; May, 2014) encourages the use of previous linguistic and cultural knowledge to learn more languages and their related cultures. The product of this process is an integrated plurilingual repertoire, which the speaker can call upon flexibly according to the needs of the context. In addition, plurilingualism takes language varieties as an integral component of this previous knowledge. While plurilingualism is not a new concept (Cenoz, 2013; Glaser, 2005), in language education it first started gaining visibility in the early working documents of the Common European Framework of Reference for languages—CEFR—in the late 1990s (Coste, Moore & Zarate, 1997/2009; Council of Europe, 1996) and later conceptualised more comprehensively in the early 2000s (Beacco 2005; Beacco & Byram, 2003/2007; Council of Europe, 2001). Thus, the plurilingual conceptual framework has been available to language educators for two decades, although we recognise that the paradigm shift is still in its early stages, and every major change needs a considerable amount of time to be successfully implemented.

Kramsch (2014) identifies the last 30 years, deeply characterised by globalisation, as the "world of late modernity" (p. 296). She contrasts it to "the modern world as we have known it" (p. 296) and stresses how in reality the difficult coexistence of these two worlds is what poses the biggest challenges to language educators: "[i]n the last decades, that world has changed to such an extent that language teachers are no longer sure of what they are supposed to teach nor what real world situations they are supposed to prepare their students for" (p. 296). The English-speaking world, in particular, is at the forefront of this dilemma. Not only is English the language of globalisation, perceived as possessing crucial economic capital (Bourdieu, 1989; Duchêne & Heller, 2012), but English-speaking countries, such as the United Kingdom, have constructed themselves as nation states; historically speaking, England was the first nation-state.

This homogenous model, integrating territory, nationality and language, has been magnified by its export to the new world during the colonial period. The longstanding ideal of the melting pot has also greatly contributed to silencing the heritage languages of immigrants and the pre-existing indigenous languages. Despite this policy of linguistic repression, nowadays North America is in reality linguistically and culturally diverse; a profusion of languages is spoken at home by millions of citizens both in Canada (Statistics Canada, 2016) and the US (US Census Bureau, 2010), including a wealth of heritage languages, the 60 indigenous languages in Canada (Norris, 2007), and the 169 Native American languages in the US (US Census Bureau, 2010). However, in both countries, heritage and indigenous languages are undervalued in mainstream education (Hornberger, 2001; Wiley & Lukes, 1996) and schools are unprepared to take advantage of such linguistic and cultural diversity, perpetuating inequalities for multilingual students (García & Kleifgen, 2010; Nieto, 2010).

Faced with this situation, the English-speaking world seems to be in search of the right conceptual framework and knowhow to cope with linguistic and cultural diversity. This translates into a frantic, and at times seemingly territorial discussion characterised by "the recent profusion of a multiplicity of overlapping terminology" (Lewis, Jones & Baker, 2012, p. 656), which, in fact, does not always result in pedagogic innovation. Oddly enough for a time of facilitated exchange, there is a lack of cross-fertilisation with other contexts that have experienced social mobility and a consequent increase of linguistic and cultural diversity early on in their history, and have therefore experimented with various forms of multilingual political entities and supranational organisations. We are referring mainly, but not exclusively, to Europe as it is the geographical area where institutional efforts to create multilingual supra-national entities have been more evident (e.g., the Council of Europe, the European Union). However, an important reminder is that in many parts of the world the daily coexistence and interaction of different languages and cultures both at the level of societies and of individuals is a stable normality. Such a normality of linguistic diversity and practice, boosted by increased social mobility, is something that calls for a new vision of the scope of language education—including in contexts where individuals see themselves mainly as monolinguals.

In applied linguistics and language education research, the past two decades have seen a shift away from monolingualism to the more open conceptualisation of language plurality. The historical prevalence of teaching languages through a monolingual framework, influenced by the works of Noam Chomsky (1965), saw proficiency in an additional language based on the native speaker model. That is, one's linguistic abilities in the additional language (second, third, etc.) were compared to the abilities of a native speaker. While not clearly defined, the native speaker was typically considered a member of a homogenous linguistic community, or, the ideal speaker of a language. The term native speaker was heavily criticised over the years by introducing the notion of heterogeneity for both speakers and communities and by moving away from what was once viewed as linguistic purity (Cook, 1999, 2015; Creese & Blackledge, 2010; Cummins, 2007; Hymes, 1972; Jenkins, 2006; Lin, 2006; Pennycook, 2010; Widdowson, 1998). This criticism opened up to a paradigm shift in language learning towards bilingualism and more recently multilingualism. However, even bilingual and multilingual teaching practices have long been perceived as the teaching of discrete languages (Wei, 2011), with little reference to languages that learners already had in their repertoire (Piccardo, 2014a/2018). In opposition to this, more holistic views of multilingualism have developed in recent years which "pay attention to the way multilingual speakers use their linguistic resources in ways that are different from the way monolingual speakers use of single languages" (Cenoz, 2013, p. 12). They also stress how these same speakers are creative and flexible in their use of multiple linguistic and communicative forms (Lüdi, 2014). Awareness of the hybridity of real-life communication, of the necessary imbalance and messiness of discourse in increasingly multilingual contexts, as well as of its potential for language education, paired with a dynamic vision of the development of learners' linguistic repertoires constitutes the basis of the philosophy of plurilingualism.

It is important to note that linguistic and cultural diversity, which is at the core of plurilingualism, is central to other *lingualisms* (Marshall & Moore, 2016). Several notions that come from different epistemological traditions feed into the concept of plurilingualism (Piccardo & North, forthcoming). To name a few: Translanguaging, pluriliteracies, code-switching, and intercomprehension. The first, *translanguaging*, involves the use of two languages as a cognitive mediating process to gain deeper understanding of and learning from content and experiences. In translanguaging, there is a focus on the functional use of languages, that is, how these languages are used for effective communication and learning (García, 2009; Lewis, Jones & Baker, 2012a; Lewis, Jones & Baker, 2012b; Sayer, 2013). The second tradition, *pluriliteracies*, includes the interrelation of languages and literacies, with an emphasis on types of literacies in sociocultural contexts, semiotics, and hybrid language use (García, Bartlett & Kleifgen, 2007). The third, *code-switching*, entails the alternation between two languages or language varieties in the context of a single conversation or even within one single sentence (Hua, 2008; Riehl, 2005). Finally, *intercomprehension* often involves interactions with two or more languages of the same family (e.g., Romance languages: Portuguese, French, Spanish, Italian, and Romanian). *Intercomprehension* encourages a user of one language to try to understand and communicate with a user of another language without translations between languages (Doyé, 2005, Araújo e Sá & Pinho, 2015). Taken together, these notions have produced significant changes and substantive alternatives to the monolingual framework, helping the paradigm shift towards plurilingualism.

Fleshing out Plurilingualism: Repertoire and Agency

While plurilingualism has been supported by language policy documents in Europe (see Council of Europe, 2001, 2006 and 2007), and other contexts (see overview in Galante, 2018), its implementation in language education, even among educational settings that support such practice, is still a challenge (Daryai-Hansen et al., 2015). Educational policies in countries across the globe often appear on paper to give value to the practice of plurilingualism; this seems to be the case in Uganda, Portugal, Australia, the UK and Brazil, just to name a few (Abiria, Early & Kendrick, 2013; Pauwels, 2014; Pinho & Andrade, 2009; Galante, in press). However, despite the good intentions and the existence of an elaborate set of objectives informed by the concept of plurilingualism presented under the umbrella term of pluralistic approaches (Candelier et al., 2007), practical application in the language classroom are still uncommon. One of the main reasons for this difficulty in translating policy into practice is a general tendency in language policy to give only theoretical approval to linguistic diversity without providing the necessary support to language teachers, which is the case of plurilingualism in some contexts.

As previously noted, one key notion of plurilingualism is that of repertoire, which relates to individual's whole linguistic and cultural experiences. The concept of linguistic repertoire does not only relate to languages and cultures as part of one's identity, but also to the emotional dimension of language (Busch, 2015), including feelings, such as happiness or sadness. Simply put, a linguistic repertoire relates both cognitive and emotional levels and includes individuals' past and future trajectories in terms of social, historical and biographical dimensions. Besides, a linguistic repertoire is not limited to the present time: Not only do plurilinguals use languages and varieties they already know but they can develop new languages and even have, so to say, the possibility of a new start either personally or professionally. Unfortunately, they may also, on the contrary, inhibit the use of a certain language due to a traumatic life experience, or cause a block in the process of learning a new language in the case of an unpleasant experience. Such hindrances are the result of being the object of (unpleasant) experiences, caused by an inability to affect events resulting in a lack of agency. Thus, in plurilingual education, helping individuals to become aware of their own linguistic and emotional repertoire and to make use of two or more languages at different levels of competence and contexts is crucial. It means supporting individuals' social agency so they can use linguistic and cultural knowledge "at their own right" (Grommes & Hu, 2014, p. 2).

Agency is thus at the core of plurilingualism, as it relates to an individual's experiences, including emotional, linguistic and cultural. These are built on both life and learning experiences, be they formal, informal or non-formal ones (Werquin, 2010). Individuals are seen as 'social agents' (Council of Europe, 2001), who are constantly operating in different culturally, linguistically and socially defined contexts and by doing so shape and modify their own individual plurilingual and pluricultural repertoire. By encompassing past, present and future of the trajectory that shapes individuals' plurilingual repertoires, plurilingualism invests social justice as it aims not only to recognise diversity—expressed in terms of linguistic and cultural differences among social groups—as an asset, but also to open up a range of possibilities to all social groups to proactively expand and modulate their competences in different languages. Thus, plurilingualism is not meant to be considered as "the privilege of a 'gifted' elite" (Beacco & Byram, 2003/2007, p. 37) but as a way of raising awareness of the value and accessibility of linguistic diversity.

Social Agents Engaged in Action-Oriented Real-Life Tasks

One of the main characteristics of the action-oriented approach, as defined in the CEFR (Council of Europe 2001), is that of agency. The CEFR vision of agency aligns with the way the term has been conceptualised in applied linguistics, where it has been associated with "the learners' capacity to make choices and change themselves and/or the environment" (Yashima, 2013, p. 5). In Second Language Acquisition, psychological approaches saw agency from the perspective of the individuals as related to their autonomy and their capacity of making choices (Oxford, 2003). At the same time, the social nature of agency is key to the sociocultural theory. In fact, "Vygotsky created a model of individuals' goal-oriented, mediated activity that generates higher mental functions" (Yashima, 2013, p. 3) and learners are seen as engaged in social practices that enable developmental processes (Lantolf & Thorne, 2006).

The action-oriented approach seeks to reconcile both dimensions, the individual and the social. In fact, it views:

> Users and learners of a language primarily as 'social agents', i.e. members of society who have tasks (not exclusively language-related) to accomplish in a given set of circumstances, in a specific environment and within a particular field of action. While acts of speech occur within language activities, these activities form part of a wider social context, which alone is able to give them their full meaning. We speak of 'tasks' in so far as the actions are performed by one or more individuals strategically using their own specific competences to achieve a given result. The action-based approach therefore also takes into account the cognitive, emotional and volitional resources and the full range of abilities specific to and applied by the individual as a social agent.
>
> (Council of Europe, 2001, p. 9)

In addition, the goal of a language learner is not simply to learn a language but to complete real-life tasks with that language: "we read in order to understand or glean information or simply for the pleasure of reading. We speak and write in order to persuade, inform, help, argue, defend ourselves, and so on." (Piccardo, 2014b, p. 17) Therefore, learners as social agents need to have the goal of the task they intend to accomplish clear in mind, what their strengths and weaknesses in relation to this task are, what resources are needed and available, and on the basis of all this they also need to make choices so they can exert their agency. Besides, they are not alone in this process. As we have seen, the CEFR emphasises the social nature of actions. Certainly not all tasks are equal; some are more social than others, however, even the most 'solitary' tasks require a form of interaction with artifacts produced by others and the outcomes of the task often have an impact beyond the individual involved. Finally, "not only is the social context in which the user/learner acts important, the user/learner's mental context is important as well. It filters and interprets the external context or situation. And the form that this interpretation or perception takes will depend on many different factors: physical, cultural, practical, cognitive, affective, emotional, etc." (Piccardo, 2014b, p. 18).

In such a perspective, plurilingualism intervenes at different levels: Different languages and varieties in learners' repertoires serve as rich resource for the accomplishment of tasks. In addition, the social interaction in a multilingual and multicultural environment contributes to the evolution and structuring of individual repertoires and the decision-making process involved contributes to raising awareness and strengthening agency. The nature of action-oriented tasks, embedded in real life, and social in nature also share many features with drama.

Drama and Social Agency

Drama is a broad concept used in language education and includes strategies and techniques from both process drama and theatre (Galante & Thomson, 2017). Simply put, process drama focuses on group-oriented tasks in which meaning is negotiated through the use of improvised language and impromptu performances (Kao & O'Neill, 1998; Moody, 2002), while theatre makes use of scripted language and is focused on the final product (Moody, 2002). Both approaches to drama can be used in complementary ways in the language classroom to emphasise particular aspects of language learning (Galante & Thomson, 2017). For example, among learners with low proficiency levels in the target language, acting out scripted role-plays can maximise practice of a particular grammatical structure as well as practice aspects of pronunciation such as intonation and comprehensibility as well as fluency. With learners who have higher levels of proficiency in the target language, discussions about particular situations and issues can occur and a scene which involves problem solving can be acted out spontaneously. Yet, when we add a plurilingual dimension to drama and theatre, more possibilities can be opened up, particularly at lower levels of proficiency, as other languages can be part of both the process and the product, as we will exemplify in the next section. More importantly, drama can explore real-life situations, create authentic interactions among people through the use of language(s), and require active participation among its players. Therefore, in this chapter we consider process and theatre as simply drama.

It is important to note that drama emphasises authentic communication embedded in a given context. Interactions among learners can be co-constructed, and learners are key players and active participants (Kao & O'Neill, 1998; Piccardo & Aden, 2014). Among many dramatic strategies, role-plays with elements of problem-solving skills help learners use language strategically and for realistic communication in which they develop speaking, listening and pragmatics in the target language (di Pietro, 1982). This realistic element typically requires learners to be agents who make mindful decisions of the language(s) to use in a given context and in specific situations. This agency can be individual or collective (Carson, 2012), that is, individuals can act alone or in groups. In language learning, this agency is reflective of tasks that can be individually or collectively performed. As van Lier (2010) emphasises, agency includes learners as individuals or as a collective group, with initiative and willingness to act, accountability for their actions and awareness of how actions affect others in a sociocultural context. This aligns well with the action-oriented approach as it centers language learning in communicatively meaningful ways, real-life situations, and with learners as social agents (Piccardo, 2014b). Taken both together, drama and the action-oriented approach to language learning interweave to form what we can call dramatic action-oriented tasks. Thus, we see dramatic action-oriented tasks as context-dependent, with authentic and meaningful communication and, most importantly, with learners as social agents.

In both Canada and the United States, where a wealth of languages and cultures are inherently typical of the society at large as well as language classrooms, it makes sense to use dramatic action-oriented tasks that promote plurilingualism. In fact, they can disrupt the "monolingual disposition" (Gogolin, 1994) existing in language education, with a positive effect on the teacher, especially on teachers who perceive themselves as monolinguals. Plurilingual agency is context-specific (Galante, forthcoming; Marshall & Moore, 2016) and refers to plurilingual and pluricultural competence "on which the social actor may draw" to communicate (Coste et al., 2009, p. 11). When language teachers allow learners' plurilingualism to emerge while performing dramatic action-oriented tasks, they provide a unique opportunity for the plurilingual dimension to be strengthened and valued. A plurilingual actor is a social actor (Coste & Simon, 2009) and will benefit from pedagogical strategies that foster this agency.

Pedagogical Practices: A Dramatic Action-Oriented Task Through a Plurilingual Lens

Following an action-oriented approach, we provide an example of a dramatic action-oriented task that was used with English as a Second Language (ESL) students enrolled in a university program in Ontario, Canada. The task described below was designed for a multilingual group of adults with upper-intermediate proficiency in English (levels B2 of the CEFR) attending a university course on Canadian culture. This was a mandatory course for first year undergraduate students whose L1 was not English and who had recently arrived in Canada. The main focus of the course was an exploration of the academic and social culture of Canada and included discussions of readings from a course pack. All of the students had international status and hailed from different countries, including Iran, South Korea, Brazil, Saudi Arabia, among others, although a vast majority was Chinese. One of the required readings discussed discrimination against foreign accents in Canada (Munro, 2003), one contained Canadian laws related to multiculturalism in Canada (Canada, 1985) and another concerned laws that grant the rights and freedoms of Canadian residents (Canada, 1982). The overall action-oriented task was introduced after classroom discussions of the three readings and presented to students through a scenario:

> Discriminatory acts happen in many societies, and Canada is no exception. These include discrimination on the basis of religion, skin color, culture, and language, among others. Despite the fact that Canada has laws to protect its residents from discriminatory acts, they may still happen in places such as schools, in the workplace, and in the public realm. Should you or anyone you know experience discrimination, it is important that you know how to act.

Six communicative language activities needed to be done for the dramatic action-oriented task to be completed. The sequence of language activities described below took a total of approximately four hours divided into three 3-hour classes. These were the steps:

1. Warm up: Students discussed the following questions in small groups: *Does discrimination against accents in your first language occur in your country of origin? Have you or anyone you know ever experienced accent discrimination in any language? How did you/people react to such comments? If having a local or foreign accent is considered normal (in language research) and something many people are proud of as it relates to their identity, why would discrimination against accents happen?* Students were given the opportunity to access their linguistic repertoire and the option to discuss these questions in any language, provided that all members of the group could be included in the discussion. Code-switching was also allowed.
2. Homework assignment: Students were asked to read Munro (2003) and highlight the discriminatory acts present in the reading *Accent stereotyping and harassment based on accent*. Then, they were asked to read the Canadian

Multicultural Act (Canada, 1985) and the Canadian Charter of Rights and Freedoms (Canada, 1982) and highlight the laws that could protect people from such discriminatory events. It was expected that students would come across unfamiliar words while reading, so they were encouraged to use inter-comprehension and translanguaging as strategies for reading comprehension. They also made use of monolingual and bilingual dictionaries and compared the English terms to words used in other languages they know and reflected on concepts.

3   Discussion: In class, students worked in small groups and discussed the discriminatory events from the reading. Once again, this discussion could be carried out in languages other than English, allowing students to use their linguistic repertoire. They were also invited to discuss personal experiences and feelings with accent discrimination in Canada, their countries of origin and other countries they had been to. This not only served for cross-cultural and linguistic comparisons but included an emotional dimension, which is integral to their repertoire. To wrap up the discussion, students were asked to refer to the Canadian laws and select the one(s) that could be used as a reasonable argument against accent discrimination, in case they ever experienced one in the future, enhancing their sense of agency and encouraging them to enact changes in their socio-context.

4   Preparing the role-play: In class, students worked in small groups and were asked to role-play an accent discriminatory situation based on problem-solving; they were given a choice of either role-playing the situations from the reading (Munro, 2003) or enacting a similar situation that had occurred or could occur to them in the future. In addition, they were asked to refer to the Canadian laws as a possible argument during the role-play. In small groups, students were social actors who took different roles and used prior knowledge of linguistic items to prepare their role-play. During the preparation, they were also given the option of using languages other than English as well as code-switching and translanguaging.

5   Presenting the role-play: Two groups of students chose to present a real situation that had occurred to one of the members of the group while the others chose a hypothetical future situation. None chose to role-play the situations from the reading. In one role-play representing a real-life situation, four Chinese students divided their roles into two university students, one office worker, and a receptionist from the Ontario Human Rights Commission (OHRC). The role-play began with two students speaking Japanese (their L2) in a university photocopy room when an office worker came in and demanded they spoke English. The argument used by the worker was "If you're in Canada, you have to speak English. Show some respect!" The two students switched to English (their L3) and tried to politely argue against the worker and said, "We're just having a conversation to practice our Japanese. What's wrong with using another language?" However, the

worker continued to demand the use of English, mocked their English accent and left the room. The two students switched to Mandarin (their L1) with one of them picking up her cellphone and dialing a number: She called the OHRC. Over the phone, the student switched to English (her L3) and explained that according to the Canadian Charter of Rights and Freedoms and the Canadian Multicultural Act, she felt they had experienced linguistic and accent discrimination and asked for advice. The telephone conversation ended with an invitation for the two students to present their case legally to the OHRC. All the students presented their dramatic action-oriented role-play in front of the class and the audience clapped after each presentation.

6 Reflection: After each presentation, the audience and the 'actors' engaged in a reflective practice; they were asked critical questions such as *How did you feel while performing this role (emotion)? Was the language used appropriate for that specific situation (linguistic choice)? Do you have any suggestions in terms of language, socio-pragmatic, content, etc.(cultural)? What consequences can we expect from this role-play (agency)?* The audience and the instructor provided suggestions for the task to be refined. Suggestions were related to both language (e.g., English grammar, pronunciation, etc.) and the problem-solving decisions about accent discrimination.

Through the completion of the steps in the dramatic action-oriented task, students activated their plurilingual repertoire and exercised their agency to act a real-life scenario, which required the use of languages in their repertoire, including the target language (English). Many students reported feeling upset when others attempt to inhibit the use of their L1—or other languages they know—and demand English only. However, they also reported that knowing about their rights and actions they can take to change this situation gave them a sense of agency and empowerment that helped affirm their plurilingual identity.

Plurilingual practice should be seen as context-specific (Galante, forthcoming) and when preparing a dramatic action-oriented task, key elements such as language proficiency levels, context, age, and topic deserve special consideration. Obviously, the task we describe here may not be compatible with all educational contexts across North America and beyond. For example, young learners who have basic proficiency levels in the target language will need to engage in less complex communicative language activities and role-play. The choice of topic also needs to be done with care, as some students may be more or less sensitive to it. Thus, while the task we describe here was appropriate for this particular context and these students, we advise that language teachers take into account their own context and reflect on their students' needs and realities.

Discussion

Plurilingualism is a conceptual framework in language education that offers several benefits. First, it has the potential to change monolingual practices, which are still present in many language classrooms, and to create new possibilities for learning languages. Learners are no longer seen as linguistically and culturally neutral individuals; instead, by acknowledging and engaging learners' existing plurilingual repertoire in classroom tasks, they can make use of their resources and advance knowledge in both language and culture. Second, plurilingualism goes beyond the exclusive use of learners' prior knowledge to include and advance knowledge of other languages and cultures not only the target one(s), particularly in multilingual classes. In fact, the knowledge learned in class can and should be transferable to social interactions with people, especially in multilingual societies where many come from diverse backgrounds. Third, because agency is at the core of plurilingualism (Council of Europe, 2001), learners are free to use strategies such as code-switching, intercomprehension, and translanguaging to advance linguistic knowledge in the target language and other languages. This freedom is emancipatory and validates learners' repertoire, as well as linguistic and cultural diversity in its entirety. Fourth, plurilingualism connects the social, linguistic, cultural, cognitive, emotional and volitional dimensions in the process of language learning, corroborating with flexibility in communicative interactions. Finally, plurilingualism in language education is congruent with many communities and societies in North America and across the globe that are diverse in nature, thus it is against cultural and linguistic homogenisation and stimulates heterogeneity.

The dramatic action-oriented task discussed in this chapter is one way to connect the concept of plurilingualism to pedagogical and real-life application and to open possibilities for learners to "adequately navigate between multiple identities without those identities becoming contradictory" (Piccardo & Aden, 2014, p. 246); after all, individuals "cannot simply 'be plural' and find a way between cultures and languages without any support or scaffolding" (Piccardo & Aden, 2014, p. 247). As previously stated, plurilingual pedagogical practices should be seen as context-dependent and tasks may take different forms from the one suggested in this chapter. It is not our intention to suggest that this task be reproduced and applied as is in other contexts. Language teachers and learners need to discuss their sociocultural context and negotiate the extent to which their plurilingualism can be harnessed and applied to real-life situations. Regardless of the context, the use of dramatic action-oriented tasks in language classrooms can harness learners' potential to use and have agency over their plurilingualism. Ultimately, these tasks do not only activate the plurilingual learner but also encourage the use of their plurilingual competence in authentic communication with others in relation to the social context.

Conclusion

The paradigm shift that plurilingualism advocates in language classes calls for a wholistic/holistic vision of what language education really means. The maze of terminology previously mentioned risks to overshadow the potential of this shift by focusing on some of the manifestations of plurilingual speakers' way of thinking and behaving. The idea that developing a linguistic repertoire requires agency and awareness provides a new impetus to both language learning and language use. As a naturally occurring phenomenon, plurilingualism is in everyone's grasp. Furthermore, by making space for all languages, the learners' language(s) of origin as well as the target second and foreign language(s), plurilingualism becomes a social justice conceptual framework as it leverages the potential that plurilingual speakers have over monolinguals in strengthening, deepening and diversifying their linguistic/cultural competences in several target languages and/or varieties as well as their general competences of knowledge, skills and know how, ability to learn, and attitudes (CEFR, 2001). However, this shift does not happen automatically only because classes are multilingual and multicultural. It requires both a maieutic attitude from teachers and adequate pedagogic tools. A plurilingual dramatic action-oriented approach provides such a tool and an effective one. It can help practitioners make the move from modernity to late modernity that Kramsch (2014) advocates by focusing on process rather than on discrete and testable skills. It means to aim at raising awareness of the value and potential of the language, to foster cognitive flexibility, to make space for metaphoric imagination and to nurture symbolic competence (Kramsch, 2009; Kramsch & Whiteside, 2008). It is the reflection on the language and its use that becomes crucial. "The goal is not just to expose students to a diversity of accents and registers, but have them critically engage with the social and political differences that they index" (Kramsch, 2014, p. 306). In this sense, the philosophy of plurilingualism supports the move from *languaging* and *translanguaging* to *plurilanguaging*, seen as a conscious, "dynamic, never-ending process to make meaning using different linguistic and semiotic resources" (Piccardo, 2018, p. 215). By doing this, it advocates more synergy among the different concepts related to language learning in increasingly diverse contexts and also focuses on the reflective, creative and critical agency of the individual learner engaged in a highly social practice.

References

Abiria, D. M., Early, M., & Kendrick, M. (2013). Plurilingual pedagogical practices in a policy-constrained context: A northern Uganda case study. *TESOL Quarterly, 47*(3), 567–590.

Araújo e Sá, M. H., & Pinho, A. S. (Eds.). (2015). *Intercompreensão em contexto educativo: resultados da investigação*. Aveiro: UA Editora.

Beacco, J-C. (2005). *Languages and language repertoires: Plurilingualism as a way of life in Europe. From linguistic diversity to plurilingual education: Guide for the development of language education policies in Europe. Reference Study.* Strasbourg: Council of Europe. Retrieved from: www.coe.int/t/dg4/linguistic/Source/Beacco_EN.pdf.

Beacco, J-C., & Byram, M. (2003/2007). From linguistic diversity to plurilingual education: *Guide for the development of language education policies in Europe. Main Version.* Strasbourg: Council of Europe.

Bourdieu, P. (1989). Social space and symbolic power. *Sociological Theory* 7(1). 14–25.
Busch, B. (2015). Expanding the notion of the linguistic repertoire: On the concept of *Spracherleben*—the lived experience. *Applied Linguistics*, *36*(4), 1–20.
Canada (1982). *The Canadian Charter of Rights and Freedoms.* Retrieved from http://publications.gc.ca/collections/Collection/CH37-4-3-2002E.pdf.
Canada (1985). *Canadian Multicultural Act.* Retrieved from http://laws-lois.justice.gc.ca/PDF/C-18.7.pdf.
Canagarajah, S. and Liynage, I. (2012) Lessons from pre-colonial multilingualism. In M. Martin-Jones, A. Blackledge and A. Creese (Eds.), *The Routledge handbook of multiingualism* (pp. 49–65). London/New York: Routledge.
Candelier, M., Camilleri-Grima, A., Castellotti, V., de Pietro, J-F., Lörincz, I., Meissner, F-J., Schröder-Sura, A., Noguerol, A., & Molinié, M. (2007). *Framework of reference for pluralistic approaches to languages and cultures.* Graz, Austria: Council of Europe.
Carson, L. (2012). The role of drama in task-based learning: Agency, identity and autonomy, *Scenario Journal for Drama and Theatre in Foreign and Second Language Education*, *6*(2), 46–59.
Cenoz, J. (2013). Defining multilingualism. *Annual Review of Applied Linguistics*, *33*, 3–18.
Chomsky, N. (1965). *Aspects of the theory of syntax.* Cambridge, MA: Harvard University Press
Conteh, J., & Meier, G. (Eds.). (2014). *The multilingual turn in languages education: Opportunities and challenges.* Bristol, UK: Multilingual Matters.
Cook, V. (2009). Going beyond the native speaker in language teaching. *TESOL Quarterly*, *33*, 185–209.
Cook, V. (2015). Where is the native speaker now? *TESOL Quarterly*, *50*(1), 186–189.
Coste, D., Moore, D., & Zarate, G. (1997). Competence plurilingue et pluriculturelle. Vers un Cadre Européen Commun de référence pour l'enseignement et l'apprentissage des langues vivantes: études préparatoires [Internet]. Strasbourg: Éditions du Conseil de l'Europe. Retrieved from www.coe.int/t/dg4/linguistic/Source/SourcePublications/CompetencePlurilingue09web_FR.pdf.
Coste, D., Moore, D., & Zarate, G. (2009). *Plurilingual and pluricultural competence.* Strasbourg: Council of Europe.
Coste, D., & Simon, D. L. (2009). The plurilingual social actor. Language, citizenship and education. *International Journal of Multilingualism*, *6*(2), 168–185.
Council of Europe. (1996). *Modern languages: Learning, teaching, assessment. A common European framework of reference. Draft 2 of a Framework proposal.* Strasbourg: Council of Europe, Modern Languages, Council for Cultural Co-operation, Education committee. CC-LANG (95) 5 rev. IV.
Council of Europe. (2001). *Common European Framework of Reference for Languages.* Strasbourg, France: Council of Europe Publishing. Retrieved from www.coe.int/t/dg4/linguistic/source/framework_en.pdf.
Council of Europe. (2007). *Guide for the development of language education policies in Europe: From linguistic diversity to plurilingual education.* Strasbourg, France: Council of Europe Publishing. Retrieved from http://www.coe.int/t/dg4/linguistic/Guide_niveau3_EN.asp
Council of Europe. (2006). *Plurilingual education in Europe.* Strasbourg, France: Language Policy Division. Retrieved from http://www.coe.int/t/dg4/linguistic/Source/PlurinlingalEducation_EN.pdf

Creese, A., & Blackledge, A. (2010). Translanguaging in the bilingual classroom: A pedagogy for learning and teaching? *Modern Language Journal, 94*(1), 103–115.

Cummins, J. (2000). *Language, power and pedagogy: Bilingual children in the crossfire*. Clevedon, UK: Multilingual Matters.

Cummins, J. (2001). *Negotiating identities: Education for empowerment in a diverse society*. Los Angeles, CA: California Association for Bilingual Education.

Cummins, J. (2007). Rethinking monolingual instructional strategies in multilingual classrooms. *Canadian Journal of Applied Linguistics (CJAL)/Revue canadienne de linguistique appliquée (RCLA), 10*(2), 221–240.

Daryai-Hansen, P., Gerber, B., Lörincz, I., Haller, M., Ivanova, O., Krumm, H. J., & Reich, H. H. (2015). Pluralistic approaches to languages in the curriculum: The case of French-speaking Switzerland, Spain and Austria. *International Journal of Multilingualism, 12*(1), 109–127.

Di Pietro, R. J. (1982). The open-ended scenario: A new approach to conversation. *TESOL Quarterly, 16*(1), 15–20.

Doyé, P. (2005). *Intercomprehension. Guide for the Development of Language Policies in Europe: From Linguistic Diversity to Plurilingual Education*. Strasbourg, France: Council of Europe. Retrieved from http://www.coe.int/t/dg4/linguistic/source/doye%20en.pdf.

Duchêne, A., & Heller, M. (Eds.). (2012). *Language in Late Capitalism: Pride and Profit*. New York: Routledge.

Galante, A. (forthcoming). Plurilingualism and TESOL in two Canadian post-secondary institutions: Towards context-specific perspectives. In S. Lau & S. Stille (Eds.), *Plurilingual pedagogies: Critical and creative endeavours for equitable language (in) education*. Toronto: Springer.

Galante, A. (2018). Linguistic and cultural diversity in language education through plurilingualism: Linking the theory into practice. In P. P. Trifonas & T. Aravossitas (Eds.), *Springer International Handbooks of Education. Handbook of Research and Practice in Heritage Language Education*. (pp. 313–329) Toronto: Springer.

Galante, A. (in press). Examining foreign language policy and its application in an EFL university program: Teacher perspectives on plurilingualism. In J. Crandall & K. Bailey (Eds.), *Global perspectives on educational language policies*. New York: Routledge.

Galante, A., & Thomson, R. I. (2017). The effectiveness of drama as an instructional approach for the development of second language oral fluency, comprehensibility, and accentedness. *TESOL Quarterly, 51*(1), 115–142.

García, O. (2009). Education, multilingualism and translanguaging in the 21st century. In A., Mohanty, M. Panda, R. Phillipson, & T. Skutnabb-Kangas (Eds.), *Multilingual education for social justice: Globalising the local* (pp. 128–145). New Delhi, IN: Orient Blackswan.

García, O., Bartlett, L, & Kleifgen, J. (2007). From biliteracy to pluriliteracies. In P. Auer & L. Wei (Eds.), *Handbook of applied linguistics, Vol. 5: Multilingualism* (pp. 207–228). Berlin, DE: Mouton de Gruyter.

García, O., & Kleifgen, J. A. (2010). *Educating emergent bilinguals: Policies, programs, and practices for English language learners*. New York: Teacher's College Press.

Glaser, E. (2005). Plurilingualism in Europe: More than a means for communication. *Language and Intercultural Communication, 5*(3, 4), 195–208.

Gogolin, I. (1994). Der monolinguale Habitus der multilingualen Schule [The monolingual habitus of multilingual school]. Münster, Germany: Waxmann.

Grommes, P., & Hu, A. (2014). Introduction. In P. Grommes, & A Hu (Eds.), *Plurilingual education: Policies—practices—language development* (pp. 1–12). Philadelphia, PA: John Benjamins.

Hornberger, N. (2001). Multilingual language policies and the continua of biliteracy: An ecological approach. *Language Policy, 1*(1), 27–51.

Hua, Z. (2008). Duelling languages, duelling values: Codeswitching in bilingual intergenerational conflict talk in diasporic families. *Journal of Pragmatics, 40*(10), 1799–1816.

Hymes, D. (1972). On communicative competence. In J. Pride & J. Holmes (Eds.). *Sociolinguistics* (pp. 269–293). Harmondsworth: Penguin.

Jenkins, J. (2006). Points of view and blind spots: ELF and SLA. *International Journal of Applied Linguistics, 16*(2), 137–162.

Kao, S., & O'Neill, C. (1998). *Words into worlds: Learning a second language through process drama*. Westport, CT: Ablex Publishing Corporation.

Kramsch, C. (2009). *The multilingual subject: What language learners say about their experience and why it matters*. Oxford: Oxford University Press.

Kramsch, C. (2014). Teaching foreign languages in an era of globalization: Introduction. *The Modern Language Journal, 98*(1), 296–311.

Kramsch, C. & Whiteside, A. (2008). Language ecology in multilingual settings: towards a theory of symbolic competence. *Applied Linguistics, 29*(4): 645–671.

Kubota, R. (2016). The multi/plural turn, postcolonial theory, and neoliberal multiculturalism: Complicities and implications for applied linguistics. *Applied Linguistics, 37*(4) 474–494.

Lantolf, J. P., & Thorne, S. L. (2006). *Sociocultural theory and the genesis of second language development*. Oxford, UK: University Press.

Lewis, G., Jones, B., & Baker, C. (2012). Translanguaging: Developing its conceptualisation and contextualization. *Educational Research and Evaluation, 18*(7), 655–670.

Lin, A. (2006). Beyond linguistic purism in language-in-education policy practice: Exploring bilingual pedagogies in a Hong Kong science classroom. *Language and Education, 20*(4), 287–305.

Lüdi, G. (2014). Dynamics and management of linguistic diversity in companies and institutes of higher education: Results from the DYLAN project. In P. Grommes & H. Wu (Eds.), *Plurilingual education: Policies—practices—language development* (pp. 113–138). Philadelphia, PA: John Benjamins.

Marshall, S. & Moore, D. (2016). Plurilingualism amid the panoply of lingualisms: addressing critiques and misconceptions in education. *International Journal of Multilingualism*, 1–16, doi 10.1080/14790718.2016.1253699

May, S. (Ed.). (2014). *The multilingual turn: Implications for SLA, TESOL and bilingual education.* New York: Routledge.

Moody, D. J. (2002). Undergoing a process and achieving a product: A contradiction in educational drama? In Brauer, G. (Ed.), *Body and language: Intercultural learning through drama*. Westport, CT: Ablex Publishing.

Moore, D., & Gajo, L. (2009). French voices on plurilingualism and pluriculturalism: theory, significance and perspectives. *International Journal of Multiculturalism, 6*(2), 137–153.

Munro, M. (2003). A primer on accent discrimination in the Canadian context. *TESL Canada Journal, 20*(2), 38–51.

Nieto, S. (2010). *The light in their eyes: Creating multicultural learning communities* (10th anniversary edition). New York: Teachers College Press.

Norris, M. J. (2007). Aboriginal languages in Canada: Emerging trends and perspectives on second language acquisition. *Canadian Social Trends*, 83 (Statistics Canada Catalogue no. 11–008).

Oxford, R. L. (2003). Toward a more systematic model of L2 learner autonomy. In D. Palfreyman & R. C. Smith (Eds.), *Learner autonomy across cultures: Language education perspectives* (pp. 75–91). New York: Palgrave Macmillan.

Pauwels, A. (2014). The teaching of languages at university in the context of super-diversity. *International Journal of Multilingualism*, *11*(3), 307–319.

Pennycook, A. (2010). *Language as a local practice*. London, UK: Routledge.

Piccardo, E. (2013). Plurilingualism and curriculum design: Towards a synergic vision. *TESOL Quarterly*, *47*(3), 600–614.

Piccardo, E. (2014a). *From Communicative to Action-oriented: A Research Pathways*. Government of Ontario and Government of Canada/Canadian Heritage. Retrieved from: www.curriculum.org/fsl/wp-content/uploads/2015/12/TAGGED_DOCUMENT_CSC605_Research_Guide_English_01.pdf

Piccardo, E. (2014b). The impact of the CEFR on Canada's linguistic plurality: a space for heritage languages? In P. Trifonas & T. Aravossitas (Eds.), *Rethinking Heritage Language Education*. (pp. 183–212). Cambridge, UK: University Press.

Piccardo, E. (2018). Plurilingualism: Vision, conceptualization, and practice. In P. P. Trifonas & T. Aravossitas (Eds.), *International handbook on research and practice in heritage language education* (pp. 207–226). Toronto: Springer.

Piccardo, E., & Aden, J. (2014). Plurilingualism and empathy: Beyond instrumental language learning. In G. Meier & J. Conteh (Eds.), *The multilingual turn in language education. Opportunities and challenges* (pp. 240–263). Bristol, UK: Multilingual Matters.

Piccardo, E., & North, B. (forthcoming). The dynamic nature of plurilingualism. Creating and validating CEFR descriptors for mediation, plurilingualism and pluricultural competence. In S. Lau & S. Stille (Eds.), *Plurilingual pedagogies: Critical and creative endeavours for equitable language (in) education*. Toronto: Springer.

Pinho, A. S., & Andrade, A. I. (2009). Plurilingual awareness and intercomprehension in the professional knowledge and identity development of language student teachers. *International Journal of Multilingualism*, *6*(3), 313–329.

Riehl, C. M. (2005). Code-switching in bilinguals: Impacts of mental processes and language awareness. In J. Cohen, K.T. McAlister, K. Rolstad, & J. MacSwan (Eds.), *ISB4: Proceedings of the 4th International Symposium on Bilingualism*. Somerville, MA: Cascadilla Press.

Sayer, P. (2013). Translanguaging, TexMex, and bilingual pedagogy: Emergent bilinguals learning through the vernacular. *TESOL Quarterly*, *47*(1), 63–88.Skutnabb-Kangas, T. (2000). *Linguistic genocide in education—or worldwide diversity and human rights?* Mahwah, NJ: L. Erlbaum Associates.

Skutnabb-Kangas, T. (2002) *Why should linguistic diversity be maintained and supported in Europe? Some arguments*. Strasbourg: Council of Europe.

Statistics Canada. (2016). Language Highlight Tables, 2016 Census. Retrieved from: www12.statcan.gc.ca/census-recensement/2016/rt-td/lang-eng.cfm.

US Census Bureau. (2010). New Census Bureau report analyzes nation's linguistic diversity. Retrieved from www.census.gov/newsroom/releases/archives/american_community_survey_acs/cb10-cn58.html van Lier, L. (2010). Agency, self and identity in language learning. In B. O'Rourke & L. Carson (Eds.), *Language learner autonomy: Policy, curriculum, classroom* (pp. ix–xviii). Oxford, UK: Peter Lang.

Wei, L. (2011). Multilinguality, multimodality, and multicompetence: Code- and mode-switching by minority ethnic children in complementary schools. *Modern Language Journal, 95*, 370–384.

Werquin, P. (2009). *Reconnaître l'apprentissage non formel et informel. Résultats, politiques et pratiques.* Paris, OCDE. www.cicic.ca/docs/oecd/rnfil.fr.pdf

Widdowson, H. G. (1998). Context, community, and authentic language. *TESOL Quarterly, 32*(4), 705–716.

Wiley, T. G., & Lukes, M. (1996). English-only and standard English ideologies in the US. *TESOL Quarterly, 30*(3), 511–535.

Yashima, T. (2013). Agency in second language acquisition. In C. A. Chapelle (Ed.), *The encyclopedia of applied linguistics* (pp. 1–7). Oxford, UK: Blackwell Publishing.

10
THE PLURILINGUAL LIFE

A Tale of High School Students in Two Cities

Brian Davy and Mei French

Introduction

This chapter considers two culturally and linguistically diverse high schools, one in New Zealand and one in Australia. Although diversity is composed differently in these schools, there are similar ways in which plurilingual practices shape the identities and learning approaches of plurilingual students, including those learning English as an Additional Language (EAL). Examples from the New Zealand site demonstrate ways in which students enact or hide their plurilingual resources. It is clear that teachers' responses to linguistic diversity significantly influence students' plurilingual practice, and the Australian study shows how teachers may reject plurilingualism, passively accept student language use, or actively engage their resources in teaching. Shifting the focus from monolingual English towards students' existing plurilingual practices is a starting point for teachers to support learning for plurilingual students. With attention to the skills and knowledge students bring, the complex relationship between language and learning, and ways in which policy and dominant practice can be challenged or adapted, teachers can develop pedagogies which engage plurilingual identities and skills in classroom learning.

The New Zealand Site

Manawa High School[1] is a large culturally diverse, co-educational, state high school situated in the west of Auckland. Around 38 per cent of the students are learning EAL, and 21.3 per cent of students are Māori for whom Māori is a heritage language. Manawa High School is a microcosm of New Zealand's largest city. In Auckland 23.1 per cent of the city's population identified as "Asian" in the 2013 Census while 14.6 per cent identified with the category "Pacific Peoples"

(Statistics New Zealand, 2013). The city's linguistic and cultural diversity has contributed to New Zealand's status as a superdiverse nation (Royal Society of New Zealand, 2013). This diversity is not, however, reflected in the teacher population of Manawa High School, where 73.5 per cent of teachers speak English as a first language. This is the socially and culturally diverse, but linguistically homogeneous milieu EAL students enter at Manawa High School.

Data from this site is drawn from a triangulation of data sources including interviews with 15 EAL students, reflexive journal entries of these students and classroom observations of EAL students' interactions with teachers and peers. The data was collected over the final two years of these EAL students' secondary schooling, a period of ongoing high stakes assessment. These methods of data collection enable a thick description (Geertz, 1973) of students' perceptions of the relationship between language and scholarly identity in their senior secondary schooling.

The Australian Site

Charity College is a girls' high school located in an area of increasing immigration in Adelaide, South Australia. With marginally below half the students speaking a home language other than English, the school boasts a higher level of diversity than the national rate of 20 to 25 per cent (Turner & Cross, 2015). Home languages include Dari, Vietnamese, Dinka and 40 other languages. Many students are proficient in three or more languages, and approximately one third formally study EAL. However, as one teacher, Dennis, observes, "Students have got all the variety, and not the teachers." 74 per cent of staff have English as a first language, and the first languages of plurilingual teachers differ from the students', including Italian, Vietnamese, Russian and Cantonese. Data from the Australian site is drawn from a multi-source ethnographic case study including student portfolios, student focus group discussions, a questionnaire completed by 35 staff and interviews with ten staff. While the broader study examines how the school's linguistic culture is constructed through student plurilingual practice and the responses of staff, the focus of this chapter is on teacher responses to plurilingualism.

The Monolingual Mindset in Education

It is important to consider these sites of diversity within their historical and social contexts. Education practices in New Zealand and Australia share a defining feature in the "monolingual habitus" identified by Gogolin in Europe (2002). This "socially dominant monolingual manner of thinking" (Benson, 2014, p. 12) has two notable features. First, languages are seen as disconnected entities, learned and used in isolation from each other (Canagarajah, 2011). In this view, an individual's plurilingual repertoire is reduced to the simple sum of its linguistic parts, for example vocabulary in two languages. Therefore, complex and interconnected plurilingual skills including metalinguistic and social abilities, remain unrecognised. Secondly, the New Zealand and Australian systems are strongly biased towards monolingual English as the medium and outcome of education (Coleman, 2012).

As Heugh (2014, p. 355) argues, "insufficient" attention is paid to plurilingual practice in society and education in these settings. Clyne (2008) lamented that the monolingual mindset stifles effective use of plurilingual resources. As such, it yields negative impacts for EAL students (Coleman, 2012). A community of practice (Lave & Wenger, 1991; Wenger 1998) centred on the dominant role of English is often the default within these institutions. When EAL students chart a linguistic course according to these norms, they seek the valued social capital of monolingual English (Bourdieu, 1991), and shape their scholarly habitus around this (Watkins & Noble, 2013). This influence suppresses the role of L1 in accessing funds of knowledge (Moll, Amanti, Neff & Gonzalez, 1992) and maintaining cultural and personal identities, and when this happens, students are often considered deficient in language and learning ability (Agnihotri, 1995; Benson, 2013, p. 284).

Recognition of the dominant role of language in education (May, 2011) by teachers is a starting point towards challenging the monolingual habitus, elevating diverse linguistic capital and manifesting a scholarly habitus that makes effective use of students' plurilingual resources. It is therefore beholden upon teachers to understand the competing influences over EAL students' language use, which can influence students to reject, hide or display their plurilingualism in different situations.

Influences on Students' Plurilingualism

Students' plurilingual practices often diverge from the language competencies expected in school (Benson, 2013, p. 289), as students draw on extensive plurilingual resources including linguistic knowledge of each language in their repertoire, the ability to make cross-linguistic comparisons, intercultural communication skills, content knowledge learned through a range of languages, and a range of cultural, linguistic and scholarly identities (French, 2016). They apply these resources to build understanding of subject content, improve academic language across their linguistic repertoire, and for classroom interaction. This complex practice illustrates the linguistic, social, academic and metalinguistic abilities that research has shown are enhanced in plurilingual youth compared to monolinguals (Cummins, 2000; de Jong, 2011). The New Zealand and Australian schools reveal various factors which influence students' language use, including students' desire to acquire English and retain their L1, their own unique schooling history and teachers' responses. These factors often clash and produce mixed messages about the roles of English and the students' own L1 in school.

Influences which Reinforce the English Language Norm

A prevailing influence on the institutional justification of monolingual approaches is the complex subject-specific vocabulary students must learn. Shanahan and Shanahan have noted the increasing specialisation of disciplinary literacy (2008, p. 44) required as students' progress through school. In a New Zealand study, Coxhead, Stevens and Tinkle examined the vocabulary requirements of secondary school Science textbooks and found that a vocabulary exceeding 15,000 English words was required to attain 97.18 per cent text coverage (2010, p. 47). When compared with an 8,000–9,000 word vocabulary required for 98 per cent comprehension of more general written texts (Nation, 2006, p. 79) such as novels, it becomes clear that the vocabulary requirements of disciplinary literacy exceed those of general literacy.

EAL students in the New Zealand school are aware of their acute needs with regard to proficiency in disciplinary literacy. Many participants feel they had greater Cognitive Academic Language Proficiencies (CALP per Cummins, 1984) in English than in their L1. In some cases this is because they had been in New Zealand schools longer than their home country's education system; in other cases because English was the medium of education in their home country.

Kathy, a Filipino EAL student, indicates she feels she has stronger academic English, "'Cause I don't really know much about my subjects in Tagalog so if I choose the one in my language it would be harder for me 'cause I don't know much words 'cause I'm used to English now." Compounding the Kathy's six years in a New Zealand secondary school, she also had much of her primary schooling in an English medium private school in the Philippines. She therefore has had little opportunity to engage in disciplinary literacies in her L1. Kathy has been educated in an environment, in both New Zealand and the Philippines, that validates the monolingual habitus. As a consequence, she has had relatively limited access to plurilingual practices in these settings and has had limited opportunity to develop L1 CALP.

Leon is another EAL student who feels he has greater CALP in English than in his L1. An international student from Hong Kong who has studied in New Zealand for three years, he states of academic vocabulary, "I don't know the words in Chinese so I'm stuck in English ... because I don't know those words in Chinese 'cause I never learned them in China." As subject-specific disciplinary literacies have become more demanding, Leon has been afforded little opportunity to utilise his plurilingual resources. The result is a consolidation of academic English and an atrophy of academic Chinese. These difficulties are often compounded by the relatively abstract nature of course content at senior levels. As the disciplinary literacy requirements become more demanding, the pedagogy becomes more decontextualised.

Moje asserts that there is a critical role for language and culture in disciplinary literacies (2007, pp. 12–13). Teachers need to become aware of the previous exposure to content EAL students have had in their L1 and the existing plurilingual resources they bring to class so that they can facilitate transfer between languages (Cummins, 2009) and assert in their pedagogy a plurilingual approach to disciplinary literacy. For example, Then and Ting (2011) found that code-switching by teachers facilitates effective understanding of science vocabulary, while Harper, Cook and James (2010) have noted that reciprocal teaching in peer language groups serves to support vocabulary understanding. In both of these students, the use of plurilingual approaches serves to enhance understandings of disciplinary literacy.

The pressure of English medium assessment practices further reinforces English language norms. In both research sites, students work towards a senior secondary certificate in their final years of high school, the National Certificate of Educational Achievement (NCEA) in New Zealand, and the South Australian Certificate of Education (SACE) in South Australia. The New Zealand Curriculum states that "success in English is fundamental to success across the curriculum" (Ministry of Education, 2007, p. 18), while in South Australia, English literacy is a capability addressed across the curriculum (SACE, 2016). In both certificates, assessment is conducted in English and often includes assessment of communication and subject-specific language.

Many NCEA and SACE subjects have complex disciplinary vocabulary requiring a high degree of academic English. Some teachers' school reports in the New Zealand research identified students as needing to build academic vocabulary and improve language structure in formal assessments. Comments such as, "Some misunderstandings of English conventions," "Needs to build his academic vocabulary" and "Her difficulties with the English language is holding back her progress in this subject" were seen in participating EAL students' reports. Comments like these reinforce a discourse among some teachers that English language learning equates to a cognitive deficit (Wigglesworth, Simpson & Laokes, 2011).

EAL students often internalise the discourse of a monolingual habitus and echo this discourse in their interviews and journals, noting that their English ability is the major obstacle to academic success. Kanda states, "I only have a problem in English. It's just a really big step between [NCEA] level 1 and level 2. English [speaking] people tend to get along well in it but I can't do it." EAL students often feel compelled to assimilate a scholarly habitus favouring English only for success in assessment. The monolingual capital of English is validated and plurilingual capital subsumed in this environment.

Influences that Induce Private Forms of Plurilingualism

The English dominant field of official schooling can be contrasted with EAL students' home and social environments. As Scarino (2008) notes, students are members of multiple lived communities, and for EAL students these are plurilingual communities. For example, Kitchen (2010) observes that New Zealand Korean students experience a breakdown of cultural and language connections. The bifurcated nature of language use creates complexity for these students. Language becomes compartmentalised as monolingual English interactions come to dominate the pedagogy of their academic life, while the language of home becomes increasingly distanced from senior secondary disciplinary literacies and English medium assessment. EAL students negotiate a complex social milieu in school when disciplinary literacies are taught in English and yet they still have private access to peers and electronic devices in which they can use their L1. Active pedagogy manifests as monolingual and yet the lived reality of these students is that they are constantly engaged in plurilingualism inside the school gate.

Manawa High School students identified a strong desire for L1 retention. Jung Min states, "since I'm Korean I kind of want to be good at it . . . I think like not forgetting who I am yeah I think that's the most important thing." Similarly, Harry states of his Cambodian, "I try and practice it often." Although Jung Min and Harry have spent the majority of their school years in New Zealand (eight and eleven years respectively), each expresses a strong desire to retain their plurilingualism.

Classroom practices, even in superdiverse cities like Auckland, often revert to dominant societal norms of communication and participation. May (2007) has noted that a linguistic hierarchy develops in social spaces, modelled along societal norms, that attaches an instrumental value to the majority language in institutions and public spaces. Conversely, sentimental value is attached to minority languages which become relegated to homes and other private spaces. In English-majority countries such as New Zealand and Australia, the instrumental value attached to English often leads to a silencing of students' L1 in forums like the classroom.

The danger here is that EAL students develop a habitus (Bourdieu & Passeron, 1990) in school based around the social attribution of capital to monolingualism. For example, Udom, a Thai international student living in New Zealand for three years states, "I never speak Thai [in class] . . . you know it's not appropriate to speak your own language." Here, Udom's learned dispositions are influenced by social norms and elevate the instrumental value of English.

Barkhuizen has questioned the monolingual norms of New Zealand schools, noting the multilingual reality of the classroom and asserting, "we should accept that in multilingual contexts people shift back and forth between languages and develop plurilingual competence" (2010, p. 13).

Influences that Encourage Active Engagement with Plurilingualism

Participating EAL students in the New Zealand study express the usefulness of plurilingual resources particularly related to assessment. Miyu, a Japanese international student, notes, "I usually make a flash-cards. I write the new vocab in English and the other side I write in Japanese . . . to remember the words; how to spell it and the meaning in Japanese." Seong, a Korean international student, expresses a similar technique for revising concepts. She states in a journal entry, "I made the word book and one side I wrote the English word and another side I wrote Korean word so it's helped me to remember those words."

Both Miyu and Seong apply their existing plurilingual repertoires to enhance their understanding of subject-specific vocabulary in both English and L1. Teachers could harness the value of these individual plurilingual resources to enrich the learning of academic content and vocabulary for other members of the students' language communities, turning individual, private, plurilingual resources into a source for collaboration.

The New Zealand EAL students who had previously learned disciplinary vocabulary in their L1, or had ongoing discussions in their L1 about academic concepts, feel more comfortable making use of their academic L1. For example, Kanda, a migrant student from Thailand who has been in New Zealand for four years, asserts, "I usually talk to my friends [in Thailand] about what I study so I try to translate that so I can talk to my friends and they can help me". Kanda makes use of collaborative plurilingual resources, giving her the access to disciplinary literacy in her L1. Kanda had been in New Zealand longer than many of the participants who do not feel comfortable with L1 academic language, retaining access to L1 resources that help her develop her academic language. This also contrasts with participants who have been in New Zealand for longer periods of time, who have perhaps lost contact with L1 peers.

Daniel, a Chinese International student in New Zealand for one year, also expresses greater comfort with academic language in his L1 than English. He, however, identifies very different reasons for this. Daniel reasons, "It's easier to understand. Like in Physics we have some explanation questions and in English I don't have some of the words so in Chinese it would be way better." Here, Daniel expresses that he has existing academic language in Chinese for Physics concepts but has not yet developed these in English. He has access to individual plurilingual resources when he thinks about concepts in his L1. He also writes Chinese translations of key terms in the margins of his English medium Physics workbook. Daniel feels making use of plurilingual disciplinary literacies, on an individual basis, can enhance his understanding of the discipline of Physics.

Clearly, when EAL students have access to plurilingual resources they feel they can develop their L1 academic language and enhance their disciplinary literacy. The disciplinary vocabulary, identified by teachers as an area of weakness, is exactly the resource that students build by drawing on their plurilingual repertoires. Crucially, it is not length of time or status as a migrant or international student that seem to be the significant factors in the students' level of comfort with academic L1. Rather, access to individual or collaborative plurilingual resources is of key significance.

Additional examples from the Australian school show how plurilingual practices contribute to collaborative learning. Selena, a Year 11 Charity College student, explains classroom talk in her home language Hazaragi, "We say a lot of, like, oh, sit down." This is a natural part of communication during busy lessons, because "like sometimes, it's harder for us to think quickly in English."

Selena also describes collaborative learning through translating and explaining ideas. "Speaking in Hazaragi with each other, it's easier, 'cause there are some words that we don't understand in English. Or we don't know how to say it in English but we know it in our language and if we talk in our language we would know what we're talking about." Selena's plurilingual practice is not limited to Hazaragi and English, as she draws on her understanding of Urdu, a lingua franca which she considers mutually comprehensible with Hindi, to support another student, "Sometimes I helped the new international student, came from India. I spoke to her in Urdu." Here, a Hazaragi-speaking student communicates in Urdu with a Gujarati-speaking student who knows Hindi, and has only just begun learning English.

These examples illustrate the complex and purposeful plurilingual practice of high school students. Although there may be no official space for plurilingual resources in these schools, students engage their repertoires privately and collaboratively to interact, learn and maintain their languages (French & de Courcy 2016, p. 167). Complex combinations of factors affect the extent to which students might reject, hide or display their plurilingual practice in the school setting. There are internal influences such as their self-concept, motivation to use different languages, prior learning and academic priorities. External factors include norms of interaction, languages available to interlocutors and curriculum and assessment policies. These factors are themselves shaped by the social and institutional culture in which English monolingual practice is dominant, and this culture is communicated to students primarily through the responses of teachers.

Teachers' Responses to Plurilingualism

Teacher responses in the Australian school suggest a continuum from rejection, through passive acceptance, to active engagement of plurilingual resources (French, 2016). Teacher actions must be seen within the context of the monolingual habitus (Windle & Miller, 2013, p. 199) which shapes teaching practice, but may be tempered by individual plurilingual experience and the classroom context, so that one teacher might respond differently at different times. With awareness of plurilingualism, teachers can incorporate strategies to support student linguistic capital in the classroom. Successful plurilingual pedagogy needs to account for affective factors, linguistic abilities, practical considerations and learning outcomes valued by both students and teachers.

Reinforcing the English Language Norm

By shaping institutional practice and personal beliefs about language, the monolingual habitus can invalidate plurilingual practices. Different manifestations of this rejection are described by Australian teachers Mary, Clare and Steve. Mary, a speaker of English and Ukrainian and experienced teacher, expresses frustration that teachers equate plurilingualism with learning deficits. "They'll come and make very generalised statements about why students can't be in their classes. But it always comes back to that argument, of, well they just haven't got the language. Except they have got the language, but it's in their own language." Teachers' attitudes and institutional approaches can position any language other than English as "no language," erasing plurilingual identities and learning skills (Blommaert, Collins & Slembrouk, 2005, pp. 197–198).

A veteran teacher, Clare is an English speaker who once studied French. She communicates to her students that speaking any language but English is not socially acceptable. "I just always say to them, 'just remember, make it, you know, not so loud. Or just . . . try the English when somebody else is around you. Then the moment somebody's gone, go for it.'" Clare also deems that English proficiency negates any purpose for home language. She reports admonishing a student, "you shouldn't be speaking another language, because your English is very good!" Clare's positioning of students' plurilingual resources as invalid reflects a view of languages outside her repertoire as "excluding, threatening or conspiratorial" (Blommaert, Collins & Slembrouk, 2005, p. 207). These interactions exemplify "policing" of students' language, even in social situations (Lo Bianco, 2010, p. 166), a compelling illustration of the monolingual habitus.

Steve, a long-serving school leader who described himself as "always trying, always failing" to learn languages, identifies that student plurilingualism can threaten a teacher's desire to understand and control student interactions. "A huge thing about this is fear . . . Staff's fear. Teachers' fear." He highlights the influence of English-based assessment practices, "The other side of it is, it's not encouraged to speak in the home language. Because in the long run, there doesn't appear to be a benefit to the stated institutional outcomes." Steve illustrates how high stakes monolingual English based assessments 'wash back' into teaching practice (Benson, 2013), threatening the use of plurilingualism as a resource.

It is apparent that rejection of plurilingual practices manifests in different ways such as denying the value of languages, constructing plurilingual practice as socially inappropriate, or excluding plurilingual practice from valued educational tasks. Rejection of plurilingualism establishes a negative feedback loop of low teacher expectations which marginalises students and creates a self image of linguistic deficiency (de Jong 2011, p. 119), and this leads to a reversion to monolingual English language norms by teachers and students. Teachers' responses are influenced not only by educational institutions such as curriculum, but also by the teacher's personal experience with and attitudes towards language. Examples of more accepting attitudes support Ellis's (2013) finding that teachers with plurilingual experience are more tolerant towards students' linguistic diversity. However, successful plurilingual strategies require more than a sympathetic teacher.

Passive Acceptance of Plurilingualism

Although rejection of plurilingualism is widespread, the majority position in Charity College is passive acceptance of plurilingual practices. Teachers in this position notice and endorse plurilingual practices, opening up a challenge to the monolingual habitus. However, the counterpart to acceptance is inaction in the classroom. The societal monolingual habitus is apparent here, as teacher training, curriculum and pedagogy do not equip teachers to support plurilingual learning. Examples from John and the staff questionnaire illustrate that teachers recognise the benefits to individual and collaborative meaning-making. Their willingness to "allow" students to engage their plurilingual repertoires is moderated by inability to devise and implement plurilingually oriented pedagogies.

John, a Russian and English speaker with extensive teaching experience, recognises the value of home languages in acquiring knowledge but does not see the teacher's role in enabling plurilingual learning:

> If hypothetically a student says, 'Mr Lennon, don't worry, I need to speak Japanese when learning physics but I will present to you perfectly well in English later on,' no objection to it. If it helps you to learn Physics and then finally you will be able to present this, your knowledge in English, excellent. And if for this you have to use a lot of Japanese, good on you, you use. But I am not able to help with this aspect. Do it yourself.

The questionnaire results also show that many staff recognise plurilingualism as a potential resource, but relegate home languages to private and low-stakes activities not linked to assessment. The graph illustrates responses to the prompt "Students should use their home languages for . . ." (Figure 10.1; n=35).

This passive position demonstrates how pervasive the monolingual habitus is in education, where even teachers who value plurilingualism are not equipped by their training, experience or imagination to support multiple languages in the classroom (Coleman, 2012). As de Jong, Harper and Coady (2013) emphasise, effective teaching for plurilingual and EAL learners requires specialised knowledge and skills.

Active Engagement: Reimagining Communities of Practice

Some teachers actively encourage plurilingual practices at Charity College. In these cases, the teachers are attentive to students' existing plurilingual practice

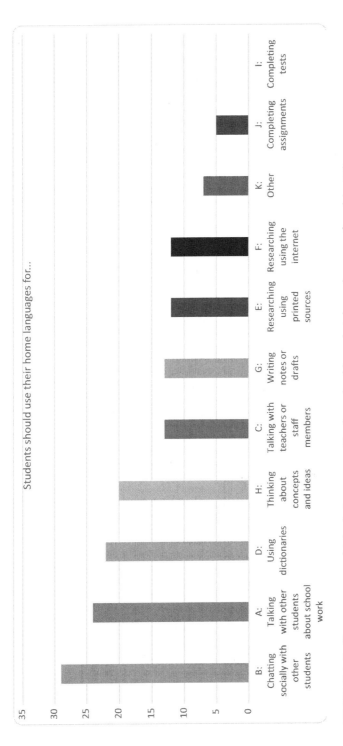

FIGURE 10.1 Staff responses to multiple choice prompt, 'Students should use their home languages for…' (n=35)

and attempt to use these opportunities to enhance learning. The monolingual habitus still shapes curriculum and institutional approaches, so that teachers must adapt pedagogy to function within existing practice and policy. Dennis, Judy and Ellie demonstrate how staff recognise the pedagogic value of plurilingual resources and seek to support these in learning and school life. It can be seen in these examples how effective plurilingual school practice must recognise students' plurilingual repertoires, understand the complex links between language and learning, and adjust pedagogy to the local context (de Jong, Harper & Coady, 2013).

In employing plurilingual software in his IT class, beginning teacher Dennis found it only benefited some students:

> I was working with this programming tool called *Scratch*, and I discovered that it suddenly worked in multiple languages, which was really cool for the Vietnamese kid in [a previous] high school. It was like, "Oh wicked we can do this in Vietnamese." And it worked alright for some of the Vietnamese speaking kids at Charity, but you give it to the Persian speaking ones and they're like, "Oh, we can't read Persian."

He laments this lost opportunity, "I thought I had this free lunch then and the idea that you can speak a language and not read or write it wasn't something I was expecting." Dennis' experience highlights the importance of understanding the skills and knowledge that constitute students' funds of knowledge, in order to coordinate plurilingual strategies with their existing repertoires.

Judy, a speaker of English, Mandarin and Cantonese, in her third year of teaching, observed two students working in Hazaragi to generate ideas for a design project. She reports, "When asked to write their responses in English, they could only express one to two points. When asked to write their responses in their own language, they came up with an additional four points." Sensitive to her faculty head's attention to assessment and curriculum requirements, Judy sought and received approval to use plurilingual brainstorming as a teaching strategy. However, most of the students rejected the option. Judy explains, "The girls didn't want to feel 'different' to everyone else."

Judy understands that the plurilingual repertoires of her students include creativity and collaboration through their home language, and she responds with an activity to engage previously hidden skills. However, the students' negative responses indicate that more work is needed to support plurilingual identity and normalise plurilingual practice by its consistent use in the classroom, so that students feel less self-conscious about making these resources public.

Plurilingual repertoires are also utilised in school business by Ellie, a careers counsellor. She had carefully selected students to assist with interpreting in family meetings:

I've had a few situations in the past where we've had a senior student who we've had permission from the family for them to be involved with interpreting and that's happened as well. But you know, it's difficult because a lot of the stuff that is discussed is confidential, so it's not an easy thing. You can't just go and pick any student to do that.

Ellie recognises students' plurilingual expertise and identifies the opportunity to apply these resources meaningfully, promoting success through careful attention to the practical and ethical requirements. It can be seen in each of these examples that, as de Jong, Harper and Coady (2013) discuss, plurilingual pedagogies must address student repertoires, teaching requirements and contextual factors.

Teacher responses to student plurilingual practice occur within the context of the monolingual habitus (Windle & Miller, 2013), and, as Ellis (2013) has shown, are shaped by prior linguistic experience. It is clear from these two sites that teachers draw additionally from a complex network of factors including teacher education, experience, institutional practices and knowledge of their plurilingual students, which yields a variety of responses. Even for teachers who value plurilingualism, the monolingual habitus of education systems and institutions impedes the conception and implementation of plurilingual pedagogies.

Conclusion

The monolingual habitus in both New Zealand and Australia shapes the educational experience of plurilingual students and their teachers. Student experiences demonstrate how plurilingual repertoires interact with personal identity, scholarly identity and approaches to learning. Application of plurilingual resources depends on factors including academic language development, contexts of language use and assessment requirements. Teachers' responses, varying from rejection, to acceptance and sometimes active engagement of plurilingual practices, are choices shaped by their own plurilingual experience, teacher training, curriculum pressures and situational factors.

Fostering students' plurilingual repertoires contributes to personal and social development, and builds a strong foundation for academic understanding and English language development. Utilising EAL students' plurilingual resources and incorporating existing cultural, linguistic and academic "funds of knowledge" (Moll, Amanti, Neff & Gonzalez, 1992) should become a pedagogical norm in our increasingly diverse classrooms. There is increasing research attention to pedagogies that support plurilingualism within linguistically heterogeneous classrooms, but this is still a developing field which calls for a responsive and creative approach. In high school settings where students may have more mature language development and independent approaches to learning, teachers can take their cues from plurilingual practices of their students, the richness of which is demonstrated by the examples in this chapter. Where curriculum, assessment and pedagogy are rooted in monolingual practice, teachers may respond cautiously within institutional expectations, or they can challenge dominant practice by actively engaging and extending the plurilingual repertoires of their students (French, 2016). In the absence of targeted pre-service or in-service training, how are teachers to develop their plurilingual approach?

The starting point is learning about our students' plurilingual resources and identities. Conceiving of a student's plurilingual repertoire not as separate languages to be switched on and off, but as an integrated, dynamic system that bears on identity and learning, is a foundation for positive plurilingual approaches (French & de Courcy, 2016). Teachers need also to understand the linguistic and social background of students, particularly those from smaller language communities (Shameem, 1997), as well as how students apply their linguistic resources (Si'ilata & Barkhuizen, 2004) within the complex nexus between language, culture and learning. Recognition of plurilingual identities will help gear pedagogy to the specific resources these students bring to New Zealand and Australian classrooms.

Teachers can build on a plurilingual mindset to demonstrate that plurilingualism is normal and useful in the classroom (Ellis, 2013, p. 457), beginning with incorporation of diverse languages in classroom routine and extend to targeted plurilingual pedagogies. As Franken, May and McComish (2007) note, teachers need to be aware of issues around supporting EAL learners' L1. This includes considering the degree of access students have to plurilingual resources and their opportunities to make effective use of these resources. Simple strategies like those seen in the Australian school may engage plurilingual resources to support the transfer and consolidation of content learning (Cummins, 2009). Students in these schools have already demonstrated how they use plurilingual resources to understand new concepts and learn collaboratively. Teachers are well positioned to improve access to these resources, and to make plurilingual strategies more explicit and less transient by acknowledging, suggesting, recording or assessing them (de Jong & Freeman Field, 2010).

Specific resources are available for teachers, such as the *Language Enhancing the Achievement of Pasifika* (LEAP) online tools created in New Zealand by Franken, May and McComish (2007) to promote Pasifika languages as a valuable educational resource. Additionally, strategies from bilingual classrooms can be adapted to draw links between students' existing linguistic and content knowledge and the English medium curriculum (de Jong & Freeman Field, 2010, p. 115). Teachers can also support their students to access community and global resources through a range of languages in research tasks (French, 2016, p. 309). There are many options for teachers, schools and education systems to promote a notion of multiliteracies and plurilingualism that "takes account of an increasing cultural and linguistic diversity" (Sandretto & Tilson, 2013, p. 2) which defines New Zealand and Australian education in the 21st century.

Teachers in New Zealand and Australian high schools are seeing increasing linguistic and cultural diversity in our student populations. The studies in this chapter make it apparent that even within monolingually focused education systems, students draw on their plurilingual repertoires in many ways which shape their identities and contribute to their academic development. Teachers have a choice of rejecting this plurilingual practice, passively accepting it, or finding ways to respond positively and actively engage plurilingualism as a tool for learning.

Note

1   School names and participant names are pseudonyms.

References

Agnihotri, R. K. (1995). Multilingualism as a classroom resource. In K. Heugh, A. Siegrühn, & P. Plüddemann (Eds.), *Multilingual education for South Africa* (pp. 3–7). Johannesburg, South Africa: Heinemann.

Barkhuizen, G. P. (2010). Plurilingualism, shedding skins and floating identities: Diversity in community language narratives. *The TESOLANZ Journal, 18*, 1–15.

Benson, C. (2013). Towards adopting a multilingual habitus in educational development. In C. Benson & K. Kosonen (Eds.), *Language issues in comparative education* (pp. 283–299). Rotterdam, Netherlands: Sense Publishers.

Benson, C. (2014). Adopting a multilingual habitus: What North and South can learn from each other about the essential role of non-dominant languages in education. In D. Gorter, V. Zenotz & J. Cenoz (Eds.), *Minority languages and multilingual education: Bridging the local and the global* (Vol. 18) (pp. 11–28). Dordrecht, Netherlands: Springer.

Blommaert, J., Collins, J., & Slembrouck, S. (2005). Spaces of multilingualism. *Language & Communication, 25*(3), 197–216.

Bourdieu, P. (1991). *Language and symbolic power*. Cambridge, MA: Harvard University Press.

Bourdieu, P., & Passeron, J. C. (1990). *Reproduction in education, society and culture*. London, UK: Sage.

Canagarajah, S. (2011). Translanguaging in the classroom: Emerging issues for research and pedagogy. *Applied Linguistics Review, 2*, 1–28.

Clyne, M. (2008). The monolingual mindset as an impediment to the development of plurilingual potential in Australia. *Sociolinguistic Studies, 2*(3), 347–365.

Coleman, J. (2012). Moving beyond an "instrumental" role for the first languages of English Language Learners. *TESOL in Context, 22*(1), 18–37.

Coxhead, A., Stevens, L., & Tinkle, J. (2010). Why might secondary science textbooks be difficult to read? *New Zealand Studies in Applied Linguistics, 16*(2), 37–52.

Cummins, J. (1984). Wanted: A theoretical framework for relating language proficiency to academic achievement among bilingual students. In C. Rivera (Ed.), *Language proficiency and academic achievement*. Clevedon, UK: Multilingual Matters.

Cummins, J. (2000). The threshold and interdependence hypotheses revisited. In J. Cummins (Ed.), *Language, power and pedagogy: Bilingual children in the crossfire* (pp. 173–200). Clevedon, UK: Multilingual Matters.

Cummins, J. (2009). Fundamental psycholinguistic and sociological principles underlying educational success for linguistic minority students. In T. Skutnabb-Kangas, R. Phillipson, A. K. Mohanty & M. Panda (Eds.), *Social justice through multilingual education* (pp. 19–35). Clevedon, UK: Channel View Publications.

de Jong, E. J. (2011). *Foundations for multilingualism in education: From principles to practice*. Philadelphia, PA: Caslon.

de Jong, E. J., & Freeman Field, R. (2010). Bilingual approaches. In C. Leung & A. Creese (Eds.), *English as an Additional Language: Approaches to teaching linguistic minority students* (pp. 108–121). London, UK: Sage.

de Jong, E. J., Harper, C. A., & Coady, M. R. (2013). Enhanced knowledge and skills for elementary mainstream teachers of English language learners. *Theory Into Practice, 52*(2), 89–97.

Ellis, E. (2013). The ESL teacher as plurilingual: An Australian perspective. *TESOL Quarterly, 47*(3), 446–471.

Franken, M., May, S., & McComish, J. (2007). *LEAP: Language enhancing the achievement of Pasifika*. Ministry of Education, Wellington, New Zealand: Learning Media.

French, M. (2016). Students' multilingual resources and policy-in-action: An Australian case study. *Language and Education, 30*(4), 298–316.

French, M., & de Courcy, M. (2016). A place for students' multilingual resources in an Australian high school. In C. Snowden & S. Nichols (Eds.), *Languages and literacies as mobile and placed resources* (pp. 153–169). Oxford, UK: Routledge.

Geertz, C. (1973). *The interpretation of cultures: Selected essays*. New York: Basic Books.

Gogolin, I. (2002). Linguistic and cultural diversity in Europe: A challenge for educational research and practice. *European Educational Research Journal, 1*(1), 123.

Harper, C., Cook, K., & James, C. (2010). Content-language integrated approaches for teachers of EAL learners: Examples of reciprocal teaching. In C. Leung & A. Creese (Eds.), *English as an Additional Language: Approaches to teaching linguistic minority students* (pp. 97–107). London, UK: Sage.

Heugh, K. (2014). Turbulence and dilemma: Implications of diversity and multilingualism in Australian education. *International Journal of Multilingualism, 11*(3), 347–363.

Kitchen, M. (2010). Vision in the New Zealand curriculum: A Korean perspective. *New Zealand Journal of Educational Studies, 45*(2), 75–88.

Lave, J., & Wenger, E. (1991). *Situated learning: Legitimate peripheral participation*. Cambridge, UK: University Press.

Lo Bianco, J. (2010). Language policy and planning. In N. H. Hornberger & S. L. McKay (Eds.), *Sociolinguistics and language education* (pp. 143–174). Bristol, UK: Multilingual Matters.

May, S. (2007). Sustaining effective literacy practices over time in secondary schools: School organisational and change issues. *Language and Education, 21*(5), 387–405.

May, S. (2011). The disciplinary constraints of SLA and TESOL: Additive bilingualism and second language acquisition, teaching and learning. *Linguistics and Education, 22*(3), 233–247.

Ministry of Education. (2007). *The New Zealand curriculum for English-medium teaching and learning in years 1–13*. Wellington, New Zealand: Learning Media.

Moje, E. B. (2007). Developing socially just subject-matter instruction: A review of the literature on disciplinary literacy teaching. *Review of Research in Education, 31*(1), 1–44.

Moll, L., Amanti, C., Neff, D., & Gonzalez, N. (1992). Funds of knowledge for teaching: Using a qualitative approach to connect homes and classrooms. *Theory into practice, 31*(2), 132–141.

Nation, I. (2006). How large a vocabulary is needed for reading and listening? *Canadian Modern Language Review, 63*(1), 59–82.

Royal Society of New Zealand. (2013). *Languages in Aotearoa New Zealand*. Retrieved from www.royalsociety.org.nz/expert-advice/papers/yr2013/languages-in-aotearoa-new-zealand/.

SACE Board of SA. (2016). *Policy update: Literacy and numeracy*. Retrieved from www.sace.sa.edu.au/documents/652891/ab3299cb-1c09-4552-801a-cb9f57a93d65.

Sandretto, S., & Tilson, J. (2013). Reconceptualising literacy: Critical multiliteracies for "new times". *Teaching and Learning Research Initiative*, 1–15.

Scarino, A. (2008). Community and culture in intercultural language learning. *Australian Review of Applied Linguistics*, *31*(1), 1–15.

Shameem, N. (1997). ESOL and first language maintenance: Language loss or language gain? A case study. *The TESOLANZ Journal*, *5*, 15–25.

Shanahan, T., & Shanahan, C. (2008). Teaching disciplinary literacy to adolescents: Rethinking content-area literacy. *Harvard Educational Review*, *78*(1), 40–59.

Si'ilata, R., & Barkhuizen, G. (2004). Pasifika student's perceptions of their L1 maintenance at home and school: Language to climb a coconut tree. *The Journal of the TESOL Association of Aotearoa New Zealand*, 22–38.

Statistics New Zealand. (2013). *2013 Census*. Retrieved from www.stats.govt.nz/Census/2013-census.aspx.

Then, D. C. O., & Ting, S. H. (2011). Code-switching in English and Science classrooms: more than translation. *International Journal of Multilingualism*, *8*(4), 299–323.

Turner, M., & Cross, R. (2015). Making space for multilingualism in Australian schooling. *Language and Education*, 782(April), 1–9. http://doi.org/10.1080/09500782.2015.1114627

Watkins, M., & Noble, G. (2013). *Disposed to learn: ethnicity, schooling and the scholarly habitus*. London, England: Bloomsbury.

Wenger, E. (1998). Communities of practice: Learning as a social system. *The Systems Thinker*, *9*(5), 2–3.

Wigglesworth, G., Simpson, J., & Loakes, D. (2011). NAPLAN language assessments for Indigenous children in remote communities: issues and problems. *Australian Review of Applied Linguistics*, *34*(3), 320–343.

Windle, J., & Miller, J. (2013). Marginal integration: The reception of refugee-background students in Australian schools. In L. Bartlett & A. Ghaffar-Kucher (Eds.), *Refugees, immigrants and education in the Global South: Lives in motion* (pp. 196–210). Hoboken, NY: Taylor and Francis.

PART IV
Plurilingualism in Higher Education Contexts

11
TRANSFORMING LEXICON, TRANSFORMING INDUSTRY

University Lecturers as Language Planners in Timor-Leste

Trent Newman

In university classrooms in Timor-Leste, as in many multilingual educational contexts throughout the world, language mixing is common practice in disciplinary teaching and learning. Technical and industry-specific terms are regularly loaned from Portuguese, Indonesian and English to fill the lexical gaps in the corpus of Tetun[1], the national lingua franca and the main language of classroom communication in Timorese tertiary institutions. This is no straightforward process, however, as a diverse range of variables affect how different lecturers in different disciplines are likely to mix their classroom language. Indeed, as I have argued elsewhere (Newman, 2018), there are significant constraints on Timorese lecturers' agency and flexibility of choice in their language practices. In particular, the educational backgrounds of Timorese lecturers, many of whom acquire their Masters and PhDs abroad, determine that they often have quite different linguistic repertoires to those of their students, sometimes making even basic classroom communication a challenge. These practical challenges for tertiary teaching and learning also exist within a wider post-conflict, post-colonial social and political climate where particular emphasis is being placed on the production of an educated workforce that can contribute to Timor-Leste's national development (RDTL, 2011). In this context, language policy and planning in education has become a hotly debated issue, with strong anti-colonial sentiment from some groups against the use of Indonesian for teaching and learning, increasing demand for English speaking workers for the tourism and petroleum industries, and pressure from the Timorese government for the increased use of Portuguese (See, for example: Carneiro, 2014; Taylor-Leech, 2013).

In this chapter, I am concerned with demonstrating how Timorese lecturers' conscious and unconscious decisions about their classroom communication constitute a kind of micro-level language planning that is intimately connected to these broader sociolinguistic complexities. In this, I follow Lo Bianco's (2010) view of language planning (LP) that goes beyond "classical definitions" that "restrict LP to overt, deliberate or conscious managerial decisions" (p. 169) and which he says limit the roles and influence of teacher voices. In a deliberate effort to amplify these voices, I explore below some examples of Timorese lecturers' explanations of disciplinary concepts that appear to become problematic when attempting to explain them to students in Tetun. To begin, I provide some background to the research that produced this data and, via some introductory analysis of one lecturer's modelling of an explanation of 'metabolism' in Tetun, I highlight some of the theoretical underpinnings of my approach to the data. I then examine three different cases of multilingual translation of disciplinary terms as recounted to me by lecturers from three different disciplines: Tourism, Community Development, and Agronomy. In my discussion of these cases, I show how the language mixing practices of these disciplinary educators are closely tied to their visions of workplace language use and of the role of the multiliterate, educated intellectual in the development of Timor-Leste. I conclude with a discussion of the implications of understanding disciplinary lecturers as language planners in developing, multilingual contexts like Timor-Leste.

Researching Timorese Lecturers as Language Planners

Having worked on a number of small pedagogy projects in the Timorese tertiary sector in 2012 and 2013, I became fascinated by how disciplinary lecturers without any training in language pedagogy are navigating these aforementioned tensions and complexities in daily classroom communication. In 2015, as part of an independent research project, I began discussions with lecturers at several institutions about how they understand the communication skills that their students need to succeed at university and to find work in their industry. I also conducted classroom observations and asked lecturers about the teaching practices and communication strategies that they employ to support their students in developing these skills. Quite often in these discussions, lecturers became focused on perceived 'limitations of Tetun' and problems with students' lack of 'scientific Indonesian' in the communication of disciplinary knowledge. These were the first indications to me of these lecturers in their professional activities as disciplinary educators acting like language planners.

Consider, for instance, the following excerpt from an interview with Professor W, an agriculture lecturer in which she models for me the difficulties that she faces in explaining scientific terms like 'metabolism' to her students. Like many Timorese lecturers, Prof. W was educated during the Indonesian occupation of Timor-Leste (1975–1999) and thus acquired her knowledge of agriculture primarily via monolingual instruction in Indonesian. Prof. W tells me that she uses a mixture of Tetun and Indonesian ('Bahasa') in order to "communicate the science" to her students, who have experienced schooling in a post-independence

Timor-Leste dominated by Tetun and Portuguese. In the transcription, I have marked Indonesian loan words with [*Bah*] in order to highlight the strategic and not so strategic moves that Prof. W makes in the mobilisation of her plurilingual resources to help students to comprehend the meaning of 'metabolism':

W: I will talk in Tetun and then add some Bahasa, right?
T: Okay.
W: Okay. Erm . . . *Ohin loron ita atu koalia kona ba metabolisme*[*Bah*]. *Metabolisme* [*Bah*] *nee katak . . . kuando buat ruma tama ita boot nia isin, depois, iha isin nee, nia prosesu nee atu berubah*[*Bah*] *husi . . . hahaan . . . ita haan . . . naan sira, depois ya*[*Bah*] *ita nia isin loron nee—ita . . . ita kunyah*[*Bah*] *tiha . . . Kunyah?* [*Bah*]—I don't know which is . . . which it mean . . .—*i depois nia tama ita nia . . . be, saida?—kakorok talin . . . tama tan ita nia usus*[*Bah*]. *Iha usus*[*Bah*] *nee, depois . . . eh, sa? iha nebaa nee proses*[*Bah*] *enzimatis*[*Bah*] *mai berlaku*[*Bah*].

[Okay. Erm . . . Today we're going to talk about metabolism[Bah]. Metabolism[Bah] is . . . when something enters your body [and], afterwards, in your body, this process is going to change[Bah] from . . . food . . . you eat . . . some meat, then already[Bah] inside your body, you . . . you . . . chew[Bah] . . . Chew?[Bah]—I don't know which is . . . which it mean . . . —and then it enters your . . . um, what? throat, then also enters your gut [Bah]. In the gut[Bah], afterwards . . . uh what?—there the enzigmatic[Bah] process[Bah] comes to apply[Bah].]

W: [*smiling*] See?

It could be argued that there is a kind of corpus planning occurring in Prof. W's use of *metabolisme*, in that she is doing the work of filling this lexical gap in the corpus of Tetun with an Indonesian word (or, more accurately, an Indonesian form of an English word derived from Greek morphology). There is also a kind of inadvertent status planning occurring where Prof. W uses Indonesian for more common words—such as 'change', 'chew', 'gut', and 'apply'—that have equivalents in Tetun. Prof. W is unlikely to be as familiar with these words in Tetun as she is with their Indonesian counterparts, signalling a dominance of Indonesian in her repertoire (indeed, she tells me directly that she does not know the Tetun word for 'chew'). However, her use of language that is overladen with Indonesian vocabulary is also a kind of silencing of Tetun in this academic domain, particularly significant given that students are likely to be much more comfortable with Tetun than with Indonesian. Prof. W is supplying students with new lexical items to describe the phenomena she wishes to teach, but she is also modelling particular kinds of language mixing in classroom and disciplinary discourse. Here enters Cooper's (1989) acquisition planning, exemplifying García and Menken's (2010) point that "acquisition planning is also part and parcel of corpus and status planning"; that all three are "more likely to occur concurrently" (p. 251).

There is a growing body of work trying to name what is happening with the kind of classroom language mixing practices apparent in Prof. W's account. In recent years there has been an excitement within educational linguistics over terms like "code meshing" (Canagarajah, 2011) and "translanguaging" (García, 2013) to describe the fluid ways that educators and students draw on their entire linguistic repertoires in classroom communication. Except for a few notable exceptions (e.g., Airey, 2011; Langman, 2014), there has been a general lack of exploration of what non-language teachers' trans- and plurilingual communication practices may signify in the context of wider social trends in education and training, and particularly in relation to higher education and workforce production. In the field of language policy and planning, there is a long history of literature on language practices constituting a form of LP and policymaking. However, so far, much of this literature has been concerned with identifying and naming certain practices as instantiations or enactments of language policy implementation, rather than examining in detail the varied and performative ways that these practices come to be constitutive of LP in institutional settings.

For instance, there has been relatively scant analysis of the pedagogical motivations or kinds of ideologically driven intentionality that may underlie common teaching tasks like translating a disciplinary or technical term. When translations are occurring from one or more colonial languages that carry academic prestige into a local creole lingua franca, like Tetun in the case of Timor-Leste, it brings into sharp focus the roles played by lecturers like Prof. W in LP processes. Langman (2014) argues that such activities constitute a kind of "engaged language planning" (p. 188), which hints at a kind of intentionality, though not necessarily one motivated by a desire to do LP *per se*. Whereas Cooper conceptualised LP as "deliberate efforts" to influence the language practices of others (1989, p. 45), researchers have subsequently shown that individual language users—educators in particular—play active roles in LP processes even though their "deliberate efforts" may be more focused on professionally and/or pedagogically motivated activities (Lo Bianco, 2010; Langman, 2014). Despite Airey's assertion that "all university lecturers are teachers of disciplinary language" (2011, p. 4), most disciplinary lecturers are unlikely to identify as language teachers, let alone as language planners, and would frame their communicative intentions in the classroom not in terms of LP but in terms of the transfer of knowledge and skills germane to their field. Recognising that LP often involves this kind of planning of the self, Lo Bianco (2010) draws on Bakhtin (1981) to advocate for a dialogical and "activity-centred approach to LP" (p. 170), specifically one focused on the professional activities of teachers as "performative action" constituting a source of LP (p. 157).

In my analysis of the three cases that follow, I attempt to get at the intentionality behind lecturers' translations of disciplinary terms by examining their own accounts of how they "take the word and make it [their] own" (Bakhtin, 1981, p. 294). Although my research has included observation of teaching and learning communication practices in classroom and supervised fieldwork settings, for this chapter I have chosen to analyse lecturers' explanations for particular translations that they believe are important for students' disciplinary learning. The focus is therefore not on observed instances of lecturers' language mixing or translanguaging practices but, instead, is on their explanations and justifications for intentional languaging moves that the lecturers themselves identify. My aim is to examine their strategic thinking behind deliberate language uses in their everyday disciplinary teaching and learning in order to better understand these as pedagogically and ideologically driven performances of LP. Towards this end, I am concerned not so much with using 'translanguaging' as a descriptive label as I am with applying it, as Mazak (2017) proposes, as a kind of lens through which to understand the transformational nature of language mixing practices in multilingual higher education settings. To understand lecturers' translingual communication practices in this way, Mazak argues, is to see them as "creative, adaptable, resourceful inventions" that "change the world . . . in a perpetual process of meaning-making" (Mazak, 2017, p. 6).

Lecturers were recruited for participation in this research project from faculties and departments related to the aforementioned industries via direct contact with three Timorese higher education institutions. The three lecturers whose stories feature in this chapter—Prof. B, Prof. K, and Prof. N—work respectively in a tourism and hospitality faculty, a community development studies department, and an agronomy department, all on different campuses within the Timorese capital, Dili. In focus groups and interviews, these lecturers were asked to share their impressions of the communication challenges faced by their students in multilingual study and work contexts particular to their disciplinary area, as well as to describe the teaching practices that they use to help their students to overcome these challenges. One of the questions that proved to be particularly productive was: *How do you explain a complex disciplinary term to students?* Many lecturers were able to respond fairly quickly and confidently to this question with a ready example. It was in response to this question that many of the explanations and justifications for particular approaches to translation came, which form the data analysed in this chapter.

The Authorial Voice of Industry: The Translation of 'service' in Tourism

For many of the lecturers whom I interviewed, the question of what communication skills Timorese tertiary students need to succeed academically and professionally spoke mainly to issues of students' comprehension of their lessons and, in particular, to the translation of difficult technical terms and industry jargon. For tourism lecturers, however, this question drove straight to the heart of what work in their field is all about. As Prof. B, a lecturer in the tourism faculty at a private technical institute (TI), put it:

The main work, the main job that tourism industry do is the service. Service. So, service including how to communicate with the tourists. So, when . . . as a tourism industry stakeholder, when we make miscommunication, means that the customer will be unsatisfied. [. . .] So, service includes always communication; how to [respond to] the different question from the tourist, etcetera.

For Prof. B, interpersonal and communication skills are what constitute the industry of tourism and hospitality. To teach students what 'service' means therefore involves teaching them this vision of workplace communication in the tourism industry, which positions the student graduate entering the workforce as "a tourism industry stakeholder", and the primary focus of their communication practices as the tourist, "the customer".

In Tetun-English dictionaries the Tetun translation for 'service' is given as *servisu*, a loan from the Portuguese *serviço* (See, e.g., Hull, 2001; Williams-van Klinken, 2008). This dictionary translation hails Tetun's origins as a creole from Portuguese colonial times and constitutes more formal corpus planning processes that have been occurring for Tetun. In spoken Tetun, however, the word *servisu* is most commonly used to mean 'work' or 'job'. Conscious of this, I sought to probe further into how Prof. B and his colleagues explained their particular understanding of 'service' to students and its distinction from *servisu* as 'work'. Their response was not an explanation but a Tetun translation drawing on an alternative Portuguese loan word:

T: *Oinsaa esplika konseitu nee?* [How do you explain this concept?] Because . . . *tanba, iha Tetun 'servisu'* . . . it can mean work, it can mean job. *Entaun, oinsaa esplika 'service' iha Tetun?* [So, how do you explain 'service' in Tetun?]
B: In Tetun, 'service'-
Others: *Atendimentu.*
B: —'*atendimentu*'.
T: //*Atendimentu?*//
B: //*Atendimentu.*// Yeah.

Atendimentu does not yet appear in any Tetun-English dictionary as the Tetun word for 'service', though it does appear as the word for 'attendance' (Hull, 2001). It does not even appear in a 2016 'Tourism and Food' glossary created by the English department at TI, where the Tetun translation of 'service' is given as *serbi* (Williams-van Klinken, da Silva, Tilman, Silva, Cardoso, Santos, & da Silva, 2016). Rather than signalling collaboration between disciplinary experts and language experts, the creation of bilingual teaching and learning resources at TI instead appears to signal competition within the institution over who has the authority to 'author' new terms in Tetun.

Consciously or not, Prof. B and his colleagues in the tourism faculty are positioning themselves as language planners in relation to the corpus of Tetun for their discipline when asserting that 'service' should be translated as *atendimentu* in Tetun. It is corpus, status, and acquisition planning happening simultaneously, informed not by linguistic expertise but by knowledge of the language used in the Timorese tourism industry and also, significantly, by a particular vision of social relations in that industry context. Given Prof. B's explanation of what 'service' means for tourism, both *servisu* and *serbi* amount to inappropriate translations: The labour-related connotations of these words being inconsistent with Prof. B's vision of what characterises the relationship between a tourist and someone who 'serves' them. *Atendimentu*, however, is etymologically linked to 'attendance' and carries connotations of being present, engaged, attentive, marking a nuanced but nonetheless significant semantic distinction from 'service' as 'work'.

While there is intentionality here—one concerned with cultures of workplace communication—it is also mixed up with the manifestation of competing institutional and national language policy discourses. In order to translate 'service' to Tetun, Prof. A might also have loaned the Indonesian word *pelayanan*, which has a meaning separate from the word for 'work' and incorporates both 'service' and 'attendance'. Like Prof. Y, Prof. A was also educated under the Indonesian education system, affording him a confidence in (if not necessarily an affiliation for) the use of Indonesian as an academic and disciplinary language. Yet, his translation, *atendimentu*, is a word of Portuguese origin. The use of Portuguese loan words over Indonesian in order to fill lexical gaps in formal and specialised uses of Tetun is consistent with an increasingly established norm of borrowing Portuguese words for 'high' registers of Tetun (Williams-van Klinken & Hajek, 2016), and also conforms to recent pressure from the Timorese ministry of education to phase out the use of Indonesian in all tertiary teaching.

On the other hand, the choice of a Portuguese loan word in this case is somewhat intriguing when examined alongside the fact that the tourism faculty at TI is in the process of moving to English-only medium of instruction. English is seen as the international lingua franca for tourism, and it is also seen as the key to competing with other countries in the region. One of Prof. B's colleagues in the TI tourism faculty tells me:

> Because next year Timor-Leste will go to the ASEAN Economic Community. In ASEAN Economic Community we should compete with the ASEAN nations. That's big competition for the economic. So . . . the students of [TI] can work in ASEAN nations—in Indonesia, Malaysia, Philippines—how to compete with them? If we want to compete with them, we should learn English. Because the ASEAN nations no . . . don't understand any Portuguese. How to compete with them? We have to learn English.

Tourism students are required to take English for Specific Purposes classes taught by the TI English Department, and regular subjects are increasingly taught in a mixture of Tetun and English. However, Prof. B does not tell me that he simply uses the English word 'service' when he explains the idea in Tetun. There *is* a word in Tetun for service, he and his colleagues all tell me quite firmly: *Atendimentu*. This translation represents an expansion and an innovation with the Tetun language that is being effected by language use in industry and confirmed by disciplinary experts. It is happening even at the very moment that English is supposed to be replacing it in that domain, and even in contradiction of LP efforts by language teachers at the same institution. This amounts to more than just the continuing use of Tetun alongside English for teaching and learning, it is the carving out of its own space and rules for its functions as a language of higher education and of disciplinary discourse socialisation.

Prof. B and his colleagues are acting as language planners in ways that significantly expand upon previous conceptualisations of LP, and particularly language acquisition planning as articulated by Cooper (1989). In moment-to-moment, in-class translations they are participating in the authoring of the linguistic culture of Tetun, developing the academic and professional registers of Tetun in line with their particular vision of what characterises ideal workplace communication in the tourism industry. They are also and simultaneously contributing to the disciplinary discourse socialisation of their students by passing on this ethics of communicative relations for their industry. Prof. B's statements about what 'service' means for the tourism industry reveal processes of LP that involve not only language ideologies but also ideologies related to workforce development. The next case shows that these sociolinguistic and sociopolitical complexities underlying the act of translation of disciplinary terms in Timor-Leste are not unique to the field of tourism. It also further reveals the significance of individual lecturers' language and educational biographies in disentangling these complexities.

The Community Becomes the Owner: Reconceptualising Teaching Sustainability

Prof. K is a lecturer in community development studies (CDS) at a public university in Dili. The handful of lecturers in his department have studied to Masters or Doctoral level via education in a range of different countries, including Australia, Indonesia, Vietnam and Portugal. These diverse prior experiences in tertiary education not only make for diverse plurilingual academic and disciplinary language repertoires among these lecturers, but they also make for differences in the development paradigm from which CDS lecturers approach the teaching of community development work. One of the key points of difference is what should be the role of the educated intellectual in the development of Timor-Leste from a CDS perspective.

Prof. K completed his Masters in Portugal and believes that the role of his students following graduation is to educate rural communities about the development opportunities available to them. Prof. K's research for his Masters dissertation examined the construction of *uma lulik*—traditional Timorese sacred houses—and their potential benefit to rural communities as tourism objects. Citing his own research on the untapped development opportunities in remote rural communities, Prof. K explained to me his reason for creating a new 'community-based tourism' subject, and the ideal end-goal of his students as graduates becoming promoters of community-based tourism in remote, rural communities:

> We have many, many tourism objects, but we still don't develop in communities in rural areas. Like I show some picture here [*pointing to where he projected the powerpoint during class*]. The [tourism] objects are in rural areas but we need to inform to community. [. . .] So they know that tourism is important. Community tourism is important.

For Prof. K, this community-centred perspective is key to sustainable tourism development. In the context of responding to my question about whether students understood this core message in his class, he tells me that many students understand 'the reality' in Timor-Leste: inadequate infrastructure, broken roads, and difficult access to and poor protection of tourism sites. However, students need reinforcement, Prof. K tells me, of the centrality of community involvement in processes of sustainable development.

According to Prof. K, students understand the concept of 'sustainability' as *kontinuitas* (Bah), or *continuidade* (Port: 'continuity'): building things and taking care of them so that they last and 'continue'. Prof. K feels that this understanding is too limited: "I think sustainability they know, but not a lot. Sustainable they know only maybe *kontinuitas*'[Bah]. Only *Continuidade* [Port]. Only that."

For Prof. K, communities need to understand the opportunities of tourism so that they take it upon themselves to construct and maintain infrastructure and to protect sites that will attract tourists. Tourism development is only 'sustainable', therefore, if it is centred on community involvement. "When we protect something about the culture, about the environment—is to continue to have [it] available. But community tourism is related to what community has. From community, to community, and for community."

Through this discursive centering of 'community', Prof. K seeks not only to correct students' understanding of 'sustainability' as 'continuity' but, moreover, to unsettle students' existing notions of the social relations that characterise sustainable tourism development. It is in this way that Prof. K reveals that he is most concerned with students imagining beyond superficial improvements to the current status quo of state-centred development, to alternative, community-centred pathways to development.

In a follow-up interview, I asked Prof. K whether he explicitly teaches this phrase "from community, to community, and for community" as a kind of translation of 'sustainability'. In response, he first corrected my effort to translate this phrase to Tetun as: *Husi komunidade, ba komunidade, komunidade nian*, asserting that the translation should rather be: *Husi komunidade, ba komunidade, komunidade mak sai nain* ("from community, to/for community, [so that] the community is the one that is the owner"). With this correction, Prof. K demonstrated his attentiveness to the key semantic distinction between my use of *nian* (a possessive marker in Tetun), which may merely communicate that community resources are involved, and his use of *mak* (a focus marker) with *sai* (the relational copular verb 'to become') and *nain* (the noun 'owner' or 'master'), which emphasises that the community should be the owner of the whole process.

That Prof. K is attentive to these subtleties between rather similar translations in Tetun exemplifies Prof. K's metalinguistic awareness as a teaching resource—what Moore and Gajo highlight as "a key asset available to plurilinguals" (2009, p. 147). Indeed, Prof. K's ability to move between English, Indonesian and Portuguese and to mobilise nuanced distinctions in Tetun in order to explain sustainability as a community-centred process shows that his pluralingualism is metalinguistic in itself, "because it calls to conjugate and to relate languages to one another, and to put them in perspective" (Berthoud, cited in Moore & Gajo, 2009, p. 147).

Prof. K told me that when talking about the concept of sustainability, that he *sempre liga ho komunidade* ("always links with community"). It appears to matter less to Prof. K which single word a student might use as a translation of 'sustainability' than whether they link this word with others to demonstrate an understanding that communities must be the authors of their own sustainable development. This approach to translation places an emphasis on meaning-making, rather than correctness of word choice, in line with Mazak's (2017) previously cited view of translanguaging in higher education. Although translation is clearly a site of key disciplinary learning in this case, it also illustrates the limitations of single word translation for rich and nuanced communication. Indeed, it fits neatly with Canagarajah's (2014) conceptualisation of communication as "translingual practice" in that it "transcends individual languages" and even transcends individual words, involving "diverse semiotic resources and ecological affordances" (p. 6). Indeed, this is why Prof. K shows pictures of community resources to accompany his explanations and takes them on field trips to villages in rural areas. A translingual view of translation—and of the LP tied up in translation—arguably incorporates all of these multisemiotic practices that Prof. K employs in order to help his students to understand 'sustainability'.

With the transfer of disciplinary knowledge via this kind of translingual translation there is also the potential for the development of students' own metalinguistic awareness and strategic language mobility. However, for this potential to be realised there needs to be conscious and strategic facilitation on the part of the lecturer—"teachable strategies of translanguaging", as Canagarajah argues (2011)—as well as collaboration with language teachers and experts for the provision of language support and towards the standardisation of disciplinary vocabulary in Tetun. The next example of disciplinary translation highlights some of the possibilities and constraints for this kind of conscious and deliberate effort.

"They Only Refer to *Moris Diak*": The Language of Farmers as an "Other Tongue"

The concepts of 'service' and 'sustainability' are evidently central to the industries of tourism and community development respectively, and are likely to appear with high frequency in disciplinary discourse. Similarly, the concept of 'growth' is so central to the field of agronomy that it is difficult to imagine having a conversation about studying and measuring the wellbeing of a particular crop without it. Prof. N, a Timorese agronomy lecturer, tells me that he learned to talk about plant development as *pertumbuhan*—the Indonesian word for 'growth'—signalling a dominance of Indonesian in his academic repertoire akin to that of Prof. Y. In Tetun, a common translation for 'growth' is *kresimentu*, from the Portuguese *crescimento*. However, Prof. N tells me that he teaches his students to use the Tetun word *moris*, meaning 'life', as a more appropriate translation for 'growth' in the context of the study of plant science in Timor-Leste.

Prof. N explained to me his choice of *moris* over *kresimentu* like this:

> *Moris*—it is like, you know, 'changing over'. . . . I think the word *kresimentu*, I think it [is] mostly applied in economic terms. [. . .] I feel quite strange when [| *laughs* |] I see like this economical term into the agriculture.

Prof. N's preference that students should use *moris* is based on substantial justifications that correspond to two different kinds of metalinguistic analysis that he is doing. Firstly, Prof. N is observing that the loan word *kresimentu* is semantically more connected to economic growth and therefore has the wrong kinds of connotations when describing and analysing plant or crop growth in agronomy. In relation to agribusiness, for example, it may be necessary to distinguish between discussion about growth in profits, and related discussion about crop growth and subsequent harvest yield and distinguishing *moris* from *kresimentu* should facilitate this. Secondly, Prof. N recognises the need for a shift in register when communicating agricultural science to rural farmers who, Prof. N believes, would not understand *kresimentu*:

> [I]f you come to, like, the people in the village, they can only tell you: "Oh, this is good growth." "*E moris diak.*" They only refer to *moris diak* [good life/growth]. They don't know what is *kresimentu*. [. . .] If you talk to them, they say: "*Oh, ida nee moris diak. Ida nee moris laduun diak. Laduun furak.*" ["Oh, this one has good life/growth. This one's growth is not so good. Not so tasty."]

This second justification by Prof. N reveals an intentionality in his use of *moris* that can be seen as a strategic example of translanguaging within a context of transglossia.

"Transglossia", as García (2013) argues, "releases ways of speaking of [and with] subaltern groups that had been previously fixed within static language identities and constrained by the modern/colonial world system" (p. 161). Other lecturers in the same agriculture faculty as Prof. N (and particularly those who have been educated in Portugal) disagree that *moris* can be used to signify 'growth', with one telling me that if farmers do not understand *kresimentu*, then they "do not speak Tetun". Prof. N, by stark contrast, is asserting that a Tetun word not only can do the work that the Portuguese loan word *kresimentu* is supposed to do, it already does it and, in fact, does it much better in terms of communicating in the contexts both of the disciplinary discourse of agronomy and also of the communicative culture of the target audience. Indeed, to talk about *moris* in the way that Prof. N explains it begins to reveal not only the limitations of *kresimentu*, but also those of the English words 'life' and 'growth'. In the lexicon of rural Timorese, *moris* does not simply refer to life as a fixed state but, more profoundly, N puts it.

Again, this is corpus, status, and acquisition planning intertwined together in Prof. N's teaching, but it is also more than that. Prof. N is not only teaching students that *moris* is more understandable for farmers than *kresimentu*, he is also teaching them that good agronomists learn the lexicon of farmers with the goal of communicating with them in their language. Consciously or not, Prof. N is challenging dominant perceptions of expertise as being located with the educated intellectual and the transfer of knowledge as one-way from agronomists to farmers. And, in doing so, he is claiming a space for the Tetun of farmers as an "other tongue" by which "other thinking" can occur to "question and transgress the coloniality of power and knowledge" (García citing Mignolo, 2013, p. 161).

Prof. N is careful to remind me that he is not a language "expert", revealing perhaps some of his hesitation to claim full authority in his translation to *moris*, but at the same time revealing his belief that the process of language development can and should be a dynamic and collaborative one, enriched by diverse voices:

> It's not: I'm the lecturer, I'm the correct one, or you are the correct one. But I also say that this is interesting—means that we are willing, you know, to develop our language. [. . .]There may be some expert of the language somewhere, but this is bringing different ideas [. . .].

Indeed, throughout our discussion of this example of *pertumbuhan/kresimentu/ moris*, Prof. N was adamant that these moments of finding translations for disciplinary language are opportunities for the development of language:

So, I think the idea is it's not a matter of either use of *moris* or *kresimentu*. I think this a good opportunity of discussion: what we do have now, and how we could find a better word in the future?

[. . .]For example, in English, for *growth*, or *pertumbuhan* in Bahasa. So, the idea is not really, you know, I won't stick on this, or stick on this, but the idea is, okay, we come . . . come and then we try. I think, either this one is correct or that one is correct, come together and then develop our language, I think and then this is the way how we learn. [. . . W]e can basically keep going until we find out which word [is] really appropriate to use for agriculture in Timor-Leste.

The problem, however, is that these kinds of discussions are not currently occurring between disciplinary experts like Prof. N, and Timorese linguists at the *Instituto Nacional Linguistica*—the government funded body responsible for developing the corpus of Tetun, which also happens to be located at Prof. N's university. At other institutions, too, there seems to be very limited collaboration on the development of technical and disciplinary vocabulary in Tetun, as evidenced by the earlier mention of the 'Tourism and Food' glossary at TI that translates 'service' as *serbi*. Opportunities for such consultative and deliberative LP are simply not being created. Instead, lecturers and experts on all sides tend to defer responsibility for initiating such discussions to someone other than themselves. Even at the classroom level, Prof. N admits that he does not usually have an explicit discussion with students about why one word may be more appropriate than another when communicating with farmers (though he may explain it in tracked changes on students' written work). This understanding, Prof. N tells me, students should be learning from their agricultural extension subject, which, incidentally, is taught by the same lecturer at NU who told me that the farmers who do not understand *kresimentu* do not speak Tetun. Thus, although lecturers' multilingual translations of disciplinary terms may be generating important innovations in the development of disciplinary language, they are also highlighting discrepancies between the plurilingual repertoires and the language ideologies of different disciplinary and language experts.

Understanding Disciplinary Lecturers as Language Planners: Some Implications

How and why is it useful to understand disciplinary lecturers like Prof. B, Prof. K, and Prof. N as language planners? To begin with, it is useful for our understanding of what constitutes language planning. If we accept Lo Bianco's performative mode of LP, then "we are all engaged in continual LP as we converse, and this personal programme of planning our subjective self is located on a continuum with the collective, public action of institutions" (2010, p. 165). The examples of multilingual translation of disciplinary terms discussed in this chapter reveal LP as a process occurring in the moment, and at the micro level, involving disciplinary lecturers' intentional as well as unintentional uses of individual words in combination with one another, as well as in combination with other semiotic resources. In translating 'service', 'sustainability', and 'growth' for their students, Prof. B, Prof. K, and Prof. N are not using lexical resources that are inherited or developed by past, expert language planners. They are innovating, and they are doing so with particular ideological visions of the social relations that underpin their professional fields. They are participating in the corpus and status development of Tetun and they are affecting the semantic placement of multiple languages within disciplinary discourse and in the communicative cultures of particular industries.

These cases also substantially expand the notion of "acquisition planning" as originally conceived by Cooper (1989). Prof. B, Prof. K, and Prof. N are not simply concerned with expanding students' vocabularies, they are acting as translators of disciplinary knowledge as well as agents of students' socialisation into academic and professional discourse communities (Duff, 2010). Thus, tied up together with the corpus and status planning that these lecturers are engaged in, their translation practices also constitute a modelling—if not always an explicit teaching—of particular mobilisations of repertoire for industry-specific communication. The focus here shifts from 'acquisition' of discrete, bounded languages, to the development of particular translingual literacies in workplace communicative cultures. Prof. B's tourism students are learning not to rely on the Tetun-English dictionaries and glossaries that tell them *servisu* or *serbi* mean 'service', and to tune in instead to the lexicon used in tourism industry settings, as well as to the social relations that characterise them. Students of Prof. K. in community development studies are developing their metalinguistic awareness; learning to link the term 'sustainability' with *komunidade*, to perceive the inadequacy of single word translations like *kontinuitas* or *continuidade*, and to find ways to augment these translations from within a community-centred approach to sustainable development. Prof. N's plant science students are learning to access an "other tongue" in communication with rural farmers and to adapt their repertoires to those of their target interlocutors, transforming understandings of expertise with the understanding that the language of farmers can and should inform the language of agricultural scientists. This expanded conceptualisation of what has been called language acquisition planning reflects an expanded view of language as a set of social semiotic resources, and of language learning as "activation" and mobilisation of students' plurilingual and pluricultural "assets" (Moore & Gajo, 2009, p. 148). These Timorese lecturers are planning their students' plurilingual repertoires for particular kinds of participation in professional discourses, and towards particular transformations of these industries.

However, the analysis of these three examples has also revealed the diverse struggles and tensions that may also constitute LP processes at this micro level.

The translation of a single disciplinary term can represent a moment of intense ideological conflict—conflict relating to language ideologies, as well as conflict relating to political and economic ideologies connected to national development, and specifically to workforce development. Ideologies of workforce development are evident in the lecturers' comments about what relationships with community and industry stakeholders should look like. Conflict is evident between individual lecturers within institutions, such as Prof. N's colleague suggesting that farmers should learn 'correct' Tetun, rather than plant scientists learning farmer speak. Indeed, translations of certain concepts can come particularly weighted with such tensions, especially if they are as central to disciplinary discourse as 'service', 'sustainability', and 'growth' are to tourism, community development studies, and agronomy respectively. For educational linguists and educators involved in multilingual higher education, these examples highlight both the centrality and the complexities of context to the teaching and learning of disciplinary language, and illustrate the constraints on, as well as the possibilities for intentionality in micro-language planning processes.

Note

1 There are multiple orthographies in use for Tetun, which disagree over the spelling of common words, including 'Tetun'(/Tetum). In this chapter I use the orthography developed by Williams-van Klinken (2008), as it is the most closely aligned with the way the lecturers who participated in this study pronounce Tetun words.

References

Airey, J. (2011). The relationship between teaching language & student learning in Swedish University Physics. In B. Preisler, I. Klitgård & A. Fabricius (Eds.), *Language & learning in the international university: From English uniformity to diversity & hybridity* (pp. 3–17). Bristol, UK: Multilingual Matters.

Bakhtin, M. (1981). *The dialogic imagination. Four essays (Edited by M. Holquist; translated by C. Emerson & M. Holquist)*. Austin, TX: University of Texas Press.

Canagarajah, S. (2011). Codemeshing in academic writing: Identifying teachable strategies of translanguaging. *Modern Language Journal, 95*: 401–417. doi:10.1111/j.1540-4781.2011.01207.x

Canagarajah, S. (2014). *Translingual practice: Global Englishes and cosmopolitan relations*. New York: Routledge.

Carneiro, A. (2014). Conflicts around the (de-)construction of legitimate language(s): The situation of Portuguese in the multilingual context of East Timor. In L. P. Moita-Lopes (Ed.), *Global Portuguese: Linguistic ideologies in late modernity* (pp. 204–221). Florence, Italy: Taylor and Francis.

Cooper, R. (1989). *Language planning and social change*. Cambridge, UK: University Press.

Duff, P. A. (2010). Language socialization into academic discourse communities. *Annual Review of Applied Linguistics, 30*: 169–192. doi:10.1017/s0267190510000048

García, O. (2013). From diglossia to transglossia: Bilingual and multilingual classrooms in the 21st century. In C. Abello-Contesse, P. Chandler, M. López-Jiménez & R. Chacón-Beltrán (Eds.), *Bilingual and Multilingual Education in the 21st Century: Building on Experience* (pp.155–175). Bristol, UK: Multilingual Matters.

García, O., & Menken, K. (2010). Stirring the onion: Educators and the dynamics of language education policies (looking ahead). In K. Menken & O. García (Eds.), *Negotiating language policies in schools: Educators as policymakers*. New York: Routledge.

Hull, G. (2001). *Standard Tetum-English dictionary* (3rd ed.). Sydney: Allen & Unwin in association with the University of Western Sydney.

Langman, J. (2014). Translanguaging, identity, and learning: science teachers as engaged language planners. *Language Policy*, *13*(2): 183–200. doi:10.1007/s10993-013-9312-9

Lo Bianco, J. (2010). Language policy and planning. In N. Hornberger & S. McKay (Eds.), *Sociolinguistics and language education* (pp. 143–174). Bristol, UK: Multilingual Matters.

Mazak, C. M. (2017). Introduction: Theorizing translanguaging practices in higher education. In C. M. Mazak & K. S. Carroll (Eds.), *Translanguaging in higher education: Beyond monolingual ideologies* (pp. 1–10). Bristol, UK: Multilingual Matters.

Moore, D., & Gajo, L. (2009). Introduction—French voices on plurilingualism and pluriculturalism: Theory, significance and perspectives. *International Journal of Multilingualism*, *6*(2): 137–153. doi:10.1080/14790710902846707

Newman, T. (2018). Policy and practicality in Timorese higher education: Lessons from lecturers in development-related disciplines. In J. Crandall & K. Bailey (Eds.), *Global perspectives on educational language policies*. New York: Routledge.

RDTL [República Democrática de Timor-Leste]. (2011). Timor-Leste strategic development plan, 2011–2030 (English version). Retrieved from https://sustainabledevelopment.un.org/content/documents/1506Timor-Leste-Strategic-Plan-2011-20301.pdf.

Taylor-Leech, K. (2013). Finding space for non-dominant languages in education: Language policy and medium of instruction in Timor-Leste 2000–2012. *Current Issues in Language Planning*, *14*(1), 109–126. doi:10.1080/14664208.2013.766786

Williams-van Klinken, C. (2008). *Word finder: English-Tetun, Tetun-Ingles*. Dili, Timor-Leste: Sentru Lingua, Dili Institute of Technology.

Williams-van Klinken, C., da Silva, H., Tilman, C., Silva, M., Cardoso, M., Santos, A., & da Silva, J. (2016). *Glosariu Turizmu no Hahaan*. Dili, Timor-Leste: Sentru Lingua, Dili Institute of Technology.

Williams-van Klinken, C., & Hajek, J. (2016). Tetu-gés: Influénsia portugés ba estrutura Tetun. In S. Smith, N. Canas Mendes, A. B. da Silva, A. da Costa Ximenes, C. Fernandes & M. Leach (Eds.), *Timor-Leste: iha kontekstu local, rejional no global / O local, regional e global / The local, the regional and the global / Lokal, regional dan global 2015 (Volume 1)*. (pp. 32–36). Hawthorn: Swinburne University Press.

12

CHALLENGING THE QUIET VIOLENCE OF A POWERFUL LANGUAGE

Translanguaging Towards Transformative Teaching in South African Universities

Monica Hendricks and Ntombekhaya Fulani

Introduction

Over the last two years, the foundations of the tertiary sector in South Africa were profoundly shaken by student protests forcibly placing their concerns on the national agenda. The student demands for the decolonisation of the curriculum, free education for all and the transformation of the institutional culture of universities together represent an urgent call for fundamental change. This chapter responds to this call in the area of language teaching. It does so by suggesting that the notion of translanguaging may be a potent force in problematising and also challenging the hegemonic position of English and hence contributing to the project of decolonisation. The chapter also raises questions about the unintended consequences of student demands for English as a medium of instruction at the former Afrikaans language universities and how these demands may affect the constitutional principle of multilingualism. Since translanguaging is an expression of multilingualism in practice, the chapter uses the case of how two lecturers (the authors of this chapter) in a multilingual team collaborate in shifting their language practices in a Bachelor of Education specialising in English Language Teaching at Rhodes University in the Eastern Cape Province of South Africa, where isiXhosa is the most spoken language (StatsSA, 2011). The main objective is to increase bilingual isiXhosa-English students' access to epistemic knowledge, by utilising their linguistic competencies in both languages.

Language(s) and Learning in University

According to Badat (2016), the university student protests constitute a multi-faceted "organic crisis" in higher education. The economic dimensions of this crisis relate to the systematic under-funding of universities and concomitant hiking of fees, resulting in the financial exclusion of poor and working-class students and growing student debt to universities, the largely state-funded National Student Financial Aid Scheme, and commercial banks. The ideological dimensions of the crisis, particularly pertinent to this chapter, were articulated in the student calls for university institutional culture to be transformed and to become more representative of national demographics and for university curricula to be decolonised.

Proponents of decolonisation advocate far-reaching change of the content of university curricula. Heleta (2016, p. 4) argues that current university curricula constitute a form of epistemic violence which erases "nearly all the linkages that black students may have with the prescribed texts, propagated narratives, debates and learning on the one side and their history, lived experiences and dreams on the other side". We suggest that English, the language of power and of higher education in South Africa, can be considered an element of curricular epistemic violence given the dissonance this privileging of English creates in the lives of students when their languages, and by implication their histories, cultures and customs are not valued.

Prominent political theoretician, intellectual and activist for multilingualism in South Africa, the late Neville Alexander's experiences at the University of Cape Town in the early 1950s (Busch, Busch and Press 2014, pp. 37–38) convey the extent to which not only languages other than English, but particular accents, were not valued at many South African universities:

> I was the only person from the countryside, and I was called the country bumpkin because . . . I had a very marked Afrikaans accent. . . . I have this very interesting memory of English, that on the one hand I was made to feel that I wasn't up to standard, and that at the same time I didn't feel sub-standard. I just felt, look here, I need to find out how to get up there at that standard, but I'm not going to change my way. I'm not going to be a different person. I think I stuck to that completely. Eventually I became one of the most bilingual people of my peer group.

Despite the reality that indigenous African languages are the home languages of the overwhelming bulk of the population (StatsSA, 2011) and that the majority nine previously marginalised indigenous African languages have had constitutionally protected official status for more than 20 years (South Africa, 1996), there is a glaring inconsistency between language in education policy and practice. Language in education policy (Bengu, 1997) advocates additive multilingualism and that all the official languages be treated as equal. Additive bilingualism would require that learners' home languages are maintained and developed throughout schooling. Yet, in most schools, the practice is that children's indigenous African home language is used as the medium of instruction for the first three years of schooling, with an abrupt switch to English as the official language of instruction from Grade 4 (Gardiner, 2008). The detrimental consequences for children's literacy and overall learning are well documented (e.g. Hendricks, 2014).

Further, the long-standing official status of Afrikaans and English means that the other nine official African languages are seldom effectively learnt by English- and Afrikaans-speakers, and are used far less in education, especially at secondary and tertiary levels, and in the print media (Hendricks, 2016). Measures such as the Incremental Introduction of African Languages (South Africa, 2013) which seeks to promote the introduction of African languages to English- and Afrikaans-speakers, and the Use of Official Languages Act (South Africa, 2012) demonstrate how far South Africa remains from "parity of esteem and equitable treatment of all official languages" (South Africa, 2012, p 10).

Despite South Africa's current multilingual context, English continues to dominate in university courses and websites; multilingualism is seldom visible in these areas of university functioning, or articulated as a demand in the recent student protests. The student #protests have effectively replaced dual English/Afrikaans language of instruction policy at some universities with English (Kunene, 2016), even though English is a historically colonial language and the home language of a minority of South Africans (StatsSA, 2011). The virtual removal of Afrikaans as a language of instruction at universities may be an issue of access, since Afrikaans is not widely understood in South Africa, but the consequence is to further the privileging of English.

This may have the unintended consequence of undermining some of the advances of indigenous African languages in university curricula, in research and as languages of instruction and scientific knowledge. In response to successive policies to promote indigenous African languages since 2002 (Maseko, 2014, p. 29), there have been a number of initiatives at a variety of South African Universities. For example, Rhodes University has a bilingual English/isiXhosa Bachelor of Education degree for teachers of the first three years of school. On the other hand, the University of Limpopo has a multilingual BA degree with some subjects taught in Sesotho sa Leboa (a dominant language in Limpopo). In the Law, Pharmacy and Education faculties of Rhodes University isiXhosa is infused on a voluntary basis while it is obligatory for all Bachelor of Journalism students to complete a semester credit in isiXhosa. Similarly, it is compulsory for all students to take isiZulu at the University of KwaZulu-Natal (Kaschula, 2013). In April 2017, Rhodes University had the first doctoral graduate who wrote his thesis in an African language, isiXhosa, (Mahlakoana, 2017) an indication that indigenous African languages are capable of moving beyond formal, but empty, official status towards more meaningful intellectualisation of isiXhosa.

Among others, academics specialising in the teaching of English (e.g. Janks, 2014; Ferreira & Mendelowitz, 2009) have interrogated the dominance of one language over others and students' differential access, both to high levels of literacy and epistemic knowledge. According to Janks (2000), privileging an already dominant language such as English adds to its power and necessarily diminishes the potential for the formerly marginalised indigenous African languages to become powerful. In the current linguistic status quo at universities, the challenge is to ensure that students achieve academic literacy in English in order to make epistemic access possible, while at the same time affirming students' linguistic (and also class, gender, regional and cultural) diversity.

In linguistically and culturally diverse USA universities, Pratt (1991, p. 34) refers to such social spaces as 'contact zones' "where cultures meet, clash, and grapple with each other, often in contexts of highly asymmetrical relations of power, such as colonialism, slavery, or their aftermaths ...". In such contested zones, Pratt (1991, p. 34) recommends that we should have what she refers to as "safe houses" which provide "places for healing and mutual recognition, safe houses in which to construct shared understandings, knowledge, claims on the world that they can bring into the contact zones".

In practice, the variety of linguistic repertoires in South African university classrooms is both daunting as well as filled with exciting prospects of discovery and enlightenment. As Ferreira & Mendelowitz (2009, p. 40) aptly observe, academics specialising in teaching English need to:

> Provide access to English within particular institutional and national constraints ... in a way that is both sensitive to the multilingual identities of our students and, while wanting to avoid a negative construction of English, nevertheless encourages a critical orientation towards its hegemonic power.

In a sense, we follow Ferreira & Mendelowitz (2009) who, in a South African course on language and identity with many bi- and multilingual student teachers, use reflexive reading and writing to create "a dynamic multilingual contact zone" in which their students write a language biography. They employ two key pedagogic strategies: "Reflexive reading ... a dialogic process that can mobilise interactions between the reader's ideas and the ideas found in the text", and writing as "a space for reflexive narrative enquiry that enables the articulation of particular identity positions" (Ferreira & Mendelowitz, 2009, p. 58).

Most translanguaging research in South Africa (e.g. Krause & Prinsloo, 2016; Madiba, 2014; Makalela, 2014 and 2015), confirms Canagarajah's (2011a) claim that mainly oral instances of translanguaging have been studied. Our case provides evidence of lecturers encouraging translanguaging in the written mode and offers a teachable strategy of translanguaging, both of which are lacking in the literature, according to Canagarajah (2011a).

The first research question was pedagogical and the second incorporated two of Canagarajah's (2011b) strategies related to writing specifically:

- How can we build on our own and the BEd students' linguistic repertoire to enhance learning and epistemic access?
- What languages, voice and interactional strategies would the BEd students use when making sense of an academic reading and given the freedom to summarise their notes in English and isiXhosa?

Translanguaging in Teaching English

Most students on the BEd in English Language Teaching course at Rhodes University are qualified teachers in rural Eastern Cape schools. While these teachers are professionally qualified, they register for this course because their initial teacher education course is outdated given the rapid curriculum change, or because of a mismatch between their initial subject specialisation and the subject (often English) that they currently teach (Reeves & Robinson, 2010). All the teachers and most of the lecturers are bi- or multilingual and speak English as an additional language. The dominant home languages in the Eastern Cape Province are isiXhosa, Afrikaans, English and seSotho (StatSA, 2011). The two lecturers involved in teaching the section of the course reported on in this chapter were an English home language speaker with rudimentary isiXhosa and an evenly proficient isiXhosa/English bilingual. While the use of two or more languages has been advocated in language in education policies for more than 20 years (Bengu, 1997; DBE, 2011), this educational aim is easy to ignore when one operates in a university context where English is the dominant language, and within a course which focuses on the teaching of English and building teachers' proficiency in English.

The course intention is to develop teachers' pedagogical content knowledge of English (Shulman, 1987). This means that there is a dual focus on:

- English content knowledge of core language skills (listening/understanding, speaking, reading/viewing, writing, grammar), basic literary studies, and related theory such as genre and critical language awareness, and;
- pedagogical knowledge of practical and procedural classroom teaching decisions including sequence, pacing and cognitive content of lessons and an understanding of learning theory and assessment.

Teachers sit in groups of about six per table and course lecturers make an effort to engage teachers dialogically in interactive tasks and activities designed to give them a lived experience of the participatory, learner-centered pedagogies advocated by the school curriculum (DBE, 2011).

During group work tasks, we have observed that the teachers often draw on their full repertoire of languages, comprising English, Afrikaans, isiXhosa and seSotho rather than simply the language of instruction, English. We encourage them to do so, based on the distinction between exploratory and presentational talk (Barnes, 1992). It is worth noting that the dominant languages the teachers speak are English and isiXhosa, while Afrikaans and seSotho are the home languages of some of their learners, and because the teachers have become used to speaking these languages with their learners, some tend to do the same with their peers in the BEd class. Since the course caters for teachers who are second language speakers of English, epistemic access entails improving their proficiency in and pedagogical content knowledge of English. Thus, the purpose of exploratory talk is to clarify ideas and understanding in pairs or groups. In this relaxed context, accurate language usage or the particular language(s) used, are not as important as conceptual and epistemic access.

In contrast, presentational talk is more formal, meant to display the speaker's disciplinary knowledge, and is usually directed to the whole class, or occurs in response to questions asked by the lecturer. Here it is important for the speaker to pay attention to accurate, grammatical English usage in order to build and demonstrate proficiency in English, and also because English is the language of assessment. We believe that encouraging students to draw on their full language repertoire during exploratory talk is useful for facilitating epistemic access and conceptual clarity, affirming of students' multilingualism and can provide a lived classroom experience of 'safe houses' (Pratt, 1991) for the teachers. This practice of encouraging students to draw on their full language repertoire as a form of scaffolding makes translanguaging an ameliorative strategy; the potential of a transformative role for translanguaging is not engaged when English remains the sole language for presentational talk and high stakes written assessment tasks. Consequently, the transformative potential of indigenous African languages in formal spoken domains and written assessment is not explored. Despite these ambivalent linguistic practices of encouraging students to draw on their full language repertoire for informal, mainly oral, tasks, but with English being the language of written tasks and assessment, we expected that students would be as willing to switch between their home language(s) and English in a written task as they are for oral tasks. Our thought was that as the task was specifically one for conceptual clarification, and not for assessment, that the students would feel free to draw on their full language repertoire.

In the students' second year, an assignment on language-in-education policy requires students to read various policy documents, research articles and newspapers articles in order to write an essay on the role of English in South African schooling. Included in a course reader are source texts such as the South African Language in Education Policy (Bengu, 1997), the distinction between Basic Interpersonal Linguistic Competence and Cognitive Academic Language Proficiency (Cummins, 1984), Ruiz (1984), Probyn (2015), Heugh (2006), and

Gibbons's (2002) genre-based language and literacy pedagogy. The essay required nuanced discussion of concepts such as additive and subtractive bilingualism, proficiency levels in a first or second language required for complex, higher order thinking to make sense of abstract, decontextualised texts, as well as relating these to teachers' own personal and professional experiences. The assignment brief read:

> Write an essay in which you discuss language in education policy and the role of English in South African education. In your discussion, refer to policy documents, language policy and educational research, language and literacy models, and your own classroom/professional experience.

We had taught students the Cornell or split-page summary, but did not specifically ask them to use it in preparation for this assignment. This form of summarising can create opportunities for epistemic access in a multilingual class, as it offers a way of extending bi- and multilingualism in writing. It involves drawing a line down the page, about one third from the left side. The wider, right side is to record notes and main ideas, while the left side is for cues: Key words, diagrams, questions. Below these two vertical columns, the student condenses the information into two or three short sentences, running horizontally across the page. While the notes in the right-hand column based on a text (or lecture) are likely to be in English, we encouraged students to use especially the left-hand column to write concepts or pose questions in a language of their choice, not necessarily English. In a sense, we hoped to extend their bilingual and multilingual practice of exploratory (and, occasionally, presentational) talk into their writing.

Two students misunderstood additive bilingualism, a key concept for this essay discussed in certain recommended academic readings, Heugh (2006) and Koch (2015). In response, we explicitly asked the two students to use both isiXhosa and English in a split-page summary to clarify their conceptual understanding of additive bilingualism so as to consider bilingualism historically in South African schooling, and in the contemporary context of their own schools. Our intention was that the split-page summary could serve as a contact zone where these students could use bilingual interactional strategies in writing to engage the concepts in the academic text written in English with their own ideas and experiences of schooling.

Drawing on their linguistic repertoires would also enable the students to insert themselves into their summaries and the texts they read. Having a choice of drawing on their linguistic repertoire meant that the students' proficiency in English was not necessarily a prerequisite for epistemic access and negotiating meaning. Their summaries, while in English and isiXhosa in two columns on a single page, were not standard split-page summaries or instances of translanguaging in writing, but a hybrid form between translation and translanguaging.

Theoretical Contestations of Translanguaging

Though Heugh (2015) states that translanguaging is theoretically contested, Baker (2011, p. 288) has defined translanguaging as "the process of making meaning, shaping experiences, understandings and knowledge through two languages. Both languages are used in an integrated and coherent way to organise and mediate mental processes in learning". In a classroom context, translanguaging is a conscious, deliberate process planned by the teacher to enable learners to take full advantage of the language repertoire of all the learners.

Empirically in South Africa, it is the case that the educational value of translanguaging has been asserted in the oral mode in educational contexts, whether in school (Probyn, 2015) or university (Madiba, 2014; Makalela, 2014), but more rarely in the written mode. Makalela (2015, p. 16) in his analysis of translanguaging in a primary school setting found that "When more than one language is used to access the same content, the learners develop a deeper understanding of the subject matter". The issue of how this 'deeper understanding' is constructed linguistically across the two (or more) languages is not clear, nor is it clear whether the teacher's pedagogy was the conscious, deliberate, planned process envisaged by Baker (2011).

Mawonga, Maseko & Nkomo (2014) provide an instance of translanguaging at university where a concept or metaphor in one language was used to explain a similar concept in another language. In a politics course, the isiXhosa expression *ukulawula ngegqudu* literally, 'to control with a stick', was used as a metaphor to explain patriarchy and paternalism in a culturally embedded way (Mawonga, Maseko & Nkomo, 2014, p. 71).

In a rare study of translanguaging in the written mode at university, Canagarajah (2011b, p. 404) found that a multilingual student writing a formal academic text employed four broad translanguaging strategies. These categories cover the basic functional grammar components of writing, namely, the contextual, personal, social, and textual:

> (a) Recontextualization strategies: Gauging the congeniality of the context for codemeshing and shaping ecology to favor one's multilingual practices; (b) voice strategies: Basing communication on one's own positionality and making textual spaces for one's linguistic strengths and resources; (c) interactional strategies: Negotiating meaning on an equal footing with readers and helping them negotiate effectively; and (d) textualization strategies: Orientating to the text as a multimodal social practice and adopting process-oriented composing strategies for effective text development.

Reflexive Pedagogy in Practice

The pedagogical issue we explored was how we could build on our own and the students' linguistic repertoire to enhance learning and epistemic access. The essay topic required the students to read South African language in education policy, some research, and in the light of this reading, to consider their own practice and experience as bi- and multilingual teachers of English to bi- and multilingual learners.

In class, given the complexity of this essay as preparation for this task, students did guided reading of key articles in groups, focusing on the structure of argument in academic writing—the claims researchers made and the nature of the evidence and research they produced to support their claims. The students also completed mind maps which they shared in class discussion to summarise and connect their understandings of the topic before they wrote their essays.

The two teachers, given the pseudonyms Gcobani (male) and Nandipha (female), were asked to write a bilingual isiXhosa-English split-page summary to clarify misconceptions in their essays (Appendix 1). Gcobani was asked to summarise Heugh (2006), while Nandipha summarised Koch (2015). However, both focused on summarising Koch. In trying to understand the decisions they made when they wrote the task, the summaries were followed up with an interview. Both teachers were asked the same questions except for one extra question that Gcobani answered concerning the fact that he decided to summarise the Koch (2015) article instead of the Heugh (2006) article.

In reflecting on this pedagogical cycle (from the design of the materials, to the essay, feedback, and students' grappling with misconceptions), transformative pedagogy (García, Johnson & Seltzer, 2016) was a helpful tool. The elements of transformative pedagogy (García, Johnson & Seltzer, 2016): Stance (teachers' standpoint and values), design (lesson planning and sequencing), and shift (teachers' ongoing decisions during a lesson) provided a means for the lecturers to interrogate not only practical aspects of their pedagogy, but also the more ideological dimensions. These are often harder to uncover when dealing with one's own language investments and bilingual vulnerabilities.

Translanguaging in Writing

When asked if writing the bilingual summary was useful in their learning, both Gcobani and Nandipha responded in the affirmative. Gcobani stated that:

> The understanding becomes deeper in your own language . . . when you come with it in isiXhosa, your own indigenous language, there is a meaning that is attached to it but I cannot fully describe what is it but the understanding just becomes better.

He might not be able to describe what it is that makes the understanding better, but his response is quite clear on the relationship between translanguaging and better chances of learning.

Below is an analysis of how Gcobani and Nandipha used their dominant language (isiXhosa), voice and interactional strategies in summarising across isiXhosa and English.

Voice Strategies

Both Gcobani and Nandipha had an opening, orientating paragraph at the start of their split-page summaries; Gcobani's was in isiXhosa, while Nandipha's was in English, which if taken as indicating their "positioning in [their] writing" (Canagarajah, 2011b) may mean that Gcobani affirms an African identity, while Nandipha affirms an aspirational English identity.

However, Nandipha's response to why she wrote her orientation to the task in English only was "I didn't think of translating even the introduction from English to isiXhosa because it was Monica [the English-speaking lecturer] that requested me to do that". This response, rather than indicating her own positioning as a writer, instead shows that she had the reader in mind when she wrote the orientation to the task.

Gcobani's response when asked why his orientation to the task was in isiXhosa was that "It was influenced by pride of being an African". Gcobani's identity seems to be the driving force behind his decisions in this writing, also illustrated in his response why he wrote a Koch summary instead of the Heugh summary "... he was more appealing to my education and of others because he was dealing more with South African education of which we are dealing with".

The Heugh (2006) article focuses on African education whereas the focus of the Koch (2015) article is South African education. In other words, Gcobani was drawn to the Koch article because he could see himself in the article and felt his voice had a better chance of coming out in the South African based article.

The voice strategy used by Gcobani in the rest of his summary provides evidence of an African, even Pan-African, identity when he refers to an African language speaker as "*Umntwana womAfrica*" (an African child). The way he refers to African language speakers uses an isiXhosa expression "*Umntwana womAfrica*" (line 12) commonly used by people with Black Consciousness or Pan-Africanist views[1] when they affectionately refer to anyone born in Africa, young or old.

On the other hand, one of Nandipha's voice strategies in English introduces a nuance in the meaning of the original text. She refers to "African children" as "kubantwana bomthonyama" (line 1), meaning "indigenous children". Although this does not necessarily change the meaning of the original text, it creates the impression that she believes that Africans are the rightful, original people of the country. Similar to Gcobani, her use of "children" rather than "learners" signals affection in her voice strategy.

In another instance, her voice strategy in the isiXhosa summary changed the meaning of the original text and was different from her English summary. Because she is an African and her home language is isiXhosa, she conflates "African language" with "Home language" even though there are 11 official languages in South Africa, two of which are not African languages. Since English and Afrikaans are also home languages, rather than referring to an African language as a home language she could have written "*Ulwimi lwesintu*" or "*Ulwimi lwaseAfrika*".

Interactional Strategies

Gcobani's interactional strategies in his isiXhosa summary involved elaboration. The elaboration strategy he used is intended to engage the reader and make things clearer to avoid ambiguity. For example, he used "*oko kukuthi*" (line 21) meaning "this means", which does not appear in his English summary.

In addition, he uses a form of personification using the isiXhosa prefix '*u*', usually reserved for people, to refer to curriculum terms and issues. The personification in his summary occurs when he refers to ANA (Annual National Assessment) as '*uANA*' and CAPS (Curriculum Assessment Policy Statements) as '*uCAPS*' (line 21). In isiXhosa, the prefix is a telling difference between a thing and a person. Since these are objects, not people, it would have been grammatically more accurate to use the impersonal prefix '*i*', '*iANA*' and '*iCAPS*'. Attaching an isiXhosa prefix before an English word is a common practice which Plüddeman (2007) refers to as "Xhosalising". Gcobani also writes '*ingxaki*' (problem) as '*uNomji*' (line 6). '*UNomji*' is a shortened version of '*uMjijiswano*' which means a bone of contention. However, this version includes the prefix '*No*' which changes it to a name and, by so doing, makes it sound like an ordinary conversation with someone or about someone. Gcobani's usage of the prefixes '*u*' and '*No*' shows an interactional strategy of summarising the article in a rather conversational manner.

When asked in the interview why he wrote "foundation phase" in an isiXhosa summary, his response was that "It was for clarification and also referring to my audience that since these are the concepts and terms that they are used it would be easy for that person to go straight to what he wants". His audience awareness and making a concerted effort to accommodate the reader are very clear in both his summary and interview and acknowledge his understanding of texts as being dialogic and interactive.

Conclusion

As lecturers, taking on the challenge of teaching about bilingualism as dynamic rather than additive (Celic & Seltzer, 2011) and modelling it in our practice requires a shift in our stance. Bi- and multiliterate isiXhosa-English teams of lecturers would need to collaborate in designing tasks, tests and teaching bilingually, and mark in teams with proficient bilingual colleagues. This shift in stance would also need to be demonstrated to students in the course delivery so that they will feel free to produce work across their language repertoire, so that the reader they have in mind won't be a lecturer who is solely an 'English specialist'.

A potential benefit of the lived experience of bringing together students' home languages and English in order to gain conceptual meaning, especially for teachers of English, is that they can draw on this in their own classroom practice. In their remote rural Eastern Cape classrooms where English is often more of a foreign language than a second language, this can only have positive learning outcomes.

For the students, the bilingual summaries created a bilingual contact zone where they used voice and interactional strategies to engage with an academic text in order to gain a deeper understanding. Tapping into their linguistic repertoires also enabled the students to insert themselves into their summaries, and to express in original ways how they would like to see themselves in the texts they read. Having a choice of drawing on their linguistic repertoire meant that the students' proficiency in English was not necessarily a prerequisite for epistemic access and negotiating meaning. It realises the possibility of Pratt's (1991) recommendation to embrace diversity in our classrooms by creating "safe houses" where our students will feel safe to draw on their linguistic repertoires without feeling that their identity is rejected because of the rejection of their languages while negotiating meaning. It is a way of redesigning the quiet but violent denial to epistemic access resulting from the dominance of English over African languages.

Appendix

Nandipha

This essay reflects on the Language in Education Policy and the role of English in South African education. Language is not just a means of communication, but also a tool that people use to express their thoughts, values and identities. Language policy supports teaching and learning of all other languages required by learners or used by communities in South Africa. If language policy is put in place, full participation in societies can be promoted. I will concentrate more on what Koch (2015) proposes with regard to language policy. Her proposal will be summarised in English as well as in isiXhosa.

NANDIPHA

English paraphrasing	Isixhosa paraphrasing	Researcher translation of Isixhosa
• Koch (2015) raises three developments as contradictions to the LiEP, namely the Incremental Introductions of African Languages	• UKoch uphakamisa imiba emithathu engquzulanayo ne LiEP eyile, Incremental Introductions of African Languages (IIAL of 2012),	• Koch raises three issues which are contradicting with the LiEP namely, Incremental Introductions of African Languages (IIAL of 2012), Annual National Assessments

NANDIPHA Continued

English paraphrasing	Isixhosa paraphrasing	Researcher translation of Isixhosa
(IIAL of 2012), the Annual National Assessments (ANA of 2011) and the Curriculum and Assessment Policy Statement (2011). • She questions the introduction of a third and compulsory language through the IIAL, which must be an African language, whereas the LiEP already provides this. • This provision does not benefit African children at all because volumes of literacy material are still written in English and Afrikaans, so a second additional African language will only add unnecessary workload on both learners and teachers. • The ANA papers are nationally controlled. Mathematics and Language tests are administered in English and Afrikaans from grade 4 to 9. • These tests therefore reinforce the exclusion of African languages as the languages of teaching and learning beyond the foundation phase. • This is a violation of childrens' language rights that are outlined	*iAnnual National Assessments (ANA of 2011) ne Curriculum and Assessment Policy Statement (2011).* • *Uphikisana nokuvezwa kolwimi lwesithathu olunyanzelisayo kwi IIAL okumele ukuba lube lulwimi lwenkobe ngelixa uLiEP ekwathetha into enye ngolu lwimi lwesithathu.* • *Olu lungiselo alwenzi abantwana abafunda ngolwimi lwesintu baxhamle kuba imiqulu encedisana nokufunda ibhalwe ngesiBhulu nesiNgesi, ngoko ukongezwa kweelwimi zesintu zesibini kwandisa umthwalo ogqithisileyo kubafundi kwakunye nootitshala.* • *Amaphepha kaANA ezibalo neelwimi abhalwa ngesiNgesi nesiBhulu ukusuka kwibanga lesine ukuya kwelethoba.* • *Ezi mviwo ke ngoko zigxininisa ekukhutshweni kolwimi lwenkobe njengolwimi lokufunda nokufundisa kumanqanaba angentla kwabafundi abaqalayo.* • *Oku kuyaphikisana namalungelo abantwana ngokolwimi njengoko kubhaliwe kumgaqo siseko womzantsi Afrika.*	(ANA of 2011) and Curriculum and Assessment Policy Statement (2011). • She disagrees with the introduction of a third and compulsory language in IIAL which is supposed to be a home language when the LiEP says the same thing about this third language • This provision does not make learners who learn in an African language to benefit because the material that helps with learning is written in Afrikaans and English, so the addition of a second additional African language adds an excessive workload on both learners and teachers. • The ANA papers of Mathematics and Languages are written in English and Afrikaans from grade four to nine. • These tests therefore emphasize on the exclusion of the home language as a language of learning and teaching in grades above the foundation phase. • This is in contradiction with the children's

continued

NANDIPHA Continued

English paraphrasing	Isixhosa paraphrasing	Researcher translation of Isixhosa
in the South African Constitution. • The third and last contradiction with LiEP according to Koch is CAPS which provides for two languages in the curriculum namely, home and first additional languages. • For African children, home language is an African language whereas for Afrikaans and English speaking children, Afrikaans and English are their home languages respectively. • The first additional language for African learners is English which also happens to be the language of learning and teaching from grade 4 onwards. • This favours English speaking learners only. African children struggle to make a change from their home language to English when they reach grade 4. • Because of what has been discussed above African children are unable to reach their high competencies in both their home language and English.	• *Umbandela wesithathu nowokugqibela ophikisana noLiEP ngokukaKoch ngu CAPS olungiselela iilwimi ezimbini kwikharityulam, ezi lulwimi lwenkobo nelokuqala olongezelelweyo.* • *Kubantwana bomthonyama ulwimi lwasekhaya lulo olwenkobo ngelixa kubantwana abathetha isiBhulu nesiNgesi zisebenza njengolwimi lwenkobo.* • *Ulwimi lokuqala olongezelelweyo kubantwana bomthonyama sisiNgesi oluphinda lusetyenziswe njengolwimi lokufunda nokufundisa ukusuka kwibanga lesine ukunyuka.* • *Oku kulungiselela abantwana abalwimi lusisiNgesi kuphela. Abantwana bomthonyama bayasokola ukwenza inguqu ukusuka kulwimi lwabo ukuya kwisiNgesi xa befika kwibanga lesine.* • *Ngenxa yokusele kuxoxiwe ngasentla, abantwana bomthonyama abakwazi ukufikelela enkcochoyini kwiilwimi zabo zenkobe nakwisiNgesi*	language rights as written in the South African Constitution. • The third and last issue that contradicts the LiEP according to Koch is CAPS that provides for two languages in the curriculum, which are home language and first additional. • For indigenous children the language spoken at home is the home language while for Afrikaans and English speakers they function/work as a home language • The first additional language for the indigenous children is English which is again used as the language of learning and teaching from grade four onwards. • This favours the English-speaking learners only. The indigenous children struggle with the transition from their language to English when they are in the fourth grade. • Because of what has been discussed above, the indigenous children cannot reach high competencies in their home languages and in English.

Gcobani

Ilwimi zase Africa kufanele zisetyenziswe eziklasini okanye emagumbini okufundela nje ngezinye zezixhobo ezingcathu zokuphuhlisa nokukhulisa izinga lemfundo eliphezulu.
African languages should be used in classrooms as one of the tools to develop and grow the level of education.

GCOBANI

English paraphrasing	Isixhosa paraphrasing	Researcher translation of Isixhosa
• In 2012 the National Department of Education proposed a policy to specifically deal with the addition and introduction of African languages in schools, of which was being piloted in schools in 2014/2015 in most provinces to kick start in 2016 until 2025 per grade. The purpose was to add the third language in the foundation phase, not only as a medium of instruction but as a subject too. This language is going to be compulsory to all learners. • The Department of Education added another LiEP called ANA in grade one, six and nine in Maths and languages. The problem is that these subjects are conducted and assessed in English and Afrikaans advantaging those learners who speak those languages at the	• Ngonyaka ka 2012 Isebe lezeMfundo lika Zwelonke lathi lanesiphakamiso somgaqo-nkqubo ozakujongana ngqo nokufakelelwa nokuziswa kweelwimi zaseAfrika ezikolweni, nkqubo leyo yayisalingwa ngo 2014 ukuya ku 2015, kumaphondo amaninzi yayizakuqala ngo 2016 ukuya ku 2025 unyaka nonyaka ukusuka kwibanga R. Injongo yayikukongeza ulwimi lwesithathu kwizinga lasekuqaleni (foundation phase) ingabi lulwimi lokufunda nokufundisa qha koko nanjengesifundo. Olu lwimi luzakunyanzeleka kubo bonke abafundi. • Isebe lezeMfundo longeze enye inkqubo-mgaqo wokufunda wee lwimi obizwa ngo ANA kwibanga lokuqàla, elesithandathu nelesithoba kwizibalo neelwimi. UNomji usekubeni ezizifundo zifundiswa zibuye zivavanywe ngesiNgesi nesiBhulu.	• In the year 2012 the National Department of Education had a proposal about a policy that would focus specifically on the addition and introduction of African languages in schools, such a programme was piloted from 2014 to 2015, in many provinces it was going to start from 2016 to 2025 year by year from grade R. The purpose was to add a third language in the foundation phase (foundation phase) not only as a language of learning and teaching but as a subject too. This language is going to be compulsory to all learners. • The Department of Education added another language learning policy called ANA in the first, sixth and ninth grade in Math and languages. The problem is that these subjects are

continued

GCOBANI Continued

English paraphrasing	Isixhosa paraphrasing	Researcher translation of Isixhosa
expense of African language speakers, for when they are assessed these two languages are used. • The third contradiction the Department of Education introduced to address the issue of African languages as language of teaching and learning was CAPS. These languages/African languages would not make the time due to the power the English and Afrikaans have in the South African society. Here home language is taken as an option to both English and Afrikaans speakers, the same with the African languages. African learners will continue to use English as a medium of instruction, compromising any chances of growing an African language. CAPS has utterly failed to address the problem of the inequality of languages.	*Nto leyo ebabeka kumnyinyiva wokuphumelela abo ezi lwimi zimbini ziluwimi lwenkobe. Yena umtwana womAfrika okungezolwimi zakhe zenkobe imenyusele amathuba amaninzi okungezi kakuhle kuvavanyo.* • *Olunye uluvo olungqubanayo olwathi lwaziswa lisebe lezeMfundo ukukhawulelana nengxaki yeelwimi zase Afrika ekufundeni nasekufundiseni ngu CAPS. Apha kuCAPS iilwimi zase Afrika azibonakali zinganalo ithuba lokugqama ngenxa yamandla nobungangamela besilungu nesibhulu ngenxa yooRhulumente bangaphambili. Apha ke ulwimi lwenkobe lusetyenziswa njengolwimi lokuzikhethela xa befuna abo besilungu nesibhulu njengakwiilwimi zeAfrika. Abafundi bamaAfrika bazakuqhubekeka besebenzisa isilungu njengolwimi lokuxhumana ekufundiseni ezikolweni. Oko kukuthi uCAPS wohlulekile ukulungisa ingxaki yokungalingani kweelwimi.*	taught and assessed in English and Afrikaans. Which means that it provides an opportunity of success to home language speakers of these two languages. This increases many chances of not doing well in assessment for he/she the African child who is not a home language speaker of these languages. • Another clashing view that was introduced by the Department of Education in addressing the problem of African languages in learning and teaching is CAPS. Here in CAPS the African languages do not seem to have the opportunity to shine because of the power and domination of English and Afrikaans because of the previous governments. Here the African language is taken as an option when the English and Afrikaans speakers want to, the same with the African languages. The African learners will continue to use English as a language of communication in teaching in schools. This means that CAPS failed in rectifying the problem of the inequality of languages.

Note

1 Robert Sobukwe (1959) offers a classic understanding of Pan-Africanism based on political allegiance rather than skin color or nationality, that Africans are: "everyone who owes his [or her] only loyalty to Afrika and is prepared to accept the democratic rule of an African majority".

References

Badat, S. (2016). *Deciphering the meanings, and explaining the South African higher education student protests of 2015–2016.* Retrieved from www.ru.ac.za/media/rhodes university/content/equityinstitutionalculture/documents/Dr%20Saleem%20Badat%20-%20The%20Student%20Protests%20of%202015–16%20Final%20Draft-10March2016.pdf.

Baker, C. (2011). Bilingualism: Definitions and distinctions. In C. Baker (Ed.), *Foundations of bilingual education and biliteracy* (pp. 1–16). Clevedon, UK: Multilingual Matters.

Barnes, D. (1992). The role of talk in learning. In K. Norman (Ed.), *Thinking voices: The work of the National Oracy Project* (pp. 123–128). London, UK: Hodder & Stoughton.

Bengu, S. M. E. (1997). *A new language policy in general and further education.* Pretoria, South Africa: Department of Education.

Busch, B., Busch, L., & Press, K. (2014). *Interviews with Neville Alexander.* Pietermaritzburg, South Africa: University of KwaZulu-Natal Press.

Canagarajah, S. (2011a). Translanguaging in the classroom: Emerging issues for research and pedagogy. *Applied Linguistics Review, 2*(1), 1–28.

Canagarajah, S. (2011b). Codemeshing in academic writing: Identifying teachable strategies of translanguaging. *The Modern Language Journal, 95*(3), 401–417.

Celic, C., & Seltzer, K. (2011). *Translanguaging: A Cuny-NYSIEB guide for educators.* Retrieved from www.nysieb.ws.gc.cuny.edu/files/2012/06/FINAL-Translanguaging-Guide-With-Cover-1.pdf

Constitution of South Africa. Act 108. South African Government. (1996).

Cummins, J. (1984). *Bilingualism and special education: Issues in assessment and pedagogy.* Clevedon, UK: Multilingual Matters.

Department of Basic Education. (2011). *Curriculum and assessment policy statement (CAPS) First additional language.* Pretoria, South Africa: Government Printer.

Ferreira, A., & Mendelowitz, B. (2009). Creating a dynamic contact zone: An undergraduate English course as multilingual pedagogic space. *English Teaching: Practice and Critique, 8*(2), 54–79.

García, O., Johnson, S., & Seltzer, K. (2016). *The Translanguaging classroom: Leveraging bilingualism for learning.* Philadelphia, PA: Caslon.

Gardiner, M. (2008). *Education in rural areas.* Johannesburg, South Africa: Centre for Education Policy Development.

Gibbons, P. (2002). *Scaffolding language, scaffolding learning.* Portsmouth, N. H.: Heinemann.

Heleta, S. (2016). Decolonisation of higher education: Dismantling epistemic violence and Eurocentrism in South Africa. *Transformation in Higher Education, 1*(1), a9.

Hendricks, M. (2014). The nuts and bolts of literacy development in English as a second language: Evidence from intermediate phase classrooms. *The International Journal of Literacies, 20*(3), 1–19.

Hendricks, M. (2016). Multilingualism, diversity and access: The future for the ISEA. In M. Hendricks (Ed.), *ISEA 1964–2014—A research institute serving people* (pp. 160–173). Grahamstown: NISC.

Heugh, K. (2006). Without language, everything is nothing in education. *Human Sciences Research Council Review, 4*(3), 8–9.

Heugh, K. (2015). Epistemologies in multilingual education: Translanguaging and genre—companions in conversation with policy and practice. *Language and Education, 29*(3), 280–285. doi: 10.1080/09500782.2014.994529

Janks, H. (2000). Domination, access, diversity and design: A synthesis for critical literacy education. *Educational Review, 52*(2), 175–186.

Janks, H. (2014). *Doing critical literacy*. New York: Routledge.

Kaschula, R. (2013, May 25). African languages key. *Saturday Dispatch*, p.15.

Koch, E. (2015). The language-in education policy—exploring the contradictions. *Izifundo, 1*, 3–5.

Krause, S., & Prinsloo, M. (2016). Translanguaging in a township primary school: Policy and practice. *Southern African Linguistics and Applied Language Studies, 34*(4), 347–357.

Kunene, F. (2016). UFS: Same racial attacks, different day. *Daily Maverick*. Retrieved from www.dailymaverick.co.za/opinionista/2016-02-26-ufs-same-racial-attacks-different-day/#.VtRHQebGpnA.

Madiba, M. (2014). Promoting co literacy through multilingual glossaries: A translanguaging approach. In L. Hibbert & C. van der Walt (Eds.), *Multilingual universities in South Africa* (pp. 68–87). Bristol, UK: Multilingual Matters.

Mahlakoana, T. (2017, April 23). PhD in isiXhosa hailed as milestone. *Sunday Independent*, p. 5.

Makalela, L. (2014). Teaching indigenous African languages to speakers of other African languages: The effects of translanguaging for multilingual development. In L. Hibbert & C. van der Walt (Eds.), *Multilingual universities in South Africa* (pp. 88–104). Bristol, UK: Multilingual Matters.

Makalela, L. (2015). Translanguaging as a vehicle for epistemic access: Cases for reading comprehension and multilingual interactions. *Per Linguam, 31*(1), 15–29.

Maseko, P. (2014). Multilingualism at work in South African higher education: From policy to practice. In L. Hibbert & C. van der Walt (Eds.), *Multilingual universities in South Africa* (pp. 28–45). Bristol, UK: Multilingual Matters.

Mawonga, S., Maseko, P., & Nkomo, D. (2014). The centrality of translation in the development of African languages for use in South African higher education institutions: A case study of a Political Science English-isiXhosa glossary in a South African university. (Special Edition) *Alternation, 13*, 55–79.

Plüddeman, P. (2007). Xhosalising Kirstenbosch. *LEAP News, 14*, 18–20. University of Cape Town: Project for the Study of Alternative Education in South Africa.

Pratt. M. (1991). Arts of the contact zone. *Profession*, 33–40. Retrieved from www.jstor.org/stable/25595469.

Probyn, M. (2015). Pedagogical translanguaging: bridging discourses in South African science classrooms. *Language and Education, 29*(3), 218–234. doi: 10.1080/09500782.2014.994525

Reeves, C., & Robinson, M. (2010). Am I 'qualified' to teach? The implications of a changing school system for criteria for teacher qualifications. *Journal of Education, 50*, 7–34.

Ruíz, R. (1984). Orientations in language planning. *Journal of the National Association for Bilingual Education, 8*(2), 15–34.

Shulman, L. (1987). Knowledge and teaching: Foundations of the new reform. *Harvard Educational Review, 57*(1), 1–22.

Sobukwe, R. (1959, April). Inaugural Speech. South African History Online. Retrieved from www.sahistory.org.za/archive/robert-sobukwe-inaugural-speech-april-1959/.

South Africa. (1996). *Constitution of South Africa.* (Act no.108 of 1996). Pretoria: Government Printer.

South Africa. (2012). *Use of Official Languages Act.* (Act no.12 of 2012). Pretoria: Government Printer.

South Africa. (2013). *Incremental Introduction of African Languages.* Pretoria: Government Printer.

Statistics South Africa (StatsSA). 2011. *Census 2011.* Retrieved from www.statssa.gov.za/census/census_2011/census_products/Census_2011_Census_in_brief.pdf.

13

FROM LINGUISTIC PREPARATION TO DEVELOPING A TRANSLINGUAL MINDSET

Possible Implications of Plurilingualism for Researcher Education

Jane Andrews, Richard Fay, and Ross White

Introduction

In this chapter, we bring together a) some lines of literature-based thinking resonant with the focus of this volume, in particular, with Kubota's (2014) reframings of pluri-/multi-lingualism; and b) some researcher reflections on a case study rich in linguistic insights re researcher praxis despite not arising from a language-oriented discipline. In this, our purpose is to consider how researcher education vis-à-vis language might support research, in diverse disciplines, which is undertaken multilingually. Bringing these ideas together also enables us to foreground an important move in our thinking about the linguistic aspects of researcher education; namely, the move from focusing on researchers' linguistic preparation for fieldwork to focusing on their development of what we, following Canagarajah's (2013) work, term a "translingual mindset".

With regard to a) above, we begin by reviewing how applied researchers have prepared themselves to engage with participants in linguistically-diverse contexts (e.g. Tremlett, 2009; Gibb & Danero Iglesias, 2017) and then consider how recent, reframed thinking about linguistic diversity—e.g. translanguaging (Blackledge & Creese, 2010) and translingual practice (Canagarajah, 2013)—may offer valuable insights for such applied researchers as they design their studies, consult diverse literatures, carry out fieldwork, undertake data analysis and interpretation, and represent their work in written and/or oral form. These two areas of literature inform the two areas of our researcher education proposals, i.e. linguistic preparation and the development of a translingual mindset.

With regard to b) above, our discussion has its roots in a body of research activity—specifically, a small network project and a large grant[1]—which focused on what we term "researching multilingually" (RM) (Holmes et al., 2013, 2016). To this end, we briefly introduce these projects before presenting the interdisciplinary *Translating Distress* (TD) case study located in the second, larger of the projects. Researcher reflections—from and on the Uganda-based fieldwork component of the TD case study—complete the coverage of what has informed our researcher education proposals.

We conclude the chapter by arguing that one way in which researcher education might become more attentive to the pluri-/multi-lingual turn would be through its contribution to the development of a translingual researcher mindset. We see this as being of value to researchers across disciplines rather than for those studies where languages might traditionally be considered as part of a researcher's toolkit (i.e. in disciplines such as linguistic ethnography, anthropology, translation studies).

Linguistic Preparation for Research

Using the term "linguistic preparation" (Fay et al., 2015), we have previously reviewed the argument—found within distinctive academic disciplines (e.g. anthropology) and areas of professional practice and study (e.g. study abroad)—that a period of time spent in a foreign language environment needs to be prepared for with appropriate language (and intercultural) learning experiences.

For the discipline of anthropology, Tremlett (2009) notes that, while language learning has been central to researchers' engagements in fieldwork, little has been published on the processes of developing linguistic competence. Rather, it seems to be assumed that, because linguistic preparation has occurred, the linguistic competence of the researcher for the particular fieldwork site concerned will successfully facilitate the research and writings based on it. Extending Tremlett's work, Gibb and Danero-Iglesias (2017) note the "silence" surrounding the impact of ethnographers' developing knowledge of languages on their research processes. Earlier, but relatedly, in reflections on the experience of fieldwork undertaken collaboratively with interpreters in the North American Arctic, the ethnomusicologist Beaudry (1997) concluded that she under-appreciated the significance of relationships mediated through languages and cultures prior to engaging in her fieldwork.

Issues of cross-cultural communication and linguistic diversity have also been problematised by scholars (e.g. Hsin-Chun Tsai et al., 2004; Watson, 2011) in health-based disciplines (including counselling). Watson (2011, p. 25) notes how "rarely addressed" are: Issues of multilingualism, including counsellors' own community language learning to support their work with their clients; and consideration of effective ways of collaboration between counsellors and interpreters. Hsin-Chun Tsai et al. (2004, p. 17) warn that, in health research, a lack of available "well trained bilingual and bicultural" staff has meant that some ethnic groups have remained under-studied. While not dismissing the "logistic and analytic challenges" of working across languages and cultural groups, they alert us to the fact that training and preparation needs for health researchers have not been sufficiently attended to.

To summarise, this brief consideration of studies from an illustrative range of disciplines (anthropology and health) reveals the value attached to linguistic preparatory work for everyone researching, collaborating and working in contexts characterised by the linguistically-diverse resources available. However, the extent to which this preparatory work is supported by well-conceptualised training courses and activities appears to be variable. Further, the anthropology-focused writings on how researchers-as-language-learners might prepare themselves for an intensive fieldwork period immersed in a particular linguistic and cultural context can be critiqued for the assumptions being made about distinctive languages used in predictable and stable ways in predictable locations. The health writing about research-practitioners-as-language-and-culture-mediators can be similarly critiqued. Such assumptions about language and languages stand in contrast to those, for example, of Kubota (2014) on the pluri-/multi-lingual turn and Heller (2012) on circulating people and circulating languages. It is to these reframed understandings that we now turn.

Moving Towards Translingual Practice in Research

Bearing in mind the above critiques, we are drawn to Heller's (2012, p. 31) image of the ways in which people in the contemporary global context make use of a set of "circulating, constructible and deconstructible resources" including languages. This way suggests to us that preparing researchers for linguistic diversity in their applied research may not be straightforward, and may involve something other than (considerable investment in) the learning of a particular language associated with a particular context and the people in it.

In sociolinguistics, applied linguistics, and linguistic ethnography, researchers report on their generation of research insights into multilingualism-in-context and demonstrate their critical awareness of their own uses of language within their research. The ways in which they do so can inform the suggested move from contextually oversimplified linguistic preparation for researchers to the development of a more nuanced understanding of the language-work. For example, Giampapa (2012), on her use of linguistic ethnography, reflects on her assumptions about her potential insider identity in relation to her heritage and those of her research participants, all Italian-Canadians. She reports on her underestimation—an echo here of the above-mentioned reflections by Beaudry—of the impact of the positionings attributed to her by her research participants, as revealed through their questions to her such as "where are you from?" (2012, p. 102). By way of a second example, in the context of a transnational language, Sámi, in northern Europe, Pietikäinen reports that adult Sámi speakers have concerns about the opportunities and motivation for their children to develop and use their indigenous language due to media influences and tourism demands, among other pressures. As a researcher who shared the languages of the adults and children in the research context, in the Finnish side of Sámiland, Pietikäinen did not need to prepare as such to enter this linguistically-diverse field of study. However, with a linguistic ethnographic framing and an intention to study an endangered language, Pietikäinen chose to approach her research participants predominantly through the visual medium of photography. Meanings about multilingualism in this context were thus generated non-verbally.

Alternative perspectives on understanding linguistic diversity in contemporary life come from sociolinguists and applied linguists of language within the global context of migratory flows (Appadurai, 1990, cited in Block, 2012, p. 51). Examples include Conteh and Meier (2015) who discuss the "multilingual turn" in language education and Blackledge and Creese (2010) who explore children in complementary schools using their languages flexibly and translanguaging together. In this chapter, given our concern for researcher education which acknowledges linguistic complexity and fluidity, we focus on Canagarajah's (2013) concept of "translingual practice". Whereas he uses translingual practice in connection with the challenges of designing language pedagogy in contemporary contexts, we argue that the concept can underpin our proposal that researcher education more effectively attends to the linguistic diversity that researchers engage with, and are part of, in the field.

For Canagarajah (2013), translingual practice is prevalent in cosmopolitan contexts and it has a purpose beyond achieving daily transactions through languages, thereby bringing in expressions of identity through language. In a similar vein to Heller (2012), and Gardner and Martin-Jones (2012), Canagarajah refers to languages as *resources* which are used purposefully by language users in a flexible way as they express who they are to those with whom they seek to develop relationships. To construct his case for conceptualising languages in use in this way, Canagarajah (2013, p. 3) analyses a song by Sri Lankan hip hop artist M.I.A., who draws upon her heritage, experiences and beliefs to rap in a way that uses languages to express her "sociocultural in-betweenness". For Canagarajah, the implication of translingual practice for language learners is that they need to develop *"co-operative dispositions and performative competence for cosmopolitan relationships"* (2013, p. 202). The suggestion is that these dispositions will take language education away from a focus on developing linguistic competence in one or more bounded languages but rather will serve to prepare language learners for more flexible uses of languages in a range of contexts. We suggest that being prepared for a fluid, contextualised use of languages, perhaps serving as an expression of identity or solidarity, will be an important aspect of researcher education for linguistic diversity. In the next section, we set out some ideas we have explored in two funded research projects which have had a focus on what we have named "researching multilingually" (Holmes et al., 2013, 2016).

Researching Multilingually

The objective of the research network project mentioned earlier was the sharing of researcher experiences in order to better understand "researching multilingually" (RM), which we defined as:

> [The ways in which] researchers conceptualise, understand, and make choices about generating, analysing, interpreting and reporting data when more than one language is involved—and the complex negotiated relationships between research and researched as they engaged with one another in multilingual sites.
> (Holmes et al., 2013, p. 297)

To this end, we analysed researcher reflections (from a range of disciplinary backgrounds) on their RM experiences noting what triggered their awareness of the possibilities for undertaking research in this way, and what informed decisions they made in designing and carrying out such research. We learned that multilingual research practice could be applied in all stages of the research process, from engagement with literatures published in a range of languages, to designing studies with attentiveness to the negotiated uses of language by all participants, and with transparency about the handling of linguistic diversity in the processing, analysing, and (re)-presentation of data. However, we also saw that, due to a combination of factors—including the global status of English in academia and research dissemination—researchers might not always make use of their own linguistic resources or those available in their contexts of study, meaning that RM possibilities might not always be taken up where they could be.

From this network project, we identified a prototypical trajectory of developing RM praxis. Thus, researchers, having experienced a triggering moment when they realise that RM is potentially an important dimension to their work (a), might systematically inform themselves about the RM possibilities and complexities (b), and consequently, might be more transparent and purposeful—on which we will say more shortly—in their decision-making about the design of their study and its operationalisation (c). This trajectory has implications for our researcher education proposals, not least because it is such researcher education which might provide the trigger needed for the informed decision-making at the heart of RM praxis. With regard to the connections between b) and c), we argued—as informed by recent ecological understandings of researcher thinking (Fay & Stelma, 2016; Stelma & Fay, 2014; and Stelma, Fay & Zhou, 2013) which focus on the concept of intentionality (akin to the ordinary meaning of "being purposeful")—that, in order to develop a purposeful sense of what RM might mean for them and their work, researchers need to consider all aspects of their linguistic engagement at all stages of their research (including engaging with written texts), and do so prior to, as well as during, their research process.

Researchers might become more informed about the possibilities for, and complexities of, undertaking their research multilingually by considering: i) Research spaces (spatiality); and ii) researcher relationships (relationality). As derived from Davcheva and Fay (2012), our thinking about the spatiality domain involves these four spaces: The researched space (i.e. the linguistic resources available in the phenomenon/context being researched); the research space (i.e. the linguistic resources available in the researcher's home, e.g. in the field and at their desk); the researcher (collaborative) space (i.e. the linguistic resources available through those with whom the researcher works); and the research (re)-presentation space (i.e. the linguistic parameters in place regarding how the research is (re)-presented and disseminated). The relationality domain concerns researchers and the relationships they develop with all those associated with their study, including participants, interpreters, translators, co-researchers, transcribers, gatekeepers and others.

The second project mentioned above—a three-year, interdisciplinary, arts-based project which followed on the network project—had two overarching aims: (1) To research interpreting, translation and multilingual practices in challenging contexts; and (2) while doing so, to evaluate appropriate research methods (traditional and arts-based) and develop theoretical approaches for this type of academic exploration. Within this project, there were five case studies, each located in different disciplinary homes (e.g. anthropology, law), focused on particular contexts (e.g. Glasgow, Gaza, Bulgaria), and each concerned with particular research questions. Taken as a set, these case studies sought to contribute to the overall aims of better understanding what it means to be researching multilingually and—bringing in a new discourse and particular type of context—to language and be languaged (see Phipps, 2011 for a discussion of "languaging") especially in contexts of pain and pressure. We were part of a separate RM Hub which was charged with supporting, working with and learning from the five case studies vis-à-vis RM praxis. The Hub's disciplinary homes lie in language education, applied linguistics, education, and intercultural communication.

This project, and especially the researcher reflections for one case study within it, has prompted us to extend and re-frame our earlier RM thinking. Whereas previously we argued for informed researcher thinking and action regarding the RM possibilities and complexities, we did so largely as framed in non-critical multilingual terms. Thus, we spoke of researchers using their "multiple languages" and of "deciding when to translate from language to another". Implicit in this discourse was the assumption that the linguistic preparation researchers might usefully undertake was to be understood from a perspective of separate linguistic systems mediated through translation and interpretation. The large project, through its over-arching discourse (e.g "What does it mean to language and be languaged?" and "What are the implications for researchers of the languaged nature of human experience?") required us to problematise the "language" element in RM (and in researcher thinking about, and preparation for, RM). This discourse in itself encouraged a move from thinking about RM through the lens of 'languages in research' to the more nuanced lens, one resonating with the ideas discussed in the literature (see Section 2 above), i.e. the lens of 'languaging (in) research'. In the next section, we explore how this discourse-prompt for our developing thinking was also underpinned by the researcher experiences of RM that the project enabled.

The Translating Distress Case Study

Translating Distress (TD), one of the five case studies within the large RM at Borders project, sought to better understand: 1) What happens when emotional distress crosses borders of geography, language, beliefs and practices; and 2) how these various borders impact on the relevance and validity of psychosocial interventions aimed at reducing this distress. It was led by a researcher (hereafter, RW) specialising in the practice-oriented discipline of Global Mental Health (GMH). One fieldwork site within this case study—the one we focus on specifically in this chapter—was in Uganda. It was explicitly located within a GMH research paradigm but, as part of the interdisciplinary ethos and ways of working of the large RM at Borders project, it also involved an applied linguist/educationalist (i.e. RF) from the project's RM Hub. This emergent interdisciplinary collaboration combined with the theorising (discussed above) to stimulate our reframed thinking about linguistic preparation and our valuing of a researcher translingual mindset. The following discussion of the fieldwork is voiced by RF and it focuses primarily on RW's public-facing blog reflections.[2] These blog entries were, in part, shaped by the daily video-diary that the research team collectively maintained. This reflective dimension of the fieldwork was encouraged not only by the overall project brief but also by RF's addition of a specific language-oriented research focus during the GMH-based fieldwork.

The fieldwork took place in the Lira region of northern Uganda, an area in which the local people have experienced major trauma and disruption during many years of war involving the so-called Lord's Resistance Army. The research involved a small team of researchers (from the Universities of Glasgow and Manchester in the UK, and Makerere University in Uganda) working with a larger team of 'local' research assistants, i.e. researchers located in, or who otherwise identified with, the Lira region, and who spoke, among other languages, Lango, the language closely associated within the Langi people who predominate in this region. The fieldwork methodology followed the DIME (Design, Implementation, Monitoring and Evaluation) approach[3] for developing and evaluating psychosocial interventions for mental health difficulties in low and middle-income countries (LMICs). This approach can be seen as recognition of, and as a response to, the ineffectiveness, inappropriacy, and epistemic injustice (Fricker, 2009) potentially arising when diagnostic measures and interventions developed in the High Income Countries (HICs) of the Global North (e.g. the UK) are transported, with little regard for methodological appropriacy (Holliday,

1994), to the LMICs of the Global South (e.g. Uganda). That the applied-research field of GMH is aware of these dangers, and that, through fieldwork methodologies such as DIME, it is addressing them, is something we appreciate; and, thus, the language-oriented reflections reported here should be seen as a strengthening of this GMH endeavour rather than a critique of it *per se*.

Notwithstanding the way in which the DIME methodology represents an operationalisation of GMH's desire for psychosocial action appropriate for the social context concerned, the understanding of "language and context" embedded in this methodology is one of separate linguistic systems (with communication between them mediated through translation and interpreting). Thus, the first phase of the DIME approach involves the rapid elicitation of local understandings of problems (affecting well-being) and identification of existing sources of support for them, local understandings elicited in (what is taken to be) the local language of the (understood as culturally-homogeneous) local population. For the Lira fieldwork, following the lead provided by the DIME approach, the research team assumed that Lango was *the* local language and, accordingly, in advance translated all the English-medium data-generation instruments into this language.

However, Uganda (including the Lira region) is a context—or, better, set of linguistically and culturally overlapping but also differentiated contexts—characterised by great linguistic diversity, and also by significant fluidity. English is the main medium of education in general as well as being the language through which most mental health professional development takes place. Therefore, it cannot simply be seen as an external language closely associated to the hegemonic epistemic flows from the Global North (even though it is the language of the DIME research manual and of the training for the local team of research assistants). Methodologically, all data collection and analysis was supposed to be conducted in Lango. However, while the research assistants were tasked with taking verbatim written notes of participants' accounts, not all of them were comfortable in Lango literacy practices as their education had been in and through English. The research assistants each possessed diverse linguistic resources above and beyond English and Lango. Therefore, Lango cannot simply be seen as *the* local language, the one in which, from a DIME perspective, the local understandings of distress and support for it were naturalistically verbalised and therefore best for research purposes. It is for such reasons that this case study generated so many language-oriented researcher reflections during the fieldwork.

Researcher Reflections

Given his language educator professional status and applied linguistics researcher home, it is perhaps not surprising that, when RF discovered a month beforehand that he would be part of the fieldwork team, he would consider—in a spirit of purposefully preparing for RM fieldwork—how best to linguistically prepare for this two-week trip to Uganda and Lira in particular. Nor is it surprising, given his central role in the RM area of research activity, that his considerations followed, in many ways, the prototypical trajectory of researchers' developing RM praxis which we discussed above. Thus, in his fieldwork journal, he notes down some of Uganda and Lira's linguistic complexities (i.e. informed thinking), and, as based on an initial appreciation of the contextual complexities, he wonders (in an exercise of transparent decision-making) which linguistic resources might usefully be added to those in English—those in Kiswahili? Luganda? Lango? Acholi? Underlying this choice lies a clear sense of purposefulness—was it reasonable that such late-in-the-day linguistic preparation (whether in Lango, Luganda, or Kiswahili etc.) for such a short-lived immersion in a fieldwork site be available for direct research purposes or, more likely, for the relational aspects supporting the research? Acting on this informed thinking, he sourced a *Lango-English: English-Lango* dictionary (as well as unsuccessfully trying to find other Lango learning resources). This proved to be an invaluable linguistic preparation tool for him and the rest of the research team (for all of whom Lango was a largely or completely unfamiliar language). But it also proved to be an essential support for the translingual practice evident in interactions with the local research assistants (and with other people that the research team interacted with in Lira), interactions through which the relationship-building on which the fieldwork rested.

While it might be that RW's involvement in the large RM project was in itself a trigger for his focus on the linguistic element in his research, it also seems that RF's investment in linguistic preparation for, and action in, the fieldwork was also a prompt for his own increased language work:

> [RF] has got great use out of his Lango dictionary so far on this trip, and has been very keen to engage with the team in Lango if and when he can. I have been trying out some words and phrases too [. . .] I also have to concede that having RF and LM in the team has increased the amount of Lango that I have been able to pick up.
>
> (blog entries, 31st March and 3rd April 2015)

He also reflects on the value of an interdisciplinary collaboration—including the presence of a language-foregrounding colleague:

> Discussions with both RF and LM have also allowed me to reflect critically on the methodology that we have been employing and sharpened my awareness around the points in the process where the use of English language training has juxtaposed with the use of Lango in the delivery of interviews and the recording of associated information.
>
> (blog entry, 3rd April 2015)

As the fieldwork progressed, and linguistic insights from it were reflected upon in the interdisciplinary dialogues within the team, RW reports on the sharpening of his language-attentive review of the DIME methodology and its operationalisation:

> It was great to have [RF]'s input on the important role that the interplay between the two main languages used in the research group (i.e. English and Lango) will have on the process that we are undertaking. It has been great to chat with him about the methodology we are using and how it makes allowances for this interplay in important ways, whilst perhaps also introducing a certain degree of rigidity to these issues also, e.g. stipulating that the process of translation should only occur at the very end of the process. Some research assistants raised the possibility that some of the participants might actually be more keen to report the problems they face in English [rather] than in Lango. . . . It will be interesting to track this in coming days.
>
> (blog entry, 31st March, 2015)

Further:

> The project and its interesting mix of training offered in English, and research materials and interviews delivered in Lango has certainly got me reflecting on the subtleties of language. I find myself making a maximum effort to maintain consistency with the words that I use to convey instructions in English. Although all of the team identify as having English as a 2nd language, I invite a Lango speaker (X) to translate and repeat the instructions. I note how conscious I am of not engaging in the process of 're-interpreting' the guidance given in the English language and the manual and the verbal instructions that I am giving the research team. This is a key point of reflection for me—issues of interpretation are not unique to the movement between languages but can also be an issue within language (particularly when moving between written text and spoken word).
>
> (blog entry, 1st April, 2015)

In their tentative use of Lango, the team might be seen as realising the simplistic view of separate linguistic systems which both the DIME methodology and the traditions of linguistic preparation encouraged. However, if that were the starting point, RW's blog entries also reveal his growing appreciation of the linguistic diversity of the context, and of the linguistic interplay between often English-medium education and GMH professional thinking and the use of local languages for expressing mental well-being:

> It is important to note that the school that we visited yesterday and the University we visited today only teach students using English. This highlights the challenges that health professionals might have [having been]

taught in a language that is not necessarily the first language of the people that they subsequently treat. I think this serves to highlight the ecological validity and potential utility of the research that we are conducting.

(blog entry, 8th April, 2015)

He had already invested significant thought in the DIME methodology but, again as prompted by the collaborative and interdisciplinary team assembled in Lira, this was given added purpose:

There is potential for uncertainty in terms of how well, or not, the methodology we are using might bear fruit in this context ... although the DIME (Diagnosis, Implementation, Methodology, and Evaluation) approach was developed by work that was led by Prof Paul Bolton (John Hopkins University) and colleagues in field trials that [were] completed in part in Uganda, this is the first time that this research team has engaged with this particular methodology.

(blog entry 31st March, 2015)

These researcher reflections—both RW's and RF's—are illustrative of the ways in which, once a language attentiveness has been triggered, researchers (including these like RW in disciplines and professions where language is not especially foregrounded) can inform their decision-making and reflect on the purposefulness of the micro-decisions of their research design operationalisation while becoming increasingly sensitive to the linguistic complexities of the contexts in which they are working. As they do so, we can not only see some aspects of a possible researcher trajectory RM but also see engagement with the challenge of linguistic preparation and the developing appreciation of the complex translingual work of value in the field.

Discussion

The data explored above challenged our thinking about researcher education for linguistic diversity in several ways. Our previous work in the Researching Multilingually network project and the papers we refer to in our brief literature review in this chapter indicate to us that more thinking and planning relating to languages in research will always be invaluable. However, from the TD case study in Uganda, we have recognised that developing an understanding of the particular context will be essential in determining the nature of the researcher linguistic preparation which will support the research. The fluidity of languages used in Lira region such as Lango and English in medical contexts, Lango in local interactions, demonstrated an overlapping use of languages which, we argue, mirrors the concept of translingual practice as set out by Canagarajah (2013). Given that each context for research will have its own particularities, it will be impossible to prescribe a curriculum for linguistic preparation for research, but we propose that supporting researchers in developing a translingual mindset which is open to their research informants and collaborators to use languages flexibly, will be an important contribution. In this definition of linguistic preparation through developing a translingual mindset, there may be any or all of the following:

a) fact finding about which languages are used, for which purposes in the country and region where the research will take place;
b) background work on the research informants and collaborators and their linguistic preferences in everyday social and work contexts;
c) background research into historical, political and geographical factors or events impacting on language uses and preferences; and
d) foregrounding of the expectations and norms of how linguistic diversity is addressed within the disciplinary and research tradition in which the research has been designed, e.g. ethnographic research or participatory action research in education, anthropology or health.

The proposed definition of achieving linguistic preparation through developing a translingual mindset is seen by the authors as a component of what we have discussed previously as researching multilingually. As such the concept of spatiality (discussed in section 4 in this chapter) can be seen to inform each of points a)-d) above and relationality can be seen to underpin point c). We argue, therefore, that researching multilingually is in operation throughout a research project and that developing a translingual mindset can be considered an important aspect of that process.

Our thinking in this chapter has been greatly stimulated by discussions across disciplinary and professional borders and we suggest that developing researcher praxis in complex and fluid multilingual contexts can be supported by insights from a range of sources. This observation could also contribute to our focus on researcher education in linguistically diverse contexts. Researchers may benefit from engaging with the practices of each other's traditions and the ways in which researchers can develop a translingual mindset appropriate to the context of their study can be shared to the benefit of other researchers.

Concluding Thoughts

In this chapter, we have reviewed the ways in which pluri-/multi-lingual communication, which is commonplace around the world, might be used to inform the distinctive language education context of researchers learning about how they engage multilingually with research collaborators, sources and participants in their specified research fields. We have drawn upon the work of Canagarajah (2013) and his concept of translingual practice being both a flexible use of shared languages and also an expression of identity as seen in cosmopolitan relationships. We propose that, for researchers preparing to work with people and ideas in linguistically diverse contexts, broadly defined, raising awareness of, and developing skills in, a "translingual mindset" will be valuable.

In the researcher reflections presented in this chapter we recognise that these researchers have developed their understanding of their own disciplinary expectations of languaging in the research context as well as the fluid uses of languages by their participants and collaborators in the specific context of the study. We propose that researcher education programs could do more to bring to the surface the linguistic and cultural diversity which could be at play in many research sites and studies. Our contribution to the focus for this book, is, therefore, that discussions of plurilingualism in learning and teaching can helpfully be applied to the distinctive case of the learning and teaching of researchers preparing for fieldwork in real world contexts.

Notes

1 *Researching Multilingually* (network) [AH/J005037/1]; *Researching Multilingually at the Borders of Language, the Body, Law and the State* project (large grant) [AH/L006936/1] www.researching-multilingually-at-borders.com.
2 https://rosswhiteblog.wordpress.com.
3 See www.jhsph.edu/research/centers-and-institutes/center-for-refugee-and-disaster-response/response_service/AMHR/ (retrieved March 1st 2017).

References

Beaudry, N. (1997). The challenges of human relations in ethnographic enquiry: Examples from Arctic and Subartic fieldwork. In G. F. Barz and T. J. Cooley (Eds.), *Shadows in the field: New perspectives for fieldwork in ethnomusicology* (pp. 83–83). Oxford, UK: University Press.

Blackledge, A., & Creese, A. (2010). *Multilingualism: A critical perspective*. London, UK: Continuum.

Block, D. (2012). Unpicking agency in sociolinguistic research with migrants. In S. Gardner & M. Martin-Jones (Eds.), *Multilingualism, discourse and ethnography* (pp. 47–60). London, UK: Routledge.

Canagarajah, S. (2013). *Translingual practice: Global Englishes and cosmopolitan relations*. London, UK: Routledge.

Conteh, J., & Meier, G. (2015). *The multilingual turn in languages education: Opportunities and challenges*. Clevedon, UK: Multilingual Matters.

Davcheva, L., & Fay, R. (2012). An examination of the research and researcher aspects of multilingually researching one language (Ladino) through fieldwork in another (Bulgarian) and analysis and presentation in a third (English). Paper presented at the 1st AHRC Researching Multilingually seminar, hosted by Durham University, 28–29 March 2012.

Fay, R., Andrews, J., Holmes, P., & Attia, M. (2015). Revisiting linguistic preparation: Some new directions arising from researching multilingually. Paper presented at the BAAL Annual Meeting, hosted by Aston University, 3-5 September 2015.

Fay, R., & Stelma, J. (2016). Criticality, intentionality and intercultural action. In M. Dasli & A. Diaz (Eds.), *The critical turn in language and intercultural communication pedagogy: Theory, research and practice* (pp. 120–146). London, UK: Routledge.

Fricker, M. (2009). *Epistemic injustice: Ethics and the power of knowing*. Oxford: University Press.

Gardner, S., & Martin-Jones, M. (2012). *Multilingualism discourse and ethnography*. London, UK: Routledge.

Giampapa, F. (2012). Authenticity, legitimacy and power: Critical ethnography and identity politics. In S. Gardner & M. Martin-Jones (Eds.), *Multilingualism, discourse and ethnography* (pp. 95–110). London, UK: Routledge.

Gibb, R., & Danero Iglesias, J. (2017). Breaking the silence (again): On language learning and levels of fluency in ethnographic research. *Sociological Review, 65*(1), 1–17.

Heller, M. (2012). Rethinking sociolinguistic ethnography: From community and identity to process and practice. In S. Gardner & M. Martin-Jones (Eds.), *Multilingualism, discourse and ethnography* (pp. 24–33). London, UK: Routledge.

Holliday, A. R. (1994). *Appropriate methodology and social context*. Cambridge: University Press.

Holmes, P., Fay, R., Andrews, J., & Attia, M. (2013). Researching multilingually: New theoretical and methodological directions. *International Journal of Applied Linguistics, 23*(3), 285–299.

Holmes, P., Fay, R., Andrews, J., & Attia, M. (2016). How to research multilingually: Possibilities and complexities. In H. Zhu (Ed.), *Research methods in intercultural communication: A practical guide* (pp. 88–102). London, UK: Wiley.

Hsin-Chun Tsai, J., Choe, J. H., Mu Chen Lim, J., Acorda, E., Chan, N. L., Taylor, V., & Tu, S-P. (2004). Developing culturally competent health knowledge: Issues of data analysis of crosscultural, cross-language qualitative research. *International Journal of Qualitative Methods, 3*(4), 16–27.

Kubota, R. (2014). The multi/plural turn, postcolonial theory and neoliberal multiculturalism: Complicities and implications for Applied Linguistics. *Applied Linguistics, 37*(4), 474–494.

Phipps, A. (2011). Travelling languages? Land, languaging and translation. *Language and Intercultural Communication, 11*(4), 364–376.

Pietikänen, S. (2012). Experiences and expressions of multilingualism: Visual ethnography and discourse analysis in research with Sami children. In S. Gardner & M. Martin-Jones (Eds.), *Multilingualism, discourse and ethnography* (pp. 163–178). London, UK: Routledge.

Stelma, J., & Fay, R. (2014). Intentionality and developing researcher competence on a UK Master's course: An ecological perspective on research education. *Studies in Higher Education, 39*(4), 517–533.

Stelma, J., Fay, R., & Zhou, X. (2013). Developing intentionality and researching multilingually: An ecological and methodological perspective. *International Journal of Applied Linguistics, 23*(3), 300–315.

Tremlett, A. (2009). Claims of 'knowing' in ethnography: Realising anti-essentialism through a critical reflection on language acquisition in fieldwork. *Graduate Journal of Social Science, 6*(3), 63–85.

Watson, V. (2011). Training for multicultural therapy: The challenge and the experience. In C. Lago (Ed.), *The handbook of transcultural counselling and psychotherapy* (pp. 17–29). Maidenhead: McGraw Hill Open University Press.

CONTRIBUTORS

Jane Andrews is Associate Professor of Education at the University of the West of England, UK. Her research interests include exploring children's perspectives on their multilingualism, researching multilingually and learning in communities and families.

Laura Ascenzi-Moreno is an Assistant Professor and Bilingual Program Coordinator in the Childhood, Bilingual, and Special Education Department at Brooklyn College, City University of New York. Her research focuses on the literacy development of emergent bilingual students, the development of teacher knowledge, and how both of these intersect with equity.

Julie Choi is a Lecturer in Education (Additional Languages) in the Melbourne Graduate School of Education. She is co-editor of the book *Language and Culture: Reflective Narratives and the Emergence of Identity*, and author of *Creating a Multivocal Self: Autoethnography as Method*.

Priscilla Angela T. Cruz has been teaching with the Ateneo de Manila University in the Philippines for over 15 years. Her research interests include Systemic Functional Linguistics, educational linguistics, language variation, and interfacing language and literature teaching. She has also been involved in the various teacher-training initiatives of her university.

Brian Davy teaches Economics and Business studies in a secondary school in west Auckland. He is also a PhD candidate at the University of Auckland. His research interests focus on the relationship between the language use and identity of English Additional Language (EAL) students at senior secondary school. Brian seeks to understand how teachers can utilise students' existing multilingualism as a resource to enhance student achievement.

Richard Fay is a Senior Lecturer (TESOL & Intercultural Communication) at the Manchester Institute of Education at the University of Manchester. His research explores intercultural communication, applied linguistics, English as a lingua franca, and researcher education.

Mei French teaches EAL in a secondary school, and is a PhD candidate at the University of South Australia. Her research into multilingual practices of high school students connects to translanguaging, pedagogy, and educational power structures. She has published work in *Language and Education* and the book *Languages and Literacies as Mobile and Placed Resources*.

Ntombekhaya Fulani is a language education lecturer at Rhodes University, South Africa. She focuses on teacher development and her research interests include multilingualism and reflective practice in language teacher education.

Angelica Galante is a PhD candidate in Language and Literacies Education at University of Toronto and recipient of a 2017 doctoral award from The International Research Foundation for English language education (TIRF). Currently, she lectures at Brock University and York University. Her research interests include plurilingual instruction and classroom research.

Ofelia García is Professor in the PhD programs in Urban Education and Hispanic and Luso Brazilian Literatures and Languages at the Graduate Center of the City University of New York. García is the General Editor of the *International Journal of the Sociology of Language* and the co-editor of *Language Policy* (with H. Kelly-Holmes). In 2017, she received the Charles A. Ferguson award in applied linguistics.

Monica Hendricks is the Director of the Institute for the Study of Englishes of Africa at Rhodes University. She teaches and coordinates undergraduate courses for teachers of English as an additional language, mostly in rural schools in the Eastern and Northern Cape Provinces. She has a long-standing interest in children's writing ability and their sense of self, and in improving pedagogical writing practices.

Rebecca Hetherington is a PhD candidate in the Melbourne Graduate School of Education at the University of Melbourne. She is interested in democratic participation and community representation in policy, and her current work combines these fields with her linguistics background to examine the effectiveness of language policy consultations in Australia.

Lara-Stephanie Krause is a PhD student at the School of African Languages and Literatures, UCT, researching translanguaging in South African township classrooms. Her MA thesis is titled *"Xhosa is my Identity, English is my Future": Complexities around Language Values and Practices at a South African Township School* (2014).

Joseph Lo Bianco is Professor of Language and Literacy Education in the Graduate School of Education, University of Melbourne Australia. As an applied linguist, his research has focused on language education policy, multilingualism and indigenous/immigrant settings in Southeast Asia and the role of language in social cohesion and conflict.

Ahmar Mahboob is Associate Professor of Linguistics at the University of Sydney. Ahmar's primary research interest is on an examination of policies, practices, and implications of language variation in local and global contexts. In pursuing this goal, Ahmar draws from and contributes to a range of linguistics and applied linguistics traditions, theories, and methodologies.

Trent Newman is a PhD candidate in Language and Literacy Education at the University of Melbourne. He has a professional background in academic literacies, language teaching, intercultural communication, and also peace education, including human rights and anti-racism education. His current work focuses on the relationship between language, education, and development.

Sue Ollerhead is a lecturer in Literacies and English as an additional language at the University of New South Wales, Sydney. She has worked in English language and literacy teaching and training in Africa, Europe and Australia. Her main interests are developing disciplinary literacies across the curriculum, learner and teacher identity in language education and translanguaging in the classroom.

Emi Otsuji is a senior lecturer in International Studies at the University of Technology Sydney. She is co-editor (with Ikuko Nakane and William Armour) of *Languages and Identities in a Transitional Japan: From Internationalization to Globalization*, and a co-editor (with Hideo Hosokawa and Marcella Mariotti) of *Shiminsei Keisei to Kotoba no kyoiku* [Constructing citizenship and language education].

Alastair Pennycook is Distinguished Professor of Language, Society and Education at the University of Technology Sydney. His most recent books include *Metrolingualism: Language in the city* (with Emi Otsuji), *Posthumanist Applied Linguistics* and *Popular culture, voice and linguistic diversity: Young adults on- and offline* (with Sender Dovchin and Shaila Sultana).

Enrica Piccardo is Associate Professor at OISE—University of Toronto and at Université Grenoble-Alpes. A specialist of the Common European Framework of Reference for Languages, she has co-authored the CEFR Companion Volume (Council of Europe, forthcoming). Her publications in different languages concern plurilingualism, the action-oriented approach and creativity in SLE.

Mastin Prinsloo is an Emeritus Professor, School of Education, UCT, researching in language and literacy studies, with a recent focus on languaging in schools. His latest co-edited books include *Language, Literacy and Diversity: Moving Words* (2015); *Educating for Language and Literacy Diversity: Mobile Selves* (2014); and *Literacy Studies* (2013).

Brendan Rigby works in the Professional Practice and Leadership at the Department of Education & Training, Victoria. His doctoral research, completed at the University of Melbourne's Graduate School of Education, is entitled *Camera Obscura: Out-of-School Children's Digital Perspectives of Literacies in Northern Ghana*. It explores how ten out-of-school children in two rural communities in northern Ghana understand and practice everyday literacies. Brendan is passionate about literacy education, participatory visual research and evaluation, global development and education systems.

Sara Vogel is a doctoral student in Urban Education at the Graduate Center of the City University of New York. A former Research Assistant for the CUNY NYS Initiative on Emergent Bilinguals, she now works at the intersection of computer science education, bilingualism, and social justice pedagogy.

Ross White is a Reader in Clinical Psychology at the Institute of Psychology, Health and Society at the University of Liverpool. His research explores the role that socio-cultural factors play in the manifestation of mental health difficulties. He is a co-editor of the Palgrave Handbook for Global Mental Health: Socio-cultural Perspectives.

INDEX

Note: *italics* indicate figures; "n" indicates chapter notes.

Aboriginal Australians *see* Indigenous Australians
Aboriginal English 57, 63
academic language 72, 132, 167, 171, 177
accents 9, 155–157, 159, 202
acquisition planning 187, 191, 192, 196, 198
action-oriented approach 152–159
Adoniou, M. 133
affordance 94
African languages 23, 202–204, 206, 209–216
Afrikaans 201, 202, 203–206, 211, 213–216
agency 13, 94, 109, 151–158
Airey, J. 188
Alexander, N. 202
Andrews, J. 13, 220–233
Arabic 75, 76, 77, 137–138; *see also* Qu'ranic
Ascenzi-Moreno, L. 12, 89–104
Ashworth, M. 3
aspiration 38–39
assemblage 10, 71–75, 86, 93–94, 100–104
assessments 169–170, 172, 173–178, 205–206

assimilation policies 3, 23, 54, 140
Attic (Ancient) Greek 78–80
Australia 3, 6, 8, 11, 22, 192; Indigenous Australians on language education in 54–66; language policy in 22–34, 58; linguistic diversity of students in 166–179; translingual innovation in 132–139, 143–144
Australia in the Asian Century report 33
Azurin, A. M. 40

Badat, S. 202
Bailey, B. 141
Baker, C. 208
Bakhtin, M. 2, 188
Barkhuizen, G. P. 170
Basque 8
Bauman, Z. 62
Beaudry, N. 221
Bernstein, B. 41
Bezemer, J. 92, 93
bilingual advantage *see* translingual advantage
bilingualism 3, 57, 74–75, 130–137, 150; higher education contexts 201, 202–203, 205, 207, 209, 211; and machine translation software 89–90, 91–104

bilingual universities 72
'bilingual voice' 137
biliteracy 92
Blackledge, A. 2, 131, 220, 223
Blommaert, J. 76, 85
Brazil 22
Busch, B. 72

Cambodian 170
Canada 3, 6, 22, 149, 154–158
Canagarajah, S. 73, 131, 166, 188, 194, 204–205, 208, 210, 220, 223, 230
Cenoz, J. 8, 56, 148, 150
China 133
Chinese 78–81, 85, 95–101, 103, 168
Choi, J. 1–14
Chomsky, N. 149
chotto-ness 76–77, 85
City University of New York, New York State Initiative on Emergent Bilinguals (CUNY-NYSIEB) project 95–96
Clyne, M. G. 27, 167
Coady, M. R. 174, 176, 177
code meshing 188
code-switching 150, 158
Cognitive Academic Language Proficiencies (CALP) 168
collaborative learning 171–172
colonial histories 38, 54–55, 57–58, 65n1, 143, 149, 190, 196
Common European Framework of Reference for Languages (CEFR) 148, 152–153, 159
communication, cross-cultural 221–222
communication practices 108, 110–111
Complementary Basic Education (CBE), Ghana 108, 111–113, 117, 119, 121
contact languages 55, 57, 58, 63, 66n2
contact zones 130, 131, 144
Conteh, J. 21, 221
Cook, V. 169
Cooper, R. 187, 188, 192, 198
Cope, B. 4
corpus planning 187, 190–191
Coxhead, A. 168
Creese, A. 2, 220, 223
Cruikshank, K. 26
Cruz, P. A. T. 11, 37–52
Cummins, J. 3, 4, 132, 138, 147, 150, 178
curricula 37, 202–203

Dagbanli (language) 108, 111–112, 114, 116, 121, 123
Danero-Iglesias, J. 221
Dant, T. 90, 94, 102
Davcheva, L. 225
Davy, B. 13, 165–180
decolonisation 201–202
de Courcy, M. 9, 172, 178
de Fina, A. 131
de Jong, E. 3, 174, 177
Dekker, D. 40
Denmark 22
Deumert, A. 89, 94
development, geopolitical 109–110, 192–197, 198
Dharug (language) 61
dialogue 2
dictionaries 156, 190, 198, 228
digital photography *see* photography
disciplinary language/literacy 168–171, 186, 187–192, 194–198, 206
distributed language view 90, 92, 104
diversity *see* linguistic diversity
double-voicedness 2
drama 153–154; action-oriented tasks 154–158

East Timor *see* Timor-Leste
education *see* higher education; language-in-education policy; mother-tongue based multilingual education (MTB–MLE); researcher education
Eisenchlas, S. 3, 23
'elite' foreign languages 3, 28, 74
Ellis, E. 7, 173–174, 177, 178
emojis 77
English as an Additional Language/Dialect (EAL/D), Australia 57, 132–134, 144, 163–171, 177
English as a New Language (ENL), USA 95–96
English as a Second Language (ESL), Canada 154–155
English for Specific Purposes 191–192
English language: higher education contexts 72, 191–192, 194, 196, 198, 202–204; in the Philippines 37, 38–40, 44–51; in researcher education 224, 227–229; students' use of 77–81, 84–85, 110, 113–118
English language learners (ELLs) 6

English language norm 3, 23, 30, 148–149, 168–169, 173–174
"English only instruction" 144

Fannin, J. 4
Fay, R. 13, 220–232
fear 173
Ferreira, A. 204
Filipino 37, 38–39, 44–51
Finnish 223
Francis, N. 54
Franken, M. 178
Freeman Field, R. 3
French, M. 1–14, 163–179
Fulani, N. 13, 201–217
funding 63–65
"funds of knowledge" 4, 6, 134–135, 139, 167, 177

Gajo, L. 194
Galante, A. 13, 147–159
García, O. 2–3, 12, 56, 63, 85, 89–104, 132, 137, 187, 196
Genesee, F. 133
Ghana 107–124
Giampapa, F. 222
Gibb, R. 220, 221
Gibbons, P. 207
Gillard, J. 33
globalisation 131, 148
Global Mental Health (GMH) 226–227, 229
Global North 226–227
Global South 110, 227
glossaries 190, 197, 198
Gogolin, I. 154, 166
Gonzalez, A. 38–39
Google Translate 89–104
grammar 44, 206, 208
Gregory, E. 131
'growth' 195–199
Gu, M. 72
Guillemin, D. 3, 23
Gurindji Kriol (language) 57

Halliday, M. A. K. 42, 44
Hammond, J. 6
Harper, C. A. 169, 174, 176, 177
He, P. 73
Heleta, S. 202
Heller, M. 222

Hendricks, M. 13, 201–217
"heteroglossia" 2, 141
Hetherington, R. 11–12, 54–66
Heugh, K. 167, 206–217
higher education: language teaching in South Africa 201–217; lecturers as language planners in Timor-Leste 185–199; see also researcher education
Higher School Certificate (HSC), Australia 24–26
High Income Countries (HICs) 226
Hokkien Chinese 78–80
home languages 3, 6–7, 9, 143, 166, 172–175, 202–206, 210–212; see also L1 (first languages); mother-tongue based multilingual education (MTB-MLE)
Hong Kong 72
Hornberger, N. H. 54–55, 92–93, 136
Howard, J. 57
Hsin-Chun Tsai, J. 221
Hull, G. 4
human-machine assemblages theory 90
Hymes, D. 111
hyperlingualism 72

identity 4, 61–63, 131, 132, 138–139, 210; see also self
ideology 27, 72, 141–142, 199
immersion 133, 135, 144
Incremental Introduction of African Languages 203
Indigenous Australians, on language education 54–66; translanguaging and 57–59
indigenous languages 23, 27, 54, 57; see also African languages; Native American languages
Indonesia 186, 192
Indonesian (Bahasa) 76–77, 185–187, 191, 194, 195
instructional language 43
Intensive English Centres (IECs), Australia 133
intercomprehension 150
internationalisation of higher education 71–72
international students 75–77
invisibility 72

isiXhosa (language) 140–143, 201, 203, 205–216
isiZulu (language) 203

James, C. 169
Janks, H. 204
Japanese 76–85
Johnson, S. 132
Jørgensen, J. 2
Joseph, J. E. 130

Kalantzis, M. 4
Karrebæk, M. 2
Kitchen, M. 170
Klein, T. 85
Kleyn, T. 56, 63
knowledge 28, 29–30; commonsense/uncommonsense 41–51; *see also* "funds of knowledge"
Koch, E. 207, 209–217
Korean 76–77, 170
Kramsch, C. 148, 159
Krause, L. 12, 129–145
Kress, G. 93
Kubota, R. 8–10, 21, 220, 222

L1 (first language) 37, 40, 136–139, 167–171; *see also* home languages
L2 (second language) 37
Lai, H. 73
Langman, J. 188
Lango (language) 226–230
language affiliation 39
language allocation 39
Language as Resource orientation 22
language diversity *see* linguistic diversity
language-in-education policy 9, 141–142, 151, 188, 191, 202–203, 206, 209; funding 63–65; Indigenous Australians on 54–66; in the Philippines 38–40
Language of Learning and Teaching (LoLT), South Africa 140
"language outcomes framework" 133
language planning (LP), university lecturers' role in 185–199
language profiles, raising 57–58
language rights 23, 62–63
language variation framework 41, 42–43
Languages other than English (LOTE), Australia 132

"learning about language" *vs.* "learning language" 42
learning "deficits" 132, 144, 169, 173
Lin, A. 2, 12, 44, 73
lingua franca 185, 188, 191
lingualisms 150
linguistic capital 172
linguistic diversity 1, 22–24, 131, 132, 134, 136, 143, 148–151, 163; in research 220, 221, 222–224, 230, 232
linguistic ethnography 222–223
linguistic hierarchy 170
"linguistic preparation" for research 220–222, 225–226, 228–230
Link, H. 92–93
literacy: multilingualism and 3–4; of out of school children in Ghana 107–124; within plurilingualism 108–109; universal primary schooling and 109–110
Literacy Engagement Framework 4
Li Wei 2, 56, 63
loan words 185, 187, 190–191, 195
Lo Bianco, J. 11, 21–34, 1846, 188, 197
local languages 37–39, 43–52
Lorente, B. 37
low and middle-income countries (LMICs) 226–227

McComish, J. 178
McFarland, C. 38
machine translation software 89–104
McKinney, C. 4
McKinnon-Kidd, M. 61–62, 65n1
MacSwan, J. 74
Madsen, L. 2
Mahboob, A. 11, 37–52
Majone, G. 28–30
Makalela, L. 72–73, 208
Makoni, S. 2
Malaysian 77
Mandarin Chinese 75–76, 78, 80
Mangonéz, L. P. 72
Māori (language) 163
Martin, J. R. 41, 44–45
Martin-Jones, M. 130
Maseko, P. 208
maths (subject) 139, 215
Mawonga, S. 208
May, S. 21, 22, 170, 178

Mazak, C. 72, 189, 194
meaning-making 90–93, 98, 174, 189
medium of instruction (MOI), of schools 40, 112, 130, 191, 201, 203
Meier, G. 21, 223
Mendelowitz, B. 204
Mendoza, F. 72
Menken, K. 187
meta-knowledge 43
meta-language 43
metalinguistics 194, 195
metaphors 208
metrolanguaging 73
metrolingua franca 79
metrolingualism 2; student repertoires 71–86
Meyer, O. 108
migration/mobility 6, 71–72, 131, 147
minority languages 8, 37, 170
Miriwoong (language) 61, 64
Moje, E. B. 168
Møller, J. 2
monolingual habitus 130–131, 164–169, 172–173, 176–177; *see also* English language norm
monolingualism 134, 136–137, 140–144, 148–150; parallel 130–131, 135–136
Montanera, M. 4
Moore, D. 1, 194
Morrison, S. 23
mother-tongue based multilingual education (MTB–MLE) 37–52; in classroom practice 44–51; and forms of knowledge 41–43; need for 40
multilingualism 1, 21–24, 110; in higher education 71–72, 74, 201, 202–203, 211, 221–223; and literacy 3–5; as term 1–2
multilingual turn 223
multiliteracy 93
multimodality 4–5, 77–84, 92–93, 108, 123
Multiple Streams Framework 28, 30–31
multivocality 2
music 75–76
Myanmar 22

Nakata, M. 54, 62, 63
National Certificate of Educational Achievement (NCEA) 169
Native American languages 149
native speaker model 149–150
neoliberalism 21, 34, 58, 63–65
"neurological impress" strategy 137–139
New Literacy Studies 108
New London Group 4
New Zealand 163–179
Newman, T. 13, 185–199
Newry, D. 61–62, 64
Nkomo, D. 208
Norton, B. 4
Ntelioglou, B. 4
numeracy 121–122

Ollerhead, S. 1–14, 129–145
Otsuji, E. 2, 12, 71–86

Pahl, K. 4
Pan-Africanism 210, 217n1
parallel monolingualism 130–131, 135–136
paternalism 206
patriarchy 206
Paulsrud, B. A. 75, 85
Pauwels, A. 72
pedagogy 2, 208–209; dramatic action-oriented tasks 154–158; *see also* translanguaging pedagogy
Pennycook, A. 2, 12, 71–86
Persian 9
personification 211
Philippines: core language issues in 38–39; mother-tongue based multilingual education in 37–52
photography, and children's literacy 107–124
Piccardo, E. 1, 13, 147–159
Pietikäinen, S. 222–223
Plüddeman, P. 211
plurilanguaging 159
plurilingual stance: problems with 8–10; teachers' uptake of 6–8; as term 5–6
plurilingual theory 148–150
plurilingualism, as term 1–2
pluriliteracy 93, 108–109, 111, 150
policy *see* language-in-education policy
polycentricity 2
polylanguaging 2
polyphony 2

Portugal 192, 196
Portuguese 187, 190–191, 194–196
power 8, 28–30, 39, 131, 136, 143
Pratt, M. 131, 204, 212
Preece, S. 72
presentational talk 206
prestige foreign languages *see* elite foreign languages
Prinsloo, M. 12, 129–145
problem-solving skills 153–154
Probyn, M. 206–207
proficiency 149–150
Puerto Rico 72

Quer, G. M. 57
Qu'ranic Arabic 110, 112, 114, 123

reading 40
refugees 133
relationality 231
repertoire, students' linguistic *see* student resources, multi/plurilingual 151–152
researcher education 220–232; *Translating Distress* case study 226–227
Reyhner, J. 54
Rhodes University, South Africa 203, 205
Rigby, B. 12, 107–124
role-play *see* drama
Rose, D. 44–45
Rowsell, J. 4
Ruíz, R. 22, 62, 206–207
rural communities 110, 111–112, 192–194, 212
rural farmers 195–197, 198

'safe houses' 204, 206, 212
Sámi (language) 222–223
SBS (Special Broadcasting Service), Australia 24–26
scaffolding 44–45, 137, 206
Scarino, A. 169
Schalley, A. 3, 23
School for Life, Ghana 111–112, 116, 118–123
Schultz, K. 4
science (subject) 168
scientific language 186–187
Second Language Acquisition 152
self 9, 117–124; *see also* identity
Seltzer, K. 132

'service' in the tourism industry 189–192, 198
seSotho (language) 203, 205–206
Shakuto-Neoh, S. 57
Shanahan, C. 168
Shanahan, T. 168
silencing 9, 149, 170, 187, 220
Singh, M. G. 33
Singlish (Chinese-Singaporean-English) 78
social agency *see* agency
South Africa 22, 72–73; language teaching in 201–217; translingual innovation in schools 141–147
South Australian Certificate of Education (SACE) 169
Spanish language 72
spatiality 231
Standard Australian English 132, 143
Standard English 130–131, 140–144
standardised testing 57, 132–133, 142
status planning 187, 191, 196, 198
Stevens, L. 166
Street, B. 108
student resources, multi/plurilingual 6–7, 151–152, 169, 170–172, 175–178; everyday language practices 75–77; and multimodality 77–84; translingual advantage 74, 77, 84–86; *see also* literacy
student use of English 77–81, 84–85, 110, 113–118
'sustainability' 192–195, 198
Syria 133, 137–139

Tagalog 38, 49
Taglish (English-Filipino) 46
target language 44–45
teachers: enactment of translanguaging pedagogies 136–137; perceptions of own linguistic resources 135–136; plurilingual stance of 6–8; responses to plurilingualism 172–177; university lecturers' role in language planning 185–199; use of students' linguistic resources 136
teacher support 151
teacher training 7–8, 143–145, 174
Teaching English to speakers of other languages (TESOL) qualifications 133

"teaching into" language 96–100, 103–104
teaching strategies 3–4, 6–7, 10, 142, 144, 176, 178
television 120–121
tertiary education *see* higher education
testing *see* assessments; standardised testing
Tetun (language) 186–187, 190–198, 199n1
Thailand 22, 171
theatre *see* drama
Then, D. C. O. 169
Thibault, P. 90, 92
Timor-Leste 185–199
Ting, S. H. 169
Tinkle, J. 168
tourism 189–192, 193, 198
transglossia 196
translanguaging 8, 72–73, 91, 131–132, 150, 159, 188–189, 194, 196, 220; as term 2; theory 55–56
translanguaging pedagogy 131–132, 143–145, 201–212; Australia school context 132–139; higher education contexts 72–73; for Indigenous languages 55, 57–65; reflexive 208–209; semiotic repertoire in 91–93, 103; South African school context 139–143; theory 56, 208; use of machine translation software 89–104; writing 208–211
Translating Distress (TD) case study 220, 226–227
translation 60, 137–138, 172, 186–198, 207; software 89–104
translingual activism 86
translingual advantage 74, 77, 84–86
translingualism 194
translingual research mindset 220, 226, 231–232
translingual research practice 220, 222–223
translingual student practices 73–75

Tremlett, A. 220, 221
truncated repertoires 76, 85
Turkey 22

ubuntu 72–73
Uganda 226–230
United Kingdom (UK) 6
United States of America (USA) 6, 29–30, 89–90, 95, 149, 154, 204
Universal Primary Education (UPE), Uganda 109–110
university lecturers, role in language planning 185–199; *see also* higher education
University of KwaZulu-Natal, South Africa 203
University of Limpopo, South Africa 203
Use of Official Languages Act (2012), South Africa 203

Van der Walt, C. 72–73
van Lier, L. 154
Vietnam 192
Vogel, S. 12, 89–104

Wallace, C. 8
Watson, V. 221
Weiss, C. 28, 29–30
White, R. 220–232
Wickert, R. 31–33
Williams, A. 131
Woods, D. 59–61
workforce development 185, 188, 190, 192, 199
workplace communication 186, 190–191
writing 208–211

Xhosa (language) *see* isiXhosa (language)

Yumplatok (language) 57

Zuckermann, G. 57